Why
Americans
Split
Their Tickets

Why Americans Split Their Tickets

Campaigns, Competition, and Divided Government

Barry C. Burden and David C. Kimball

The University of Michigan Press
Ann Arbor

In memory of
David W. Kimball Jr.

First paperback edition 2004
Copyright © by the University of Michigan 2002
All rights reserved
Published in the United States of America by
The University of Michigan Press
Manufactured in the United States of America
⊗ Printed on acid-free paper

2007   2006   2005   2004   4   3   2

A CIP catalog record for this book is available from the British Library.

Library of Congress Cataloging-in-Publication Data

Burden, Barry C., 1971–
Why Americans split their tickets : campaigns, competition, and divided
government / Barry C. Burden and David C. Kimball.
ix, 205 p. : ill. ; 24 cm.
Includes bibliographical references (p. 183–198) and index.
ISBN 0-472-11286-4 (alk. paper)
1. United States. Congress—Elections.   2. Divided government—
United States.   3. Party affiliation—United States.   4. Voting—
United States.   5. Presidents—United States—Election.
I. Kimball, David C., 1966–   II. Title.

JK2271 .B9155   2002
324.973—dc21   2002005413

Contents

Acknowledgments

We are in the midst of a unique period of American history in which the competitive balance between the two major political parties at the national level appears infinitesimally close. Vermont Senator James Jeffords's decision in May 2001 to leave the Republican Party ended a short-lived period of unified GOP control of national government and restored a form of divided government. We are thankful for this competitive balance between the parties because it highlights the subject of this book. In such a competitive environment, ticket splitters (or swing voters, as some call them) demand close scrutiny since they determine the electoral fortunes of the two major parties even though such voters appear to be declining in number.

Unlike some other projects, this book has several sources of inspiration. First, both of us were intrigued by the presence of divided government in the 1980s and 1990s yet not convinced by journalists' conclusions about its sources. As political science caught up with the real world, we tracked the emerging literature on ticket splitting and divided government. This literature began to raise intriguing questions about voter motivation and election mandates. So the second source of inspiration was the ongoing scholarly debate about whether divided government was a result of strategic split-ticket voting. We frequently turned to Morris Fiorina's *Divided Government* since it presented all sides of the argument in a congruent yet controversial style. That book and Fiorina's other works continue to make us think about important political phenomena. Third, at Ohio State University we separately did graduate work on aspects of the larger project. Kimball's dissertation was a direct study of ticket splitting using National Election Study data, while Burden's dissertation focused on position-taking by congressional candidates, a related phenomenon. Finally, we were introduced to Gary King's solution to the ecological inference problem by a combination of King's instruction and our own reading and experimentation. Ticket splitting seemed a natural application for the new technique. Thus, we decided to embark on this book. We hope that the result is a constructive reflection of these influences. Note that this is a truly collaborative project and our names are listed alphabetically.

Almost all of the analyses presented in this book are new. However, an early and shorter statement of our main arguments, based on data from the 1988 elections, appeared in the *American Political Science Review* (Burden and Kimball 1998). We are grateful for the advice of editor Ada Finifter and reviewers of this early report of our research.

This book was written over a period of several years while both of us finished graduate school and began careers as academics. For their many comments over the past several years, we thank Laura Arnold, Larry Baum, Paul Beck, Bill Bianco, Janet Box-Steffensmeier, Aage Clausen, Mo Fiorina, Paul Frymer, Jim Garand, Paul Goren, Tim Johnson, Gary King, Dean Lacy, Bryan Marshall, Rich Pacelle, Harvey Palmer, Phil Paolino, Pat Patterson, Katherine Tate, Herb Weisberg, Gerald Wright, and Chris Zorn. Bianco and Garand in particular provided useful comments on the entire manuscript. We are especially thankful for the faculty and graduate colleagues in the Department of Political Science at Ohio State University. We both have fond memories of our time in Columbus in the mid-1990s.

One or both of us also presented preliminary results of this research to groups at George Washington University, Harvard University, Louisiana State University, Ohio State University, Southern Illinois University at Carbondale, the State University of New York at Stony Brook, and the University of Kentucky; at several professional meetings; and to the Central Intelligence Agency. Participants at all of these locales assisted us by providing fresh criticism on a project with which we were too familiar at times. We extend our appreciation to them.

We also benefited from collegial benevolence in more practical ways. Data were provided by Gary Jacobson (presidential election results and early campaign spending data), Gary King (House election results), Jeff Milyo (challenger quality), Keith Poole (NOMINATE scores), and Peter Radcliffe (campaign expenditures). Richard Winger of *Ballot Access News* filled in the gaps in our knowledge of ballot format changes. Kimberly Allen and DuBose Kapeluck of LSU and Chris Owens, Thomas McCauliffe, and Katherine McAndrew of SIU provided us with quick research assistance in the later stages of writing. Brady Baybeck assisted in last-minute mapmaking. Finally, Gary King's ecological inference technique and accompanying software made it possible for us to conduct the statistical analyses that speak to our argument. We thank him for contributing statistical advances that improve our substantive work. Folks at the University of Michigan Press were especially patient and helpful. We appreciate the help of Jeremy Shine and Kevin Rennells.

Finally, we are extremely thankful to our families. Our parents helped nurture an interest in politics and supported us at every stage of our education. We owe a special debt to our wives, both of whom are named Laura and both of whom made great sacrifices so that we could complete this project. Looking back, we realize that it is not possible to thank them enough since they managed to produce a whopping five children during the gestation period of this book. Burden did it the old-fashioned way— one at a time—while Kimball had three wonderful kids all at once. We dedicate this book to all of our children.

CHAPTER 1

Contemporary American Politics and Divided Government

In late 1995 and early 1996, Democratic President Bill Clinton engaged in tense negotiations with Republican congressional leaders in an effort to produce a balanced federal budget. While the negotiations generated considerable acrimony on both sides, they did not yield a long-term budget agreement. In fact, the federal government shut down for nearly 30 days between November 1995 and January 1996 when negotiators failed to agree on short-term resolutions to continue funding the government. A divided national government did not help matters. The budget battle revealed stark philosophical differences between Republicans and Democrats over budget priorities and the role of the federal government. The negotiations also had a stop-and-go quality, as each party pulled away from the bargaining table at different points during the process, each time professing its good faith while heaping blame on the other side.

The government shutdowns, partisan bickering and brinkmanship, blame avoidance, and elected officials' failure to reach an agreement on an important national problem clearly did not sit well with American citizens. Public approval of Congress and its leaders sunk to new depths at the end of 1995 (S. Patterson and Kimball 1998). And while conventional wisdom may hold that the budget standoff enhanced Clinton's stature at the expense of that of congressional Republicans, the president's approval ratings also dipped during the budget dispute (Moore 1996).[1] One national survey taken in December 1995 found that a plurality believed that continued divided government would be worse than would be unified government under either party (Lang, Lang, and Crespi 1998). When the president and Congress agreed to pass temporary continuing resolutions in January 1996 that would keep the government open through the November election, both sides proclaimed that the American electorate would have to decide which party better reflected the country's spending and revenue priorities. The implication was that the budget stalemate would motivate voters to choose sides in the upcoming elections.

Nevertheless, less than ten months later, American voters maintained the same pattern of divided government by reelecting President Clinton and returning Republican majorities in the House and Senate. Clinton won reelection by a larger margin than he had garnered in 1992 at the same time that the Republican Party gained two seats in the U.S. Senate. In fact, all of the major players in the budget talks of 1995–96 (with the exception of Bob Dole, who resigned from his Senate seat to run against Clinton) retained their positions after the November 1996 elections.

Why would voters choose the same divided government configuration again after it seemed to fail so miserably in the winter of 1995–96? Do voters prefer divided government and policy stalemate? That is the conclusion reached by some observers. No less an authority than Bill Clinton has remarked that "a lot of time in our history the American people would prefer having a president of one party and the Congress the other" (Broder 1996). The mainstream press offered similar explanations for the 1996 elections, concluding that the outcome was a mandate from the voters for bipartisanship and compromise in Washington (Lang, Lang, and Crespi 1998). The following is a representative example.

> Americans took the fork by voting for Bill Clinton but then decided
> to reduce their risks by retaining Republican majorities in both
> Houses. The public seeks bipartisanship, conciliation, and compromise
> rather than confrontation (remember the public fury at the shutdown
> of government in 1995). In this divided government it understands
> that the only way for either side to achieve anything is by working and
> negotiating with the other. (Zuckerman 1996)

We find it odd that the media would interpret the 1996 elections as a mandate for bipartisanship and compromise after the reelection of all but one of the central players who had failed to compromise during the government shutdown.[2] In any case, the perpetuation of divided government in 1996 once again demands that we explain why millions of people divide their votes between the two major parties.

This book examines the underlying causes of divided voting behavior in American national elections. Why do some voters split their ballots by selecting a Republican for one office and a Democrat for another? Why do some voters switch parties from one election to the next? We define *divided voting* broadly to describe citizens who divide their votes between the two major parties either on the same ballot in one election or across elections. Under this definition, ticket splitting is a particularly salient and important form of divided voting, though we will often use the terms interchangeably throughout the rest of the book.

Divided government and ticket splitting are features that define the past forty years in American politics. Divided national government has been more common in the last half of the twentieth century than in any other period of similar duration in American history (see table 1.1).[3] While divided government dominated 20-year intervals before the Civil War and during the "period of indecision" in the late 1800s (Fiorina 1996), the United States has had divided government for 28 of the past 34 years (including 2002).

Similarly, the last half of the twentieth century has seen more president-Congress ticket splitting than other times in American history. See figure 1.1, which displays the percentage of split congressional districts in each election since 1900 (i.e., districts carried by a presidential candidate of one party and House candidate of another party) and the percentage of major-party president-House ticket splitters since 1952.[4] For roughly 30 years, citizens have been demonstrating relatively high levels of independence from the major parties and the political system more generally in the United States, although voters have become more partisan in the 1990s (Bartels 2000; Hetherington 2001). This independence is manifested in split-ticket voting in national elections, which rose from about 15 percent in the 1950s to almost 30 percent in the 1980s, although there was a sharp decline in major-party ticket splitting and congressional districts with split president-House outcomes in the last three presidential elections. Second, there has been a rise in the number of independents

TABLE 1.1.   Control of National Government, 1826–2000

Period	Unified	Divided
1826–1900	22	16
1902–1950	21	4
1952–2000	9	16
Total	52	36

Note: Entries are numbers of elections producing the outcome.

Source: Silbey 1996; Stanley and Niemi 1999.

and a drop in strong party identifiers since the 1950s.[5] More recently, independent voting behavior blossomed in the form of Ross Perot's 19 percent share of the presidential vote in 1992. And in 1996, the movement for the presidential nomination of Colin Powell—a man whose background and apparent policy views do not fit neatly into either party platform—was surprisingly popular. Recent surveys even suggest that a majority of Americans support the formation of a third party (Moore and Saad 1995; Saad 1995; Tollerson 1995). Something is causing voters to forsake loyalty to one of the major parties, and we need to understand this phenomenon.

There are several reasons why these voters are a critical part of the current U.S. political landscape. First and foremost, divided voting behavior is important because it contributes to divided government, a situation in which control of government institutions is shared by more than one political party. The presence of divided government has several important consequences for public policy and the representative nature of American government. Second, divided voters—especially those who switch from one party to another—contribute to the volatile and unpredictable nature of the American political system. For example, few if any observers predicted that the Democratic Party would lose control of both houses of Congress in 1994, only two years after finally winning all three elected branches of national government. Third, it is important to understand the causes of divided voting behavior because political campaigns try to target those voters who are capable of supporting either party. In the sections that follow, we briefly discuss each of these implications of divided voting.

DIVIDED GOVERNMENT AND ITS CONSEQUENCES

Until recently, divided government in the United States typically occurred after a midterm election, when the president was not up for election and his party simply lost seats in Congress (Fiorina 1996). This suggests that the electoral system was at least partly responsible for creating divided government. However, divided government has been created or perpetuated in six of the past nine U.S. presidential elections, and divided government has become the norm during the past few decades. Government has been divided in 28 of the last 34 years (from 1969 through 2002). The 2000 elections ushered in a brief period of unified Republican national government (until the defection of Sen. Jeffords) only by the narrowest of margins. By way of comparison, divided government existed during only 8 of the 34 years before 1969.

As we will show, the current era of divided government coincides with

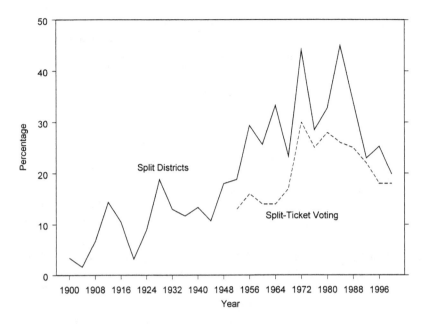

FIG. 1.1.   Split district outcomes and presidential-House ticket splitting in the United States, 1900–2000

a greater frequency of divided voting behavior. The presence of divided
government undoubtedly results from the shifting and divided allegiances
of many voters. If every voter cast a straight party ballot, never abstained
from any contests, and regularly supported the same party, then divided
government simply would not occur.

   We have consciously chosen to limit our subject matter to divided voting and divided government in the United States. This makes the mater-
ial more tractable and allows us to test several competing explanations
within the context of a single political system. It is worth acknowledging,
however, that the definition of divided-party government may be
expanded to include configurations found in parliamentary systems. In
particular, a coalition government is often included as a variant of divided
government. The new view among those who study comparative institutions is that "when the executive does not control a legislative majority in
a parliamentary democracy, minority government is, in effect, divided
government" (Laver and Shepsle 1996, 269).

The sources of divided control are more diverse in parliamentary sys-tems as a result of strategic voting and coalition formation (Laver and Shepsle 1996), though the outcomes are analogous to split-party control in the U.S. According to this view, divided government could exist in a parliament even if a majority government was formed as long as the ruling party exhibits an internal division that parallels the legislative-executive structure (Laver 1999).[6]

Although useful cross-national comparisons are possible, we believe that divided governments in parliamentary and presidential systems are not entirely comparable since the latter are facilitated by the fact that executives and legislators are elected to separate institutions and often even on separate ballots. If American voters are purposely splitting their tickets to produce divided outcomes, then the strategic aspects of voting in parliamentary systems might appear in the U.S. system as well. While there are plentiful and fruitful comparative connections to be made, we leave them for other scholars and future research.

In this book we are primarily concerned with the relationship between divided voting (especially split-ticket voting) and divided government—a focus on the causes of divided government. Though we shall not explicitly analyze the consequences of split-party control, the normative implica-tions of divided government are part of what motivates our study. A grow-ing research area seeks to determine whether government performance and public policy outcomes differ under unified versus divided party con-trol. The unwritten but conventional wisdom in the 1980s was that divided government produced some unpleasant side effects, such as leg-islative gridlock, party posturing, and huge budget deficits (e.g., Sundquist 1988). Despite these beliefs, the initial empirical studies turned up little evidence that divided government differs substantially from its unified counterpart. More recent studies have refined this literature, and some effects of divided control have been identified. Here we briefly review this literature to provide an up-to-date accounting of research findings. We divide the subject into three major areas of interest: lawmaking, account-ability, and budgeting.

Lawmaking

Though scholars have considered the effects of divided government on lawmaking in a theoretical way, Mayhew's *Divided We Govern* (1991) was the first and is still the definitive empirical study of the legislative effects of split-party control. After carefully identifying all of the significant laws passed between 1946 and 1990, Mayhew concludes that "unified versus divided government has probably *not* made a notable difference during the postwar era" (179).

Mayhew's findings remain central to debates about the effects of divided government; however, several criticisms of his study have recently appeared. Among other faults, Mayhew considers the quantity but not the quality of legislation that was passed (Fiorina 1996). It might be that presidents and congressional majorities of different parties produce less coherent, less meaningful policies but do so with the same frequency as unified governments do. In addition, Mayhew relies on counts of legislative "supply" rather than "demand," ignoring legislation that fell short of passage. The number of important bills passed might not vary with party control, but periods of divided government could require more legislation because they indicate that American society is experiencing what Fiorina calls "chronic societal strain" (1996, 8). A substantial and growing number of studies develop alternative measures of legislative productivity, and all find that divided government impedes legislative output (see, e.g., Binder 1999, 2001; Bowling and Ferguson 2001; Coleman 1999; Edwards, Barrett, and Peake 1997; Howell et al. 2000; cf. Krehbiel 1998).[7]

Despite empirical findings contrary to Mayhew's thesis, several other theoretical treatments agree that government remains productive even when the congressional majority does not share the president's party label (Brady and Volden 1998; C. Jones 1994; Krehbiel 1998). These studies tend to argue that the degree of gridlock depends on the exact configuration of policy preferences of elected officials in both branches of government, rather than on party control. Government goes on doing or not doing the nation's business in periods of divided and unified control. The steady flow of legislation, especially the demanding annual budget and bill renewals, dampens any natural differences between regimes.[8]

There is no doubt, however, that divided government increases interbranch conflict, which manifests in the form of more presidential vetoes (Cameron 2000; Groseclose and McCarty 2000; Kernell 1991; Rohde and Simon 1985; Woolley 1991), diverging budget projections by the two branches (Engstrom and Kernell 1999), less congressional delegation of authority to executive-branch agencies (Epstein and O'Halloran 1996), weakened presidential control over trade policy (Lohmann and O'Halloran 1994), and delayed confirmation of executive-branch (McCarty and Razaghian 1999) and judicial (Binder and Maltzman 2002) nominations.[9] In addition, although divided governments might continue to produce legislation, they are more confrontational than cooperative because presidents in these situations are more likely to appeal directly to the public rather than to Congress for support (Kernell 1997). Some conclude from these indicators of interbranch conflict that divided government is more likely to produce incoherent and ineffective policies (Kernell 1991; Schick 1993; Sundquist 1988, 1993) and damage presidential and congressional approval ratings (Groseclose and McCarty 2000; Durr, Gilmour, and Wolbrecht 1997; S. Patterson and Caldeira 1990). Indeed, several scholars have examined the effect of divided government on the quality of legislation, particularly in the realm of budgetary policy.

Budgeting

Budgetary politics have become increasingly important in Washington, and much policymaking is now done via spending bills, especially large omnibus legislation, which is more common in periods of divided government (Krutz 2001; Mayhew 1991). Since budgeting has become Congress's most important activity, it is reasonable to examine the budgetary process to locate some of the most prominent and recurring consequences of divided control.

Several scholars have noted a link between deficits and divided control of government at the national (Poterba 1994; Schick 1993; cf. Barro 1991) and state levels (Alt and Lowry 1994). The huge increases in budget deficits and the national debt in the 1980s are often attributed to the inability of Republican presidents Ronald Reagan and George Bush to work with stubborn Democratic congresses (McCubbins 1991; Peterson and Rom 1988; Sundquist 1988). According to this argument, both parties wished to spend money in their preferred areas—the military for Republicans and social welfare for the Democrats—without increasing taxes, thus leading to annual deficits and a growing debt. Others dismiss this possibility because many divided governments (such as those in the 1950s and late 1990s) produced surpluses (Fiorina 1996). Indeed, the divided governments produced by the 1994 and 1996 elections drafted the first balanced budget plans in more than 30 years. Until terrorist attacks, a recession, and a large tax cut intervened, the federal government ran generous surpluses based on the spending plan agreed to by the Clinton administration and the Gingrich-Lott Congress.

Though deficits might not be a direct product of divided government, there is evidence that budgetary patterns are more erratic when parties must work together across institutional divides. In particular, federal budgets are more subject to rapid changes under divided government as a result of lack of consensus over budget priorities (Bryan Jones et al. 1997; also see J. Cox, Hager, and Lowery 1993 in terms of budgetary roles). Similarly, there is evidence at the state level that recessions are more likely to lead to deficits when the upper and lower legislative chambers are controlled by different parties (Alt and Lowry 1994). Finally, there is theoretical work indicating that changes in partisan control, particularly divided control, lead to partisan business cycles that alternatively emphasize inflation and unemployment (Alesina and Rosenthal 1995). Thus, several studies suggest that while divided and unified government might not differ significantly in their output during periods of normal politics, economic aberrations and other shocks to the system are better handled by a government controlled by one party than by two.

Accountability

If divided government has undesirable effects on the legislative process and government policy, one obvious question is which party (if any) is blamed for these problems. Here, however, another problem appears. Divided control makes it difficult for citizens to assign responsibility for government performance to one party or the other, causing some confusion and uncertainty for voters (Fiorina 1992; Jacobson 1991; Sundquist 1993; cf. Norpoth 2001). For example, fewer voters know which party controls each chamber of Congress during periods of divided government (Bennett and Bennett 1993; Segura and Nicholson 1999). This confusion and uncertainty appears to depress voter turnout when government is divided (Franklin and Hirczy de Miño 1998).

More importantly, divided government reduces government accountability because voters have difficulty making attributional inferences about the causes of government acts. For example, voters are less likely to punish incumbent governors and state legislators for poor economic conditions when different parties control different branches of state government (Leyden and Borrelli 1995; Lowry, Alt, and Ferree 1998). Voters are better able to reward or punish a party when that party enjoys unified control of government.

The president's party nearly always loses House seats in midterm elections, but divided government conditions this regularity. Divided government helps candidates of the president's party in midterm elections because attribution of blame (and perhaps praise) is difficult (Nicholson and Segura 1999). Over the past 14 midterm elections, the president's party has lost an average of 11 additional House seats when government was unified rather than divided. The 1994 and 1998 midterm elections provide stark examples of this difference. When the Democrats last enjoyed unified control of government, in late 1994, they lost 53 House seats and 7 Senate seats in the midterm elections and became the minority party in Congress. In contrast, the 1998 midterm elections took place against a backdrop of divided government, and the president's party gained five House seats.

Some argue that divided government encourages leaders to be irresponsible since they realize that blame is not likely to be cast solely on them (Sundquist 1988). This remains an open question in our minds, though not an unlikely by-product of divided control. For example, after the budget stalemate and unprecedented government shutdowns in late 1995 and early 1996, public opinion was initially undecided about whether congressional Republicans or the Democratic president bore more responsibility. Though public sentiment eventually turned against the Republicans, it was not obvious a priori that this would occur. The expected lack of accountability might have emboldened both sides, although each side took a chance by resisting compromise in the hopes that the other party would be blamed. A different process defines the good times. When the economy is doing well, the nation is at peace, and neither party is involved in scandal, voters are likely to reward incumbents of both parties by returning them to office on Election Day. Thus, the relationship between accountability and divided government has different effects depending on whether the public acts, in Key's (1966) terms, as a god of vengeance or of reward when voting retrospectively (Downs 1957; Fiorina 1981).

Conclusions about Consequences

This brief review of the consequences of divided government indicates that scholars have appropriately refocused their research questions in this area over time. Instead of asking "Does divided government matter?" we now ask "Under what circumstances and to what degree does divided government matter?" The overly simplistic comparison of unified versus divided government suggests that American national politics is dichotomous in nature, but the electoral and legislative coalitions that make (or do not make) policy in this country are much more complex (see M. Smith 1997 on state welfare policy). Inattention to such subtleties probably explains inconsistent findings in some of the early work on divided government.

To take but one example, some landmark studies of roll-call voting in

Congress found that "party voting" and other forms of partisanship were more intense under unified government (Brady, Cooper, and Hurley 1979; S. Patterson and Caldeira 1988). The argument, based on observation of real-world politics, was that the majority party can be more cohesive when it controls both the executive and legislative branches. In contrast, Rohde (1991) has noted that partisanship increased dramatically in the 1980s despite (or perhaps because of) the presence of conservative Republican presidents and liberal Democratic congressional majorities. Thus, the relationship between divided government and the intensity of partisanship on Capitol Hill is more complex than previously thought. Indeed, a recent divided government swung from the most extreme form of gridlock (government shutdown in 1995 and 1996) to remarkable legislative success (a balanced budget and budgetary surpluses) just a few years later.

Divided government has real consequences for American politics, some of which we have reviewed to demonstrate why the causes of divided government are so important to understand. The degree to which voters are thinking about consequences when casting their ballots gets to the heart of electoral motivation and voter mandates. Whether voters prefer divided or unified government, it is necessary to understand why one or the other is in place at a given time. Though blanket statements about the effects of divided government are not always advisable, some empirical regularities indicate that party control matters in two important ways. First, under divided government, policymaking is less predictable and more conflictual. Second, divided government reduces voters' ability to hold political parties responsible for government performance. That is an unpleasant combination of consequences, even if the flow of legislation is unaffected by party control. If voters are strategically splitting their votes to produce divided government, then perhaps these consequences are intended. If, conversely, ticket splitting and divided government are not the result of strategic voters but the by-products of other forces, then reforms should be considered to reduce the chances of divided government or at least minimize its unintended consequences.

THE VOLATILE NATURE OF AMERICAN POLITICS
Recent elections have dramatically changed the composition of the U.S. national government. The 1992 election brought the first Democratic president in 12 years, yet only 2 years later, Republicans won control of both houses of Congress for the first time in 42 years. But by 1996, in another turnabout, Bill Clinton had recovered sufficiently to win reelec-

tion handily. Two years later, Clinton's Democrats gained congressional seats, an unusual midterm occurrence. Finally, the 2000 elections brought another surprising change. Despite peace and economic prosperity at home and President Clinton's high job-approval ratings, the Republicans took back the White House, though George W. Bush had negative coattails in Congress.

Another sign of volatility is the tremendous amount of turnover in Congress in the past six years. More than half the members of the 104th House of Representatives were first elected in the 1990s. The number of first-time winners in three consecutive House elections in the 1990s is instructive: 110 in 1992, 86 in 1994, and 74 in 1996. This is the largest number of newly elected members entering the House of Representatives since the 1940s (Jacobson 2000b). Finally, the 1992 elections produced a shift in party control of 49 House seats, and more than 55 House seats switched parties as a result of the 1994 elections.

The public popularity of the leaders of both parties more closely resembles a roller-coaster ride than the steady voyage one might imagine for leaders of a relatively long-standing and peaceful democratic nation. For example, President George Bush's approval ratings reached record high levels shortly after the Gulf War before plummeting to extremely low levels before the 1992 election. President Clinton has experienced his own highs and lows in opinion polls, though not of the same amplitude as his predecessor. Even Newt Gingrich and Bob Dole saw their approval ratings drop suddenly and substantially in the span of one year following the Republican ascendance to majority status in Congress (S. Patterson and Kimball 1998).

The leaders of both parties have been humbled by the transitory nature of public approval and electoral success in contemporary American politics. In this climate, elected officials seem unwilling to advocate bold policy changes for fear of overreaching and then suffering at the hands of the voters. Without a booming economy producing greater than anticipated government revenues, one wonders if Republican and Democratic officials could have ever reached an agreement on a balanced budget plan. If more voters displayed party loyalty, the U.S. political system would experience fewer dramatic short-term changes, and politicians might not be so apprehensive about innovative policy proposals.

SWING VOTERS

It is important to understand the reasons for divided voting behavior because doing so will help make sense of the swing voters who are important targets of political campaigns. As Beck (1999, 28) explains, it is common to decompose American voters into "two electorates—one partisan and ideologically polarized, the other nonpartisan, sometimes even antipartisan." Party loyalists can usually be counted on to support the same party in every election, without much stimulation. In contrast, swing or switcher voters are increasingly the focus of sophisticated campaign strategies designed by professional consultants (Goeas and Tringali 1993; Hodgett and Tarr-Whelan 1997; Kitchens and Powell 1994). Most straight-ticket voters are loyal partisans who have generally made their voting decisions long before Election Day, even before the official campaign has started (A. Campbell et al. 1960). Significant campaign resources are devoted to identifying and targeting independent-minded voters who remain undecided as the campaign nears its end (Boyd 1986; De Vries and Tarrance 1972; Key 1966; Maddox and Nimmo 1981). Since the partisan component of the electorate is closely divided between Republicans and Democrats, the swing voters (who often turn out to be ticket splitters) often make the difference in national elections and are the main source of the recent volatility in American electoral politics. Thus, explaining the factors driving divided voting behavior will ultimately lead to a better understanding of the causes of divided government and the sources of electoral volatility in American politics.

OVERVIEW OF THE REST OF THE BOOK

The past decade has produced a flurry of research on ticket splitting and divided government. In chapter 2, we review various theoretical perspectives and empirical evidence on the causes of ticket splitting, and we outline our theory of divided voting. In contrast to those who posit that voters strategically split their votes to balance party control of government, we argue that divided voting is a by-product of other forces, especially the competitiveness of congressional contests and the blurring of ideological differences between the major political parties. Divided government, we argue, is more the sum of many local decisions than a single national mandate for bipartisanship.

Any empirical study of the causes of ticket splitting must begin with accurate estimates of the frequency of this behavior. These estimates must use the congressional district or state as the unit of analysis because these electoral units collectively produce unified or divided government. Variation in split-ticket voting rates across districts cannot be analyzed without such estimates. Earlier studies have used two other approaches. The first relies on aggregate election data but suffers from the well-known "ecological fallacy" that invalidates individual-level inferences from aggregated data. In fact, ecological measures typically underestimate the frequency of ticket splitting and so are biased, a point that we will illustrate in more detail in the next chapter.

A more common approach has been to analyze self-reports of voting behavior from national postelection surveys such as the National Election Study (NES). Survey data are useful for analyzing trends since the 1950s but cannot provide estimates of ticket splitting within districts and states because of the small number of cases drawn from each electoral unit. Surveys are also prone to misreporting problems because of social desirability and other artifacts of the interview process. As an alternative to these two approaches, in chapter 3 we use King's (1997) solution to the ecological inference problem. This approach uses data from election returns, thereby avoiding the misreporting problems of surveys. By using a sophisticated statistical method to draw individual-level inferences from aggregate data, we are working between the individual and aggregate levels. We extend King's basic model to account for voter roll-off in congressional races and use surveys to validate our national estimates. The chapter also highlights the substantial variation in ticket splitting across districts by using several different types of districts as case studies. Later, we conduct parallel ecological and individual-level analyses to allay the concerns of readers who are skeptical of inferences based solely on aggregate data.

Chapter 4 analyzes ticket splitting in presidential and House races, as has been the focus of most work in this area. Using our district-level estimates from every House election from 1952 to 2000, we seek to explain why voters in some districts are much more likely to split their ballots than are voters in other districts. Because we have a time series that begins when ticket splitting became more frequent, we can assess changes in the relative influences of these determinants over time. We begin by showing that the greatest rise in ticket splitting in the 1970s and 1980s results primarily from more voters choosing Republican presidential candidates and Democratic House candidates simultaneously, which we label RD voting. Using this as a dependent variable in several analyses, we find that variation in levels of RD voting across districts can be explained by a simple model. Most ticket splitting occurs because of the relative qualities of the competing congressional campaigns, particularly the amounts of money spent. Also, RD ticket splitting is more likely in districts with Democratic incumbents and in the South. The fact that these district-level variables have remarkable influence suggests that most ticket splitting is the unintended by-product of local factors.

Voters choose candidates from opposite parties not because of the different parties per se but because reasonable reactions to local candidates produce such behavior. We cast considerable doubt on policy balancing theories, which argue that voters consciously split their tickets so that the parties will cooperate to produce moderate policy. Using several measures of candidate and party ideology, we find that voters are not more likely to split their tickets as the candidates move farther apart, as balancing arguments contend. Instead, blurring boundaries between the parties makes cross-party voting more common. In particular, incumbent representatives can encourage ticket splitting by positioning themselves closer to the policy preferences of the opposite party. Estimating separate regression equations for each election year in our data set, we find a striking pattern: the effect of incumbency has grown over time, while regional effects have waned. An understanding of the literature on congressional elections thus moves a long way toward understanding the causes of divided government.

Chapter 5 turns to a broader definition of divided voting across presidential and midterm congressional elections. As other scholars have reported, divided governments before the 1980s were usually produced in midterms. The regular loss of House seats by the president's party sometimes resulted in divided control, though single-party government was often restored in the next presidential election. This pattern is probably not intentional, as we have defined it, because many other factors shape midterm voting. Midterm elections have historically been more likely to produce divided government and have been explained using theories associated with "surge and decline" and "strategic politicians." Using the new ecological inference technique on transition tables, we assess the number of voters who switch parties when voting in presidential and then midterm elections. While we still find little support for the notion that ticket splitting is intentional, rates are much higher in midterm elections, when voters have further dissociated presidential and congressional elections.

Though ticket splitting in House elections is the focus of most studies, a puzzle remains at the senatorial level. In House races, the incumbency advantage underlies most vote defection and thus most ticket splitting. This should not be the case in senatorial elections, where incumbency is less potent and seats are more vigorously contested. Yet the number of divided state delegations—states with senators of different parties—rose dramatically in the 1970s and 1980s, only to fall in the 1990s. To understand this behavior more thoroughly, in chapter 6 we estimate levels of ticket splitting across all president-Senate races from 1952 to 1996, as we did with the House. There we find that incumbency and the South play small roles in determining RD ticket splitting, if only because the Senate was Republican controlled during the height of divided government in the 1980s. Most important again is campaign spending, which serves as a cue as to the quality of the candidates. Further, we find no evidence that voters are intentionally balancing within Senate delegations.

The final chapter of the book briefly summarizes our findings into a more coherent framework for understanding ticket splitting theoretically. We highlight the abrupt shifts from RD government in the early 1990s to unified Democratic control in 1993 to the reverse DR pattern in 1995. We explore what these changes mean for government responsibility, political realignments, and the maintenance of political parties. We also forecast the frequency of split-ticket voting in the future and the likelihood of divided government during an era in which ideological differences between the two major parties have sharpened.

Explaining Divided Voter Behavior

The prevalence of divided government in recent decades and concerns about its consequences have prompted scholars to attempt to explain its causes. These theorists can be separated into two groups: (1) those arguing that citizens strategically split their votes to create divided party control of government, and (2) those arguing that structural features of American elections, as well as short-term electoral forces, both of which have nothing to do with voters' motivations, account for the presence of divided government. For the latter group, divided government occurs "accidentally," a by-product of the peculiar features of the American political system and its campaigns rather than a purposeful effort to make divided government. For the former group, voters—or at least some voters—intentionally create divided government. The following sections review what these arguments say about divided voting behavior.

STRUCTURAL EXPLANATIONS

Many explanations of divided voting note that structural features of American elections make it relatively easy for citizens to split their votes between the major political parties. These explanations usually begin by pointing to the constitutional separation of powers in the United States. By separately electing executives and legislators, there is always a chance (depending on the relative abilities of the candidates, the relevant national and local issues, and the strength of competing parties) that the collective outcome of an election is divided government. By comparison, divided outcomes like these are simply not possible in pure parliamentary systems because the major party (or coalition) runs government from the legislature. In addition, the United States has staggered terms for different offices. Midterm congressional elections, which lack presidential races, often produce different results than do presidential elections. The midterm

17

SPRING CREEK CAMPUS

electorate is smaller and more partisan than the electorate in presidential elections (A. Campbell 1960; J. Campbell 1993; cf. Jacobson 1992; Sigelman and Jewell 1986; Wolfinger, Rosenstone, and McIntosh 1981), and (with notable exceptions, as in 1998) the president's party almost always loses seats in midterm elections. Thus, it should not come as a surprise that divided government is more common in countries with staggered elections and terms for different offices (Shugart 1995).[1] As recent American national elections have demonstrated, consecutive presidential and midterm elections often occur under different conditions, with quite different results.

Another systemic factor is the Australian ballot, a state-controlled voting mechanism that provides voters with anonymity. The Australian ballot was instituted in most states at the end of the nineteenth century, and like some other Progressive reforms, the new ballot reduced the intimidating power of party machines and made it easier for voters to eschew straight party ballots (Rusk 1970). Prior to the ballot reform, political parties provided the ballots, and a voter had little choice but to select an entire slate of party candidates. The Australian ballot listed candidates of all parties on one ballot, allowing voters to choose candidates from different parties. The opportunity was only slowly exploited by voters, a majority of whom has always cast straight tickets. Though all states have now moved to government-produced ballots, some still facilitate straight party voting by providing a ballot device allowing voters to cast a straight party ballot in one stroke. Voters in states where the ballot offers a straight party option are less likely to split their tickets than citizens in states that do not provide a straight party mechanism (Burden and Kimball 1998; A. Campbell and Miller 1957; McAllister and Darcy 1992). We find some evidence for this argument in our analyses, though political factors outweigh these structural design issues.

A number of structural arguments try to explain long-term Republican dominance of presidential elections and Democratic control of Congress (neither of which seems now to hold true). For example, some explanations of the recent Democratic grip on the House of Representatives point to gerrymandering (J. Campbell 1996) and incumbency advantages in securing campaign financing and media access, in providing constituency service, and in availability of office perks. However, several pieces of evidence cast doubt on the notion that the Democrats enjoy an unfair advantage in House elections (Fiorina 1992; Gelman and King 1990; Jacobson 1992; Lockerbie 1999). First, the gerrymander thesis is discredited by the fact that Republicans received fewer total House votes than Democrats in every election from 1952 to 1992 (Fiorina 1992).[2] Moreover, Democrats outperformed Republicans in open-seat contests during the same period (Jacobson 1990b). In contrast, Fiorina (1992, 1994) argues that the trend toward professionalized state legislatures helps explain the relative weakness of Republican legislative candidates. As the argument goes, citizen legislatures are more attractive to Republicans because they allow one to serve without giving up a lucrative career (which is more often found among potential Republican candidates). To use the economic terminology, Republicans face higher opportunity costs than do Democrats when putting careers on hold to serve in a professionalized legislature that requires full-time participation.[3]

One might also turn to the executive branch for explanations. Some suggest that the Republicans are more successful at winning the presidency because they are better able to minimize intraparty conflict at the nomination stage (Mayer 1996; Wattenberg 1991a, 1991b). The Republican coalition is more homogeneous, and Republicans select more of their convention delegates through a winner-take-all process, which means that the party's nomination tends to be clinched earlier in the primary season. This allows the GOP nominee to sets his sights on the general election before the Democratic nominee does. However, divisive primaries are usually caused by poor candidates, unfavorable national conditions, or salient controversial issues (Wattenberg 1991a, 1991b).[4] In short, though asymmetries in the divisiveness of party nominations might not directly cause divided government, differences in presidential candidate success are probably a contributing factor.

To some degree, divided government occurs by design. The American constitutional system was created with several checks and balances to prevent one group from imposing its will on the rest of the country—what James Madison called the "mischiefs of faction" (*Federalist Papers*, no. 10). These same checks and balances often thwart one-party dominance. However, the U.S. electoral system makes divided voting possible, not probable. The current electoral system (including a popularly elected Senate) has been in place since the early twentieth century, yet divided government did not occur regularly until the 1950s and did not become the norm until the 1970s and 1980s. The government's formal structure has not changed, but its campaigns and elections have. It is still necessary to explain why voters increasingly took advantage of the system to split their votes between the two major political parties and why fewer have done so in the last ten years.

Ultimately, the voters select the government. It is no accident that the postwar period of divided government coincides with a surge in split-ticket voting, though we will argue that the relationship between the two phenomena is not as direct as is commonly assumed. Ticket splitters are still a clear minority of voters, although they play a pivotal role in determining the partisan configuration of government. While structural features of the American electoral system make divided voting possible, a sufficient theory of divided government must provide an explanation of voter attitudes and motivations as well as other short-term features of election campaigns that produce divided voting behavior.

SHORT-TERM ELECTORAL FORCES

A class of explanations emphasize short-term forces that vary from one campaign to the next. These forces produce divided voting behavior independently of any individual motivation or desire for divided government. In particular, these explanations focus on campaign issues and candidate qualities as important factors.

For example, Petrocik's (1991) "issue ownership" thesis begins with the premise that each party has a reputation for handling certain issues well and others not so well (see also Petrocik and Doherty 1996). Democrats might be viewed by the public as the better party to address unemployment and health care, while Republicans may be viewed as better at handling crime and national security. Ticket splitting then occurs when the salient issues in the presidential campaign advantage one party while the salient (usually local) issues in congressional campaigns favor the opposite party. Which issues the parties dominate might vary considerably over time (Downs 1957; Norpoth and Buchanan 1992). This explanation does not require voters to desire divided government but merely to choose the candidate whom they favor on the most salient campaign issues. The argument relies on current national and local conditions as well as candidates' ability to raise particular issues successfully and distance themselves from their national party.

This argument differs only in subtle ways from Jacobson's (1990b) notion of "institutional matching," which posits that voters tend to favor Republican presidents because GOP strengths—in economics and foreign policy—conveniently match the qualities expected in a strong president. Similarly, Democrats excel at distributive and social welfare issues such as education and the environment, so their issue emphases are more likely to match the institutional expectations for members of the House of Representatives. We shall subsequently return to the topic of institutional matching.

DIVIDED VOTING AND PARTISAN DECLINE

Studies that locate split-ticket voting within the recent era of partisan decline place more emphasis on candidate features than on issues as the relevant short-term forces producing divided voting. Many scholars focus on performance-based evaluations of presidential and congressional candidates as crucial aspects of the voting decision. Thus, many by-product explanations of divided voting start by noting the decline of party attachments in the electorate. Flagging party loyalty enables candidate traits, events, and other short-term forces to influence the voting decision.

Advances in media coverage and campaign technology, reduced party control over nomination procedures, and an increased focus on constituency service have helped produce a candidate-centered politics in which voter attachments to parties are weaker than in earlier times (Cain, Ferejohn, and Fiorina 1987; Jennings and Markus 1984; Norpoth and Rusk 1982; Wattenberg 1998). The party-decline perspective views split-ticket voting and divided government as two among many indicators of partisan dealignment (Burnham 1970; Nie, Verba, and Petrocik 1976; Wattenberg 1998). As figure 1.1 showed, between 1950 and 1980 presidential coattails diminished as election results within the same constituency for presidential and subpresidential contests became more independent of one another (Beck 1997; Cummings 1966; Ferejohn and Calvert 1984; Wattenberg 1998), although presidential coattails have grown stronger in the 1990s (Jacobson 2001).[5] Both split-ticket voting rates and the number of split districts—where the presidential candidate of the winning House candidate's party did not carry a plurality—increased drastically over much of the postwar era. It is important to keep in mind that ticket splitting has not increased monotonically over time even though the last clear realignment in the 1930s continues to move further into the past. The decline of mass party attachments removes a barrier to split-ticket voting, but other forces are also needed to provide the impetus for ticket splitting.[6]

Abundant evidence shows that ticket splitting is abetted by weakened party attachments (Beck et al. 1992; A. Campbell and Miller 1957; Garand and Lichtl 2000; Maddox and Nimmo 1981; McAllister and Darcy 1992; Soss and Cannon 1995; Sigelman, Wahlbeck, and Buell 1997).

Strong partisans are simply less likely to split their ballots than are independents and weak partisans. The link between strength of partisanship and ticket splitting receives circumstantial support from the fact that president-House ticket splitting increased at the same time the proportion of strong partisans in the electorate declined.[7] Weaker partisan ties in the electorate enable other short-term forces to play a bigger role in voter decision making.

One important short-term factor in voting decisions involves the experience, resources, personalities, and other traits of the candidates. This is reflected in the widely varying levels of competition in congressional races. The presidential campaign offers two visible candidates, so lack of competition is uncommon in presidential races.[8] Most party identifiers who split their tickets do so by defecting from their identified party in congressional races (Brody, Brady, and Heitshusen 1994; Kimball 1997), so any study of divided voting should focus on congressional elections. The least competitive congressional races feature unopposed candidates. In districts where a congressional candidate runs unopposed, voters of the opposite party must either defect and vote for the unopposed candidate or leave that part of the ballot blank. As a result voters will split their ballots simply because their party did not field candidates for every office on the ballot (Bloom 1994).

A less extreme example of unbalanced competition involves incumbency. Incumbents often face weak, unknown opponents in House elections, partly as a result of the officeholders' ability to raise early campaign money to scare off quality challengers (Box-Steffensmeier 1996). Consequently, partisan defections in House elections are skewed toward the incumbent by a substantial margin (Mann and Wolfinger 1980). Thus, voters might divide their votes simply because their party's candidate is running against an entrenched incumbent. Not surprisingly, split-ticket voting is more common in districts with incumbents running (Alvarez and Schousen 1993; Born 1994; Burden and Kimball 1998; Garand and Lichtl 2000; McAllister and Darcy 1992). Thus, several recent studies of divided voting merely include a measure of incumbency to account for candidate quality in congressional races (Born 2000a, 2000b; Forgette and Platt 1999; Mebane 2000; Scheve and Tomz 1999).

However, something is missed when incumbency is accepted as the sole explanation for why citizens might cross party lines to cast split ballots. Incumbency is a blunt measure of the level of competition in House contests, because some incumbents face strong challengers while others face relatively unknown challengers and still others face no opponent at all.

We will later consider more precise indicators of the level of competition or intensity in congressional elections, which prove to be powerful predictors of divided voting. Because these factors' explanatory power outweighs incumbency, we are further convinced that not solely incumbency per se but candidate quality induces divided voting.

Other evidence links ticket splitting more directly to voter evaluations of candidate qualities and name recognition. For example, when the most visible candidates in different races come from different parties, voters are more likely to split their ballots (Beck et al. 1992). Similarly, voters who distinguish candidates and their issue positions from party stereotypes are more likely to split ballots (Soss and Canon 1995). More generally, voters who report a heavier reliance on candidate factors as the basis for voting decisions are more likely to split tickets (DeVries and Tarrance 1972; Maddox and Nimmo 1981).[9]

Finally, voters who are cross-pressured by some combination of issue positions, party identification, and candidate evaluations are likely ticket splitters (Brody, Brady, and Heitshusen 1994; A. Campbell and Miller 1957; Mattei and Howes 2000; McAllister and Darcy 1994). A voter who prefers the issues associated with one party might also be attracted to a candidate of the opposite party because of nonpolicy considerations such as personal history or government experience. In addition, partisans whose issue preferences differ from their party's platform—for example, a hawkish Democrat or a pro-choice Republican—are often likely to split their ballots (Brody, Brady, and Heitshusen 1994). In national elections, ticket splitting usually results when an effective congressional candidate exploits such cross-pressures by appealing to voters of the opposite party (Mattei and Howes 2000, 405n.15).

Election campaigns are contests of competing candidates and messages. In separate races, candidates from different parties often enjoy substantial advantages in name recognition and the ability to reach voters. Advantages in campaign spending, incumbency, electoral experience, career history, and the like are often critical in local elections. As a result, sincere voters who simply look for the "best" candidate in each contest could find themselves casting a split ballot in the absence of any strategic motive to produce divided government.

Policy Balancing

In contrast to the accidental, candidate-centered explanations of divided voting, some theorists argue that citizens purposefully divide their votes to achieve specific policy outcomes or representational arrangements. This

view holds that voters are more government oriented than candidate oriented because their main concern is with the overall composition of the
government after the election is over. Voters think about multiple races
simultaneously rather than considering each office in relative isolation.
This reasoning is neatly summed up by the following voter: "I've liked having split control in Washington, D.C.," said Susan LaFramboise, an insur-
ance adjuster from Poulsbo, Washington. "I just think you get a little more
well-rounded vote on things" (Verhovek 2000).

A prominent explanation for divided voting behavior is that some citizens purposefully vote for divided government to balance party control of
the government and achieve policy moderation (Alesina and Rosenthal
1989, 1995; Fiorina 1992, 1996; Ingberman and Villani 1993; Lacy and
Niou 1998; Lacy and Paolino 1998; Mebane 2000; Scheve and Tomz
1999; C. Smith et al. 1999; Tarrance and DeVries 1998). We label this
explanation "policy balancing." Policy balancing explanations of divided
government recently have gained in standing. Among political scientists,
Alesina and Rosenthal (1995), Fiorina (1992, 1996), and Mebane (2000)
have made the strongest defenses of this explanation. For example,
Alesina and Rosenthal argue that "middle-of-the-road voters seek to balance the president by reinforcing in Congress the party not holding the
White House. This balancing leads, always, to relatively moderate policies
and, frequently, to divided government" (1995, 8).

A balancing, government-oriented approach to voting is most common
among economists. More than half of the 60 leading U.S. macroecono-
mists surveyed shortly before the 1996 election wanted divided government to continue (*Economist* 1996). Though we suspect that a minority of
political scientists would feel the same way, some voters clearly endorse
this view as well. Following the 1996 presidential election, Albert Bersticker of Cleveland concluded, "I'm glad Republicans kept the House and
Senate. It forces Clinton to be less liberal and the Republicans to be less
conservative" (Gleckman 1996). Of course, accepting the outcome of an
election once it is known is quite different than pursuing that same outcome before the election has taken place.

Journalists and other political observers have joined the policy-balancing
camp. Many reacted to the 1996 election by concluding that voters wanted
to perpetuate divided government.[10] Two eminent political pundits, Robert
Samuelson and David Broder, reached the following conclusions.

> Divided government is no accident. It may be the only way voters can
> retain some control over their leaders. . . . If you don't trust either

party fully—and may share some views of both—you can hope that forcing them to bargain will create policies closer to your preferences than having either party dominate. . . . This best describes, I think, what happened in 1996." (Samuelson 1996)

[T]he voters reelected the Republican Congress to keep the pressure on Washington to balance the budget within the next few years. They put Clinton back in office in order to see that his priorities—which are also their priorities—remain at the top of the list. (Broder 1996; see also Tarrance and De Vries 1998)

Even politicians have suggested that voters want divided government. Representative Jim Leach (R-IA) has observed that "there is an instinct in the American body politic to favor checks and balances" (quoted in Sundquist 1993, 9). In the 1996 elections, many Republican congressional candidates campaigned on the idea that they would serve as a check on President Clinton (Berke 1996). In the final week of the campaign, the Republican Party aired the controversial "crystal ball" television advertisement, which conceded the presidential race to Clinton and urged viewers to vote for Republican congressional candidates to keep an eye on Clinton. As noted earlier, President Clinton defended his less-than-forceful campaign efforts on behalf of other Democratic candidates by arguing that the American public sometimes prefers to have one party control Congress while the other party holds the White House (Broder 1996).

Even William Safire delighted on the eve of the 2000 election that "conflicted" voters like himself have great opportunities to act purposefully in creating divided government. He advised voters to do just this. Fortunately, he noted, "our system offers us an opportunity to hedge our bets. . . . It's called splitting your ticket." He goes on:

If the lurch to the right or the left troubles you, don't participate in it. Instead, vote for a Republican president and Democratic Congress, or vice versa. Splitting the difference creates as much energy as splitting the atom. . . . Make the deals that keep the nation's legislative battles between the 35-yard lines. Resist the tyranny of the majority. If the nation's course is to be changed, it should be eased around gently, not yanked about by a party and an executive all too sure of themselves. (Safire 2000)

Policy-balancing explanations for divided voting clearly have captured the imaginations of many important political observers, yet it is crucial to point out an alternative, although related, hypothesis that is consistent with intentionality but for different microlevel reasons. Some scholars argue that people split their votes in sincere attempts to select the closest candidates on an ideological spectrum (Frymer 1994; Frymer, Kim, and Bimes 1997; Grofman et al. 2000). A common example is a moderately conservative voter in the South who votes for a Republican presidential candidate (instead of a liberal Democrat) and a moderately conservative Democrat for the House (instead of a very conservative Republican). This is sincere voting rather than strategic balancing, even though the two opposing processes yield similar outcomes. In the 1970s and 1980s, split-ticket voting was most common in the South because Democratic candidates for Congress have been able to position themselves near the conservative end of the ideological spectrum, while Democratic nominees for president often fail to do the same. The important point is that voters might split their ballots for ideological reasons that have nothing to do with a desire for divided government. Without knowledge of candidate locations, however, the two explanations are often observationally equivalent.

Empirical support for the balancing model is scattered. One piece of supportive evidence is the consistent finding (notwithstanding the 1998 elections) that the president's party loses seats in Congress in midterm elections (Alesina and Rosenthal 1989; Erikson 1988). However, other nonbalancing explanations (such as the increased motivation of voters with negative evaluations of the president) can account for this empirical regularity.[11] There is additional evidence that moderates are more likely to split their ballots than are ideological extremists (Fiorina 1996; Garand and Lichtl 2000; McAlister and Darcy 1992; cf. Alvarez and Schousen 1993; Bloom 1994; Born 1994; Brody, Brady, and Heitshusen 1994). This, however, does not prove that moderate voters split their ballots strategically to produce divided government and middle-of-the-road policies.[12]

Several studies have used individual-level survey data to identify voters with the motivation to engage in policy-balancing behavior. Many of these attempts have failed to find evidence supporting policy-balancing theory (Alvarez and Schousen 1993; Beck et al. 1992; Born 1994; Forgette and Platt 1999; Kimball 1997; Mattei and Howes 2000; Petrocik and Doherty 1996; Sigelman, Wahlbeck, and Buell 1997; Soss and Canon 1995). Others, however, find that expectations about party control of one branch can motivate voters to support the other party in other races (Lacy and Paolino 1998; Mebane 2000; Scheve and Tomz 1999; C. Smith et al. 1999).[13] Examinations of the relationship between party polarization and ticket splitting in recent elections produce evidence that is hard to square with the balancing model: voters who perceive sharp differences between the parties are least likely to split their ballots (Born 1994; Garand and Lichtl 2000; Kimball 1997; Mattei and Howes 2000; Petrocik and Doherty 1996; Soss and Canon 1995). However, it is likely that loyal and ideologically extreme partisans are the ones who perceive the greatest policy differences between the two parties.

If ticket splitters are politically sophisticated, as the policy-balancing theory requires, one would expect that interest in politics should be positively associated with ticket splitting. However, some evidence suggests a positive relationship (Maddox and Nimmo 1981), some indicates a negative relationship (Born 1994; A. Campbell and Miller 1957), and still other evidence finds no relationship at all (Garand and Lichtl 2000). Using demographic and attitudinal variables as proxies for sophistication have not succeeded in depicting split-ticket voters as particularly attentive and interested in politics.

The policy-balancing model also offers a crucial prediction: ticket splitting should increase with party polarization. Fiorina goes so far as to call this "probably the most important point" in his balancing argument. "When the parties are relatively close, near the center of gravity of the electorate, ticket splitting declines. When the parties move away from each other . . . they open up a large policy range in which ticket splitting is the voter response" (1996, 81).

Thus, policy balancing theory clearly predicts that ticket splitting is more common when there is greater ideological distance between the two political parties and their candidates. On the surface it seems illogical for moderate voters to prefer extreme candidates, but the balancing intuition makes it plausible. The more that candidates offer "choices," the more voters prefer an "echo." It seems to explain, for example, that ticket splitting and divided government were common in the 1980s precisely because Republicans and Democrats were so ideologically distinct.

We examine this hypothesis in more detail and find that the opposite actually holds—ticket splitting is more common when the political parties converge toward the middle of the ideological spectrum. In other words, it is easier for voters to cross party lines when they do not have to travel far along the ideological spectrum.

The balancing model has also been used to explain the rising number of split U.S. Senate delegations (Alesina, Fiorina, and Rosenthal 1994; Fiorina 1992; Lacy and Niou 1998). Again, the evidence appears mixed. One study finds that senators running for reelection receive a larger share of the vote when the sitting senator is from the opposite party, even after controlling for other variables (Schmidt, Kenny, and Morton 1996). However, a separate study finds that the party of the sitting senator does not affect the outcome in contested Senate races (Segura and Nicholson 1995).[14]

The Senate studies point out a conceptual puzzle in policy-balancing explanations for divided voting behavior. Are voters trying to produce divided government or simply divided representation? Put differently, are voters trying to balance party control of different branches of government, or are they trying to balance the policy positions of their elected representatives in Washington? Balancing theories generally posit the former rather than the latter, although voters have more influence over the latter than the former. Voting for senators from different parties will help produce divided representation, but it will not create divided government as it is traditionally defined.

There are also theoretical reasons why strategic balancing is unlikely. Here we note just some of the arguments that challenge the notion of policy balancing. First, when parties (or candidates) offer voters similar platforms, voters are apt to rely on nonideological considerations such as candidate traits, which are likely more evenly distributed across the parties than are candidate policy positions. Naturally, when voters choose on the basis of candidates rather than parties or issues, the chances of ticket splitting are likely to increase. That is, when the electorate is presented with ideological "echoes" rather than "choices," voters must turn to nonideological dimensions of candidate evaluation because policy differences are no longer useful for distinguishing candidates (Key 1966; Page 1978).

Second, when political parties are close ideologically, it is easier for candidates to steal issue positions typically held by the other party. Downs (1957) points out that parties in a two-party system are motivated to equivocate and allow their platforms to overlap to attract as many voters as possible, recalling the "issue ownership" and "issue trespassing" notions introduced earlier. Conversely, when parties polarize, candidates will have more difficulty credibly making crossover appeals to voters from the other party, so divided voting probably decreases.

Finally, Fiorina and other proponents of balancing are not necessarily wrong in stating that some voters wish to balance the parties. Rather, balancing-oriented voters who resist the deterrents discussed previously are probably few in number and can seldom act on their wishes. Real-world constraints, particularly the uncompetitive nature of many congressional districts, hinder voters' ability to pursue a balancing strategy even if they desire to do so.

Matching Institutional Responsibilities with Party Strengths
Another strategic explanation of split-ticket voting argues that different offices elicit different criteria for voting decisions, although it is similar to the balancing model in that voters weigh the policies and competencies of the two parties. As has already been explained briefly, Jacobson (1990b, 1991) proposes that voters split their ballots to resolve conflicting preferences for expensive government programs and low taxes (for a similar argument using a formal theory framework, see Zupan 1991). Split-ticket voting tends to feature Republican executives and Democratic legislatures because voters match party strengths with perceived institutional responsibilities. Specifically, voters tend to look to the Republican Party to manage the economy (in terms of efficiency and low taxes) and foreign affairs. However, the Democratic Party is better at ensuring distributional fairness, protecting programs from spending cuts, and dealing with the unintended consequences of the market system. Meanwhile, voters want the president to impose some collective responsibility on the federal government because they tend to hold him responsible for national problems, such as the economy and foreign policy. Conversely, people expect Congress to look out for the little people by taking care of particularized problems and distributing local benefits. Jacobson (1990b) argues that acting on such contradictory values allows voters to have their cake and eat it too.

Though the coupling of a Democratic president and Republican Congress in the 1990s discredits institutional-matching theory, there is some evidence to support the more flexible issue-ownership argument. For example, the 1994 congressional elections seemed to hinge on issues such as crime, taxes, and welfare reform, which are more amenable to Republican candidates. However, one problem with the issue-ownership explanation is that congressional campaigns are often devoid of issues (Jacobson 1992; Mann and Wolfinger 1980). In addition, candidates' ability to thrive on issues "owned" by the opposite party (as Bill Clinton has with crime, trade, and welfare reform and George W. Bush has with Social Security and education) weakens the theory's applicability (Norpoth and Buchanan 1992). Our explanation for divided voting behavior, discussed subsequently, will pay closer attention to the qualities and resources of individual candidates, particularly at the congressional level.

Jacobson provides some aggregate opinion data to support each of the four claims about public perceptions of the parties and branches of the federal government. However, polls often show that public images of the parties and their relative advantages in handling particular problems vary over time, depending on the performance of the government (also a weakness of the issue-ownership thesis). For example, in May and June 1995, the Republican Party was seen as better at handling the budget deficit. By the end of the year, however (in the midst of government shutdowns), a healthy plurality chose the Democratic Party as the best at handling the deficit (Saad 1995).

It is true that different issues are associated with voting decisions in presidential and House campaigns (Alvarez and Schousen 1993; Morgan 1995; Petrocik 1991, 1996). Performance evaluations associated with presidential elections tend to gravitate toward national issues such as the economy and foreign policy (Fiorina 1981; Miller, Wattenberg, and Melanchuk 1986). At the same time, the role of national issues in congressional elections has decreased, while constituency service and district benefits have become more important (Cain, Ferejohn, and Fiorina 1987; Fiorina 1989). Also, voters tend to view their own representative as closer to the ideological middle than the representative's party is (Brady 1993). Thus, congressional incumbents are often able to separate themselves from their party's positions on national issues (Fiorina 1989; Mayhew 1974).

However, no evidence has yet demonstrated that individual voters who hold the required mix of conflicting preferences and perceptions of the parties split their tickets more often than others. More importantly, Jacobson's model fails to account for instances where voters elect a Democratic executive and a Republican legislature, a pattern seen at the national level and in several states during the 1990s.

Voter Alienation

A weaker form of the balancing thesis, the governmental degeneration hypothesis, argues that voters split their tickets because they do not trust either party with complete control of the levers of power (Fiorina 1992, 1996). People who are disenchanted by corruption, greed, and incompetence among U.S. politicians divide votes to create stalemate so that neither party can use the government for corrupt ends. In this formulation, public cynicism or alienation does not derive from ideological considerations or policy positions. Citizens who do not trust either party with the full reins of power may divide their votes with the hope that each party will check the worst habits of the other.

The recent cohabitation of high levels of public cynicism about politics with continued divided government has attracted scholars to the voter alienation hypothesis. For example, a text on the 1996 elections states,

> The venerable American concepts of separation of powers and checks and balances have taken such a hold in the American political culture that we have apparently come to accept divided government as the best guarantee against abuse of power by one party. In fact, a political culture that exhibits ever-increasing levels of political distrust toward elected officials and alienation from the political system might also be expected to show high levels of comfort with divided government. (Jackson 1997, 44)

However, this idea has not been extensively tested, and most attempts to do so have failed. Some measures of alienation and distrust correlate with higher rates of ticket splitting (Born 1994; Fiorina 1992; Garand and Lichtl 2000); others do not. There is apparently no relationship between measures of political efficacy and ticket splitting (Alvarez and Schousen 1993; Born 1994, 2000b; Garand and Lichtl 2000; Mattei and Howes 2000). Furthermore, there is little evidence of any relationship between the familiar National Election Study (NES) "trust in government" items and ticket splitting (Born 1994; Jacobson 1991; Mattei and Howes 2000; cf. Garand and Lichtl 2000).[15]

Summary

The foregoing discussion should make clear that there are many potential reasons why citizens divide their votes between the two major parties. Many of these alternative explanations emanate from fundamentally different premises. Competing explanations of divided voting differ in the assumed level of information the voter possesses. At one extreme, theories emphasizing party identification, ballot format, and candidate name recognition require relatively little information about policy positions when voting choices are made. At the other extreme, policy balancing explanations assume that voters roughly know the ideological center of gravity in each party, the party affiliation of each candidate, and which party controls each branch of national government. Somewhere in between, models of sincere proximity voting assume that voters know something about the policy positions of the competing candidates.

Our approach to this subject begins with the premise that voting decisions are influenced by forces at three levels of aggregation. National forces (the state of the national economy, presidential performance, and most importantly for us, the relative ideological positions of the major political parties) shape voting choices. At another level, contest-specific forces (campaign resources, issue positions, and other traits of competing candidates) influence voting decisions. Finally, at the level of individual voters, several political attitudes and perceptions (especially toward the two parties) are important factors.

In the existing literature on ticket splitting and causes of divided government, individual-level factors have been subjected to the closest scrutiny, contest-specific factors have been less carefully scrutinized, and national forces have been almost neglected. Several studies demonstrate that candidate quality (especially incumbency) fosters ticket splitting. We argue that it is necessary to move beyond incumbency and consider other candidate characteristics (especially campaign spending and issue positions) that often induce ticket splitting. In addition, several studies indicate that political parties in national government have become more homogeneous and distinct from one another in ideological terms over the last twenty years (Poole and Rosenthal 1997; Rohde 1991). Aside from policy-balancing theories, studies of ticket splitting have not considered the implications of changes in party positions.

In addition, we argue that forces at all three levels of aggregation interact to produce ticket splitting. As indicated previously, candidate traits such as name recognition and personal appeal often induce ticket splitting. However, we believe that voters who blur or ignore policy differences between the political parties are most influenced by such candidate traits. Thus, when more voters come to believe that there are no significant policy differences between the parties, the number of potential ticket splitters increases.

Voters' perceptions of the major parties do not form in a vacuum but arise in response to the recorded positions of each party's elected officials and platform. As we show in chapter 7, as the national parties have moved farther apart on the ideological spectrum, the number of voters who see important differences between the parties has increased substantially. As a result, more voters today are apt to rely on ideological considerations than did so in the early 1970s, when ideological distinctions between the parties were more ambiguous. There is empirical evidence to support this view of issue voting. When competing candidates offer similar or ambiguous policy proposals, voters often rely on character assessments and personal traits of candidates (Asher 1988; Page 1978). In contrast, ideological con-

siderations have a stronger influence on vote choice when opposing can-
didates take clear and contrasting policy positions (Abramowitz 1981; A.
Campbell et al. 1960; Downs 1957; Page 1978; Wright 1978; Wright and
Berkman 1986).

In sum, Key's "echo chamber" metaphor for the electorate guides us in
understanding divided voting behavior. Key states that "as candidates and
parties clamor for attention and vie for popular support, the people's verdict can be no more than a selective reflection from among the alternatives
and outlooks presented to them" (Key 1966, 2). When political parties
move apart on the ideological spectrum and offer more meaningful
choices, voters respond by selecting one of the parties across several different races. When the parties and their candidates move toward the ideological center and blur their differences, the response from the electorate is
often equally vague: ticket splitting and divided government. Clarity from
the parties begets clarity from the voters; confusion begets confusion. Thus,
as we illustrate in chapter 6, it is no surprise that the highest rates of ticket
splitting occurred in the 1970s, when ideological distance between the parties was at its smallest. In addition, the recent decline in ticket splitting
coincides with the national parties' renewed ideological polarization.

Explanations of divided voting and divided government have aggregate
and individual-level predictions. Even though the aggregate implications
of ticket splitting (states and districts with split results in different races)
form the building blocks of divided government, most studies examine
divided voting only at the individual level (cf. Grofman et al. 2000). We
aim to correct this oversight by focusing more on the aggregate implications of divided voting.

A NEW APPROACH TO THE
STUDY OF TICKET SPLITTING

Most academics study voting behavior by sifting through survey data.
Much can certainly be learned from survey data, and we also rely on them
to better understand electoral behavior. However, there is an important
disadvantage in basing conclusions solely on analyses of survey data. For
the most part, those who examine survey data, where the individual is the
unit of analysis, tend to restrict their search exclusively to individual-level
explanations for human behavior. What this means for research on ticket
splitting and divided government is that most studies focus on individual
characteristics that lead some voters to split their ballots. For example, sur-

vey-based studies examine whether ticket splitters prefer divided government or whether ticket splitters have weak psychological attachments to a
political party.

In contrast, journalists and pundits rely on national election results and
thus gravitate toward nationwide forces, such as election mandates, to
explain election outcomes. When the 1996 election produced divided
government, many pundits simply reasoned that the voters must have
wanted it that way. This is a circular argument and a misleading way to
look for voter mandates. In fact, even in elections that produce divided
government, straight-ticket voters remain a huge majority, even among
those who say they prefer divided government (Petrocik and Doherty
1996).

While individual characteristics and national trends are important,
local contextual factors that help explain why people split their tickets
have been lost. Specifically, more attention should be paid to the nature of
the candidates running for Congress in each state and district.[16] From this
perspective, divided government is accidental, at least on the part of voters. Survey data have uncovered the fact that most people split their ballots by defecting from the party they typically support in the congressional
contest (Brody, Brady, and Heitshusen 1994; Kimball 1997). This leads us
to suspect that some voters split their ballots simply because they do not
have an appealing choice in the congressional contest.

Based on rich literature on congressional elections, several characteristics of the congressional contest might well explain this unintentional
form of ticket splitting. First, there will be no contest at all in some districts. If a Republican voter resides in a district where the Republican
Party does not field a congressional candidate, the voter would have little
choice but to select the Democrat or abstain from voting in that race. This
is not a trivial point, because roughly 70 House seats (15 percent of the
total) were uncontested in each election in the 1980s; during the 1960s
and 1970s, the number of uncontested House seats was closer to 50, still
more than 10 percent of all races (Wrighton and Squire 1997).

Second, in contested races, candidate quality can be compared by measuring the amount of money spent on the campaign. A campaign is a contest of competing messages, and congressional candidates spend most of
the money they raise on some form of advertising. Candidates who spend
a lot more money than their opponents are likely to be more visible to voters, who will be more familiar with the richer candidates' messages. Again,
voters often choose a candidate from the opposite party in congressional

contests because the nominee from their own party is relatively unknown and spends little money on the campaign. This is also not a trivial point— in most House races, one candidate outspends the other by at least a two-to-one margin (after excluding uncontested races). Money is important because it buys access to voters, from candidate travel to staff salaries to mass mailings to television advertisements. The importance of candidate quality and spending in congressional elections has been thoroughly documented (Jacobson 2001; Mann and Wolfinger 1980), yet studies of split-ticket voting have not examined these matters as carefully.[17]

Third, incumbency confers certain advantages, beyond an enhanced ability to raise campaign funds, in congressional elections. By diligently attending to constituent-service needs and federal projects for the district, members of Congress can develop a personal appeal to voters that crosses party lines. Incumbents enjoy other advantages, such as franked mail and free media coverage, that also help increase visibility and popularity back home.

Finally, congressional candidates can encourage ticket splitting by positioning themselves ideologically closer to the other party's voters.[18] Bill Clinton is well known for this maneuver at the national level (as is perhaps George W. Bush), but for years many House Democrats (particularly in the South) won reelection in Republican-leaning districts by crafting records that included moderate to conservative positions on some important local or national issues. More generally, congressional candidates can encourage ticket splitting by taking positions at odds with their national party (Frymer 1994) or by shifting attention away from issues at the center of the presidential campaign (Petrocik and Doherty 1996). Though some ticket splitting is facilitated by presidential politics, we believe that congressional candidates have more room to maneuver because of the more parochial and less competitive nature of their elections.[19]

To examine these characteristics of the congressional contest, we redirect our focus toward the state or congressional district as the unit of observation and then ask why ticket splitting is more common in some places than in others. It is important to study ticket splitting at the state and district levels because election outcomes are determined by aggregating votes within these electoral units (Wright 1989). Voters within these geographical boundaries, not the national population, determine the composition of Congress and the Electoral College. Our approach allows us to link divided voting directly with divided outcomes because we can compare levels of ticket splitting to the election outcome in each state or district.

At a rudimentary level, we expect that the degree of competitiveness varies widely across districts but is closely tied to the frequency of ticket splitting. We assert that most split-ticket voting is driven by defections of partisans voting in lopsided congressional races. Simple analysis of the NES data seems to confirm this claim. From 1972 to 1996, just 18 percent of voters split their tickets in districts with open seats; in contrast, 25 percent split tickets in districts with an incumbent running. Ticket splitting was also much higher in uncontested districts (36 percent) than in contested districts (23 percent). These simple aggregate statistics reinforce our belief that ticket splitting has local origins. Indeed, in presidential elections over the past 40 years, partisans (including independent leaners) who split their tickets were much more likely to defect to the other party in the House race than in the presidential election. Since 1980, more than 70 percent of president-House splitters defected from their identified party in the House contest.[20]

The following example shows what we have in mind. Table 2.1 and figure 2.1 compare four neighboring congressional districts in Central Illinois in the 1988 elections. These districts cover the middle of the state— they exclude the Chicago suburbs to the north and the St. Louis suburbs to the south. Because of their close proximity, these districts share a lot in common. All four Republican-leaning districts went for George Bush in the 1988 presidential contest and for Ronald Reagan in 1980 and 1984. In addition, all four districts have remarkably similar demographic characteristics. Roughly 95 percent of each district's population is white, and all have sizable rural areas and similar median incomes and home values. However, the four districts did not produce similar election outcomes in the 1988 House races. The first two (the 15th and 18th) elected Republicans to the House, remaining consistent with the presidential outcome, but the other two districts (the 19th and 20th) contributed to divided government by electing Democrats to the House. The rather obvious reason that the 19th and 20th districts produced split outcomes is that almost half of the Bush voters in these two districts split their ballots by selecting the Democratic candidate in the House contest. By contrast, there was little ticket splitting on the part of Bush voters in the other two districts.

This leaves us with the question of why ticket splitting was so much more common in the 19th and 20th districts. It seems unlikely that a principled preference for divided government was more common among the voters of the 19th and 20th congressional districts than among voters in

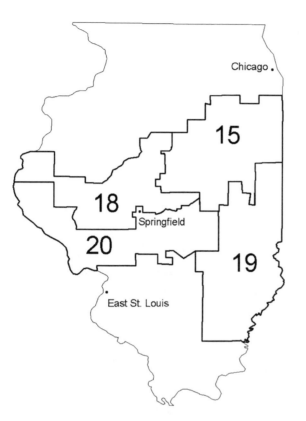

FIG. 2.1. Four congressional districts in central Illinois (1988)

neighboring districts. Rather, the nature of the congressional contests explains the variation in ticket splitting across these districts. The races in the 19th and 20th districts featured Democratic incumbents who greatly outspent their Republican challengers, while the contests in the 15th and 18th districts featured Republican incumbents who outspent their opponents. In addition, ticket splitting was more prevalent in the 18th than the 15th because Robert Michel (the incumbent in the 18th district) faced a spirited challenge from a candidate who spent more than $200,000 on the general election campaign. In addition, the Democratic incumbent in the 20th district (Richard Durbin) attracted Republican voters (and ticket splitting) by crafting a roll-call record that placed him slightly to the right

TABLE 2.1.   Election Outcomes in Four Illinois Districts, 1988

District	Presidential Winner	House Winner	Estimated Ticket Splitting Among Bush Voters
15	Bush (R)	Madigan (R)	8%
18	Bush (R)	Michel (R)	20%
19	Bush (R)	Bruce (D)	43%
20	Bush (R)	Durbin (D)	46%

Note: The source of ticket-splitting estimates in the final column is explained in chapter 3.

of the average Democrat in Congress. Using a model of ticket splitting that emphasizes characteristics of the congressional contest, we are able to explain much of the variation in ticket splitting and election outcomes from one geographical unit to the next. While the voters' preferences vary across districts and are partly responsible for differing outcomes, candidates' positions and qualities matter more. Rather than a national mandate for bipartisan policymaking, ticket splitting has fundamentally local roots that are shaped indirectly by the ideological positions of the national parties.

This, in a nutshell, is what we will examine in more detail in this book. To learn why divided government exists, it is necessary to understand why some districts produce split outcomes and others do not. And if we want to know why some districts produce split outcomes, we need to understand why ticket splitting is more common in those districts. Before saying more about the methodology and moving on in later chapters to our substantive findings, we will clarify some of the terminology that has already been used and will continue to appear throughout the book. These terms are used frequently in the literature but without common definitions, so it is important to consider more precisely what we mean by them.

The Meaning of Ideology

We will often use the term *ideology* to describe the public position that a candidate, elected official, or other political actor adopts. An ideology is essentially a location or set of views on political issues that is available for the taking. It is not necessarily an actor's personal ideology. Though personal values and public positions probably overlap considerably (Burden, Caldeira, and Groseclose 2000; Downs 1957; Erikson 1990; Mayhew 1974; Rohde 1991), we make no unnecessary assumptions about candidates' belief systems or internal ideal points. We refer to *ideology* and *positions* and *locations* interchangeably as an individual's public policy reputation or tendency. Citizens infer candidates' ideologies from party labels and actions— roll-call votes, position papers, speeches, endorsements, alignments, and so on—made by the candidates and by other relevant political actors.

In general, we mean candidate ideology to be the positions that candidates adopt along a unidimensional (liberal-conservative) political spectrum. A *position* can be thought of as "the public enunciation of a judgmental statement on anything likely to be of interest to political actors" (Mayhew 1974, 61), akin to Rohde's (1991) definition of "operative preferences." If voters' decisions are based in part on ideology, candidates' public positions must matter more than their personal values. We will use several proxies for ideology derived from roll-call voting data and mass surveys. None is perfect. Fortunately, the results are robust across different measures, so we are confident about our conclusions concerning ideology and ticket splitting.

The Meaning of Intentionality

Though the reasons that voters cast split tickets are many, the theories available to explain their motives conveniently boil down to the two camps we have described. The distinguishing feature between these two theoretical viewpoints is whether voters are seen as acting strategically to produce divided government. One camp posits that split-ticket voting is a purposeful or intentional attempt to create divided party control of government. Voters have in mind the postelection configuration of officeholders and act to increase the chance that parties share governmental control. The major alternative is what we call an unintentional theory of divided government. By *unintentional* we do not mean to say that voters accidentally or even carelessly vote split ballots. Individual votes are made deliberately. Voters might even be "in search of moderation," to use Fiorina's terminology, but they vote sincerely in each race. Voters who split their tickets in an unintentional way might even be aware that they are increasing the likelihood of parties sharing power, but the reasons for their votes lie somewhere other than in the motive to create divided government.

CONCLUSION

In this chapter we have presented alternative explanations for why ticket splitting and divided government are such regular features of American

politics. We argued that divided government is largely an accidental creation, a by-product of lopsided congressional races around the country that
foster split-ticket voting. Ticket splitting is thus not a purely bottom-up
phenomenon because voters play only an intermediate role, translating
the campaigns that face them in November into the governments taking
office in January. At the same time, divided government has local rather
than national roots since the variability needed to create it is found in the
campaigns waged in states and districts that vary widely in their competitiveness. Ideology often matters in congressional elections, but it is
trumped by the strengths of candidates' messages and works in a way consistent with the traditional proximity spatial model rather than policy balancing theory. Institutional features such as ballot formats and cultural differences also can matter, but the relative strengths of congressional
candidates' campaigns vary and matter more. It is no accident that ticket
splitting increased dramatically in the same years that the incumbency
advantage gained clout and campaign fund-raising and spending became
more important. Though Americans have become more accepting of
shared party control over recent decades, it would be a mistake to interpret
divided government as a national mandate. Even grand political battles
between a legislature of one party and an executive of another are the
product of the dictum that "all politics is local."

CHAPTER III

Measuring Ticket Splitting

The secret ballot is viewed as sacred in the United States, and the Progressives were right in believing that private votes are highly insulated from undesirable political influences. However attractive the secret ballot might be politically, though, it is a severe hindrance to those who wish to study geographic voting patterns. In particular, the secret ballot makes it difficult to determine split-ticket voting rates within various geographic boundaries in the United States. The key variable of interest in this study is the level of ticket splitting within each district and state. We want to know why the percentage of voters who split their ballots is higher in some areas than in others. Thus, a prerequisite for our analysis is to know (or at least estimate accurately) the proportions of straight- and split-ticket voters in each jurisdiction. This is more difficult than it sounds.

The Australian ballot generally prevents researchers from ever knowing the true level of ticket splitting. This point cannot be overstated. At the level of the individual voter, researchers are not permitted to know how Americans vote. There is no perfect solution to the problems that the secret ballot creates.[1] In this chapter we discuss the voting literature's two dominant approaches to ticket splitting and indicate the ways in which we depart from them.

For studies of ticket splitting, it is crucial to know how many voters split their ballots—usually by selecting one party for president and another party for Congress—to understand why voters do so. Accurate estimates of ticket splitting and its determinants will help in understanding the extent to which divided government is the will of the voters. This research question is a continuing one in studies of electoral behavior. Unfortunately, the data used to address it have not been up to the task. Two types of data—aggregate election results and individual survey responses—have been commonly used. While they are informative in a variety of research settings, they are not entirely satisfactory in this endeavor. As we demonstrate in this chapter, aggregate data are inappropriate because they induce the ecological inference problem, and national survey data are inadequate because of small district sample sizes and misreporting by respondents. Here we consider both of these traditional approaches and then demonstrate why the method we implement is an improvement. The method is King's (1997) ecological inference technique, which allows us to use aggregate data to draw more accurate conclusions about individual-level relationships than had previously been possible. Before outlining this approach in detail, we will consider the alternatives. Because this chapter considers a number of complex statistical issues, readers more interested in the substantive results may wish to skip to chapter 4. However, we believe that the methods used to estimate ticket splitting should be scrutinized if results are to be accepted, so we have devoted this chapter to describing the methodological choices we made.

INDIVIDUAL DATA

As with other voting studies, analyses of ticket splitting rely primarily on survey data. The National Election Study (NES), for example, routinely asks a sample of Americans how they voted in the most recent elections. These studies have been informative for examining some of the determinants of ticket splitting and trends in split-ticket voting at the national level over several decades. Indeed, we use some NES data in this book. However, survey data suffer from several limitations. First, data simply do not exist prior to the 1940s. Despite the sophisticated survey techniques available today, reliable interview data will never exist from the first 150 years of U.S. electoral history.

There are also problems with contemporary data. It is difficult to parcel representative national survey samples into smaller units of aggregation such as states or voting districts. Because of the number of cases required for such an analysis, it is often unfeasible to use a national survey to compare voting behavior in different congressional districts or states (Voss, Gelman, and King 1995). Furthermore, a representative national sample does not usually consist of a representative group of voters from each state or congressional district. The NES interviews about 2,000 people each election year, so few respondents come from the same states and even fewer are drawn from the same House districts. Even the Senate Election Study (SES), which sampled within each state, garnered only about 50 voters per state. The small number of observations makes statewide estimates inefficient, if estimable at all. Though survey data can estimate the proportion of split-ticket voters nationally, it is virtually impossible to do so at the district or state level.

Compounding the problem of small, unrepresentative district samples is the potential for people to report inaccurately their voting behavior (Abramson and Claggett 1986; Silver, Anderson, and Abramson 1986; Wright 1990). Estimates based on survey responses are only unbiased if respondents accurately report their voting behaviors.[2] Studies suggest that the NES overstates support for the winning congressional candidates (Wright 1990) and incumbents (Box-Steffensmeier, Jacobson, and Grant 2000; Eubank and Gow 1983; Gow and Eubank 1984) by as much as 10 percentage points. This phenomenon results from forgetfulness (a time effect), social desirability pressures (a bandwagon effect), or a question wording artifact (Box-Steffensmeier, Jacobson, and Grant 2000; Jacobson and Rivers 1993; Wright 1990). To the extent that incumbency contributes to ticket splitting, the proincumbency bias means that the NES may overestimate the extent of split-ticket voting in national elections, at least in the 1980s (Wright 1990). Thus, NES surveys estimate higher levels of ticket splitting than do national exit polls from the same election.[3] And this bias may compound the one associated with turnout: reported voter turnout rates are higher in the NES than in actual elections, and this difference is growing with time (Burden 2000). These problems result from a combination of misreporting and declining response rates that leads to unrepresentative samples. Thus, at a minimum, a study of voting data at an aggregated level is a worthwhile supplement to self-reported voting patterns derived from surveys.

AGGREGATE DATA

Aggregate election data have also been used to examine split-ticket voting. Studies of historical voting patterns in the United States have relied on election returns because of the absence of early survey data. Burnham's (1965) classic work on American political realignment analyzes split-ticket voting as an indicator of large-scale political change. His measure of split-ticket voting is the difference between the highest and lowest Democratic percentages of the two-party vote among races within each state. Among others, Cummings (1966) used the measure extensively in his study of congressional and presidential elections, and Rusk (1970) employed it to demonstrate the effects of moving from partisan to Australian ballots in the early 1900s.

While the aggregate difference measure might have been the best available at the time, Burnham admits that this indicator of ticket splitting is "measured rather crudely" (1965, 9). The aggregate difference measure is the product of two underlying processes, ballot roll-off (in which voters in one contest fail to record a vote in another contest) and ticket splitting. While both underlying processes reflect the failure of voters to support a straight party ticket, ticket splitting is a stronger version of disloyalty to a party.

Rusk points out two additional flaws in the aggregate difference measure. First, "since the measure is an aggregate difference figure, it would not detect mutual crossovers between the two parties" (1970, 1224); second, differences in the types of elections being held in the states the same year threaten interstate comparisons, the "race composition factor" (1970, 1225). Though the race composition factor is a concern, the ramifications of the mutual crossover problem are more immediate. Even if two states had the same contests on the ballot, Burnham's measure is invalid because voters who split their ballots in opposite directions cancel out one another. For example, if the Democratic presidential and congressional candidates in a district each got 45 percent of the popular vote, a value of zero might mean that no split-ticket voting occurred (as Burnham, Cummings, and Rusk assume) or, at the extreme, that all voters split their tickets (Cowart 1974). There are thousands of microlevel processes that could lead the same macrolevel observation.

Though much could be happening at the individual level, aggregate data cannot reveal it, a consequence of the ecological fallacy that has plagued social science for decades (Achen and Shively 1995; King 1997; Robinson 1950). In cases where there is no ballot roll-off or roll-off does not fall disproportionately on the voters of one party, the Burnham-Cummings-Rusk (BCR) measure captures the net effect of ticket splitting and thus represents the lowest possible amount of total ticket splitting (Cowart 1974). Thus, the BCR measure almost always underestimates the true level of split-ticket voting (Bain 1996; Gitelson and Richard 1983), and the potential for bias is highest when the BCR measure indicates little or no apparent ticket splitting (Cowart 1974). Even if these inference problems were minor, which they are not, the BCR measure is not adequate for our purposes because it does not reveal the direction of ticket splitting. Using the BCR convention, each district gets one number that represents the total percentage of voters who choose candidates of different parties on the same ballot. This artificially dichotomizes a rather complex choice set.

Another commonly used aggregate measure of ticket splitting is the "two-office split-result" (Feigert 1979; Gianos 2000)—different parties winning a plurality of votes in different contests within the same jurisdiction. For example, as in figure 1.1, the number of congressional districts with split results in presidential and House voting is used as an indicator of split-ticket voting (Cummings 1966; Jacobson 1990b; Wattenberg 1991b). Using split districts as a measure of ticket splitting assumes that a difference in party outcomes for two offices in the same voting district is evidence of widespread ticket splitting, which is not necessarily the case. Feigert (1979) shows that using the two-office split-result technique produces inaccurate estimates of split-ticket voting, and he instead finds a high correlation between split districts and ballot roll-off. In fact, Feigert recommends the use of ecological inference techniques to further study ticket splitting. Ecological inference techniques frequently have been employed to examine "voter transitions"—the extent to which voters switch parties from one election to the next (Achen and Shively 1995; Gosnell 1937; King 1997)—but ecological inference has rarely been used to examine ticket splitting (cf. Johnston and Hay 1984; Johnston and Pattie 2000).[4] In some ways, the split-district indicator is less informative than the BCR difference measure because the split-district indicator collapses all amounts of ticket splitting into a single dummy variable.

A more desirable approach would permit the estimation of the direction and prevalence of microlevel actions based on the available macrolevel outcome data. This has been problematic because of the looming ecological fallacy. With the development of more sophisticated solutions to the ecological inference problem, however, it is possible to produce estimates of the proportions of voters casting split tickets that avoid the problems described previously. We use aggregate data, so survey misreporting is not a concern because voters are not interviewed: only their collective (and anonymous) votes are needed. In addition, King's method deals with the ecological inference problem by yielding both point estimates and standard errors. Earlier methods could produce the former but not the latter, and the point estimates were often wrong (Achen and Shively 1995). Before turning to estimation itself, we will briefly describe the ecological inference problem and the data used.

CLARIFYING THE PROBLEM

The general ecological inference problem may be conceptualized as a standard contingency table with some missing data. The marginal frequencies of the table are known since they are aggregate data, but the cell frequencies remain unknown. Table 3.1 lays out the ecological inference problem in estimating ticket splitting, using 1988 election results from Maryland's sixth congressional district as an example. Since the presidential contest usually appears at the top of the ballot and is the more visible race, for convenience we assume that voters make their presidential choices first. They need not actually do so; this assumption merely guides how we later present the results. Voters then have three options in the congressional races that appear farther down the ballot: (1) vote Democratic, (2) vote Republican, or (3) abstain.[5] From election returns, we know how many voters in Maryland's sixth district chose George Bush in the presidential contest (158,808), and we know how many voters selected Beverly Byron, the Democratic candidate for the House of Representatives (166,753), but we do not know how many of the Bush voters split their ballots by also selecting Byron, although many presumably did so since each candidate carried the district by a hefty margin. Similarly, we have reason to believe that slightly more than 20,000 presidential voters rolled off by not casting a vote in the House race, but we do not know whether abstention in the House contest was more prevalent among Bush or Dukakis voters.[6] Thus, the challenge is to use the known information from this district and many others to estimate accurately how many Bush and Dukakis voters cast split ballots.

King's (1997) approach to ecological inference combines the insights of two long-standing methods: the method of bounds (Duncan and Davis 1953) and ecological regression (Goodman 1953, 1959). We will briefly describe these two approaches before introducing King's synthesis.

Method of Bounds

The method of bounds makes use of the known aggregate information to create intervals that must include the true values of the unknown quanti-

TABLE 3.1.   Voting in Maryland's Sixth Congressional District, 1988

| Presidential Voting Decision | House Voting Decision | | | Total |
	Byron (Democrat)	Halsey (Republican)	Abstain	
Democrat	?	?	?	82,781
Republican	?	?	?	158,808
Total	166,753	54,528	20,308	241,589

ties. In the example in table 3.1, we are able to put deterministic bounds on the cells' quantities without using any statistics. At one extreme, if all 158,808 Bush voters chose Byron in the House contest, then 100 percent of the Bush voters split their ballots. At the other extreme, if all 82,781 Dukakis voters chose Byron, then the remaining votes for Byron (83,972) must come from Bush voters. In this second scenario, roughly 53 percent of the Bush voters (the lowest percentage possible) split their ballots. Thus, the method of bounds illustrates with certainty that between 53 percent and 100 percent of Bush voters in Maryland's sixth congressional district split their ballots in the 1988 House election. Similar calculations indicate that between 0 percent and 66 percent of the Dukakis voters in Maryland's sixth district split their ballots in the House contest.

The main advantages of the method of bounds are that it makes use of known information and produces bounds that must be correct. The main disadvantage is that the deterministic bounds might not be as informative as one would like. As a result, analysts often extend the method of bounds by incorporating additional assumptions about the unknown quantities of interest (Achen and Shively 1995).

Ecological Regression

To introduce ecological regression and King's method, we will provide some basic mathematical notation for the ecological inference problem (see table 3.2). We now express the known data and the unknown quantities as fractions of voters. The known aggregate quantities for district i in table 3.2 are denoted by capital letters, including the fraction of voters who select Dukakis (X_i), the fraction of voters who select a candidate in the congressional contest (V_i), and the fraction of voters who choose the Democratic congressional candidate (T_i). We also know the total number

TABLE 3.2. Ecological-Inference Notation for District i, 1988

Presidential Voting Decision	House Voting Decision				Fraction of all Voters
	Democrat	Republican	Vote (subtotal)	Abstain	
Democrat (Dukakis)	β_i^b	$1 - \beta_i^b$	λ_i^b	$1 - \lambda_i^b$	X_i
Republican (Bush)	β_i^w	$1 - \beta_i^w$	λ_i^w	$1 - \lambda_i^w$	$1 - X_i$
Fraction of voters	T_i	$1 - T_i$	V_i	$1 - V_i$	1

of voters in the presidential contest (N_i). We have retained most of King's (1997) notation to make it easier for interested readers to consult his book and software to replicate our analysis.[7]

The purpose of ecological inference is to use these aggregate quantities to estimate several unknown proportions, denoted by Greek symbols. They are the fraction of Dukakis and Bush voters who also vote in the congressional contest (λ_i^b and λ_i^w, respectively) and the fraction of Dukakis and Bush voters who choose the Democratic congressional candidate (β_i^b and β_i^w, respectively). Since we are interested in ticket splitting, our main concern is with the left half of table 3.2. The proportion of Bush voters who split their tickets by selecting a Democrat for Congress is denoted by the fraction β_i^w. The fraction of Dukakis voters who split their ballots by voting Republican in the congressional race is $1 - \beta_i^b$. If we momentarily ignore voter abstention in the House contest to simplify this example, the Democratic share of the House vote can be expressed by the following equation:

$$T_i = \beta_i^b X_i + \beta_i^w (1 - X_i) \tag{3.1}$$

β_i^b and β_i^w are unknown, while T_i, X_i, and $(1 - X_i)$ are known for each observation (congressional district). Thus, Goodman (1959) proposed regressing T_i on X_i and $1 - X_i$ under the assumption that the unknown parameters are constant across the aggregation units. The main insight of Goodman's regression is to pool all of the observations and thus borrow strength from all of them. If the constancy assumption is met, the regression equation will produce reasonable estimates of the aggregate quantities of interest and run through most of the points in a scatter plot of T_i by X_i. Goodman's regression yields the following equation based on our 1988 House election data:

$$T_i = 1.154X_i + .085(1 - X_i) \tag{3.2}$$

Though the standard errors associated with the parameter estimates are small (around .007), the coefficients themselves are clearly off the mark. Based on the Goodman estimates, one would conclude that just 8.5 percent of Bush voters voted for a Democratic House candidate and that an impossible 115 percent of Dukakis voters chose a Democratic House candidate. Goodman's ecological regression method often predicts proportions outside the [0,1] interval, an impossible result. Even if estimates from Goodman's regression are within the unit interval, they may still fall outside the interval determined by the method of bounds, since Goodman's regression makes no effort to ensure that its estimates fall within the range of values determined by the method of bounds. And even if the aggregate estimates produced by Goodman's regression fall within the deterministic bounds, they tell us nothing about district-level quantities of interest since ecological regression requires an additional assumption that these parameters are constant across districts.

King's Method

Though other methods improve on Goodman's regression and the method of bounds (Achen and Shively 1995), King's approach is attractive in part because it appears to be the first to combine the insights of both earlier methods. For example, King (1997) takes the deterministic information provided by the method of bounds into account before estimating individual-level parameters. More specifically, King combines the method of bounds with a random coefficients variant of ecological regression.

King's ecological inference technique involves a combination of procedures. It begins by using the method of bounds to restrict estimates of β_i^w and β_i^b, the cell quantities of interest in table 3.2, to a narrower region than the [0,1] interval (Duncan and Davis 1953). These narrower bounds are identifiable because of the accounting identity in equation 3.1, and they increase the amount of information that can be used in a subsequent statistical model.

King's method then posits a probabilistic distribution of the quantities of interest that assumes that β_i^w and β_i^b are distributed truncated bivariate normal (TBVN), conditional on X_i. The bivariate normal distribution is bell shaped, but the TBVN distribution is truncated to ensure that it is confined to the unit [0,1] interval. Thus, King relaxes the Goodman assumption that the two unknown quantities of interest are constant across all observations. Rather, King assumes that the two unknown quantities vary around a single mode (the values of β_i^w and β_i^b that represent the peak of the bell-shaped distribution). Thus, the TBVN assumption posits that the observations have something in common.[8]

In the third major step, King's method uses the available aggregate data to estimate five parameters that define the shape of the TBVN distribution for β_i^w and β_i^b (via a maximum likelihood function). The TBVN distribution is defined by the vector ψ, which includes means and standard deviations for β_i^w and β_i^b as well as the correlation between β_i^w and β_i^b (hence five estimated parameters).

Finally, King uses statistical simulation in conjunction with the hypothetical TBVN distribution to estimate the unknown quantities for each observation (as well as standard errors to indicate the level of uncertainty associated with each parameter estimate). Basically, the simulations record where each observation (electoral unit) cuts through the TBVN distribution estimated in the previous step. The means of the simulated distributions of β_i^w and β_i^b are used as point estimates, and standard errors are based on the variation in the simulated values. This is a real benefit because earlier ecological inference methods suffered from an inability to report levels of uncertainty associated with point estimates (King, Keohane, and Verba 1994).

In addition to the TBVN assumption, King's method relies on two important assumptions. First, as in other methods, King assumes that there is no aggregation bias in the data, meaning that the estimated quantities are not correlated with the X variable. Second, King assumes the absence of spatial dependence in the data (that is, that the T variables are not correlated across units after conditioning on X). In the following sections, we discuss King's method and its assumptions in relation to data we use for much of the empirical analyses in this book.

DATA AND METHOD

Many of the analyses presented in this book use King's ecological inference technique and program to produce estimates of ticket splitting for each state or congressional district. The estimates of ticket splitting are then used in a series of analyses to compare our ecological estimates to other estimates of ticket splitting and to examine why ticket splitting is so common in some places and nonexistent in others.

Our estimation of ticket splitting using King's method is a two-stage process that divides table 3.2 into two two-by-two tables that are analyzed separately. First, we estimate the fraction of Democratic and Republican presidential voters who also cast a vote in the House contest (the right half of table 3.2). Then we use those estimates, along with the other known aggregate quantities, to estimate ticket splitting (the left half of table 3.2).[9] It is important to first control for ballot roll-off in the congressional contest because voters who abstain from the congressional race cannot split their ballots. In addition, if there are partisan differences in roll-off (for example, if Democrats are more likely to roll off), then aggregate measures of ticket splitting that fail to account for roll-off (such as the BCR indicator) are biased.[10]

One important decision we faced involved the treatment of uncontested congressional races, which occur infrequently in Senate contests but are common in House elections. On the one hand, these cases clearly differ from the others. For example, when a Republican runs unopposed for Congress, all Democratic presidential voters must either abstain from the House race or split their tickets. Making ecological inferences in these districts is not challenging. In addition, ballot roll-off in uncontested congressional races is much higher than in contested races (Burden and Kimball 2001). On the other hand, uncontested congressional races certainly contribute to overall levels of ticket splitting. As a result, we used only contested districts in the likelihood maximization stage of ecological inference.[11] The idea was to base the TBVN distribution on the large majority of districts that featured House candidates of both major parties. This is not the same as removing the uncontested districts from the data set. Observations that are selected out of the likelihood maximization stage are included in the simulation stage and thus are included in all aggregate estimates. This allows us to set aside the uncontested contests without dropping them from the data, so that the uncontested House races still figure into aggregate (that is, national) estimates of ticket splitting.

King's ecological inference technique has its share of critics. As with all ecological inference techniques, King's method is not perfect. It has been occasionally criticized for having unrealistic distributional assumptions and poor guidance for diagnosing and correcting for aggregation bias (Cho 1998; Cho and Gaines 2001; Freedman et al. 1998; McCue 2001; Rivers 1998).[12] We have taken several steps to address problems in applying King's technique to estimate ticket splitting.

One potential problem is the likely presence of aggregation bias in our data (Burden and Kimball 2001; Cho and Gaines 2001). Aggregation bias occurs when an unknown quantity of interest (β_i^b or β_i^w) is correlated with X_i. In our case, if the frequency of ticket splitting among Democrats is imagined to decline as a district becomes more Democratic, then aggregation bias is present. Given that congressional districts are often drawn for partisan purposes on the basis of voting patterns, aggregation bias should be expected (King 1997, 46–53). Aggregation bias causes Goodman's regression to produce biased ecological inferences. Though King's method has been shown to be far more robust to aggregation bias than previous methods (King 1997, chaps. 11–13), the problem still must be taken seriously. Fortunately, King's method allows the user to correct for aggregation bias by extending the basic method to include covariates in the estimation. A covariate is chosen so that β_i^w and β_i^b are independent of X_i after conditioning on the covariate. Thus, one seeks a covariate that is correlated with the quantities of interest (β_i^w and β_i^b) and whose presence in the estimation removes the correlation between X_i and the quantities of interest.

Thus, one of the choices users of King's method must make is selection of covariates. This is a specification issue much like decisions about which variables to include and exclude on the right-hand side of a regression equation. Including a covariate in the estimation is also a way to control for violations of the other two major assumptions in King's method. For example, a covariate can be used to account for more than one mode in the bivariate distribution of β_i^w and β_i^b (a violation of the TBVN assumption) or to allow the distributions of β_i^w and β_i^b to vary across geographic regions (a violation of the spatial independence assumption).

For many of the elections analyzed in this book, we use a South dummy variable as a covariate to account for possible violations of the assumptions of King's basic method. Over the past 40 years (the period covered by this book), the South has been the locus of a gradual realignment from Democratic dominance to parity between the parties and even Republican majorities in some states. Since the southern realignment began in presidential contests well before Republicans made gains in southern congressional races (Aistrup 1996; Brunell and Grofman 1998; Bullock 1988; Frymer 1994; Frymer, Kim, and Bines 1997), we suspect that the process generating the observed election results in the South differs from the rest of the country. In addition, ballot roll-off in congressional races is more frequent in the South. Because of the unique nature of voting patterns in the South, we reason that aggregating votes may conceal more ticket splitting in the South than in other regions.[13]

The choice of a covariate is not to be made lightly. We selected the South as a covariate after careful consideration of the voting literature as a way to control for possible violations of the assumptions of King's basic ecological inference model. As it turns out, estimating ticket splitting without a covariate produces similar results (Burden and Kimball 1998; Cho and Gaines 2001; Burden and Kimball 2001). In addition, the use of other justifiable covariates produces similar estimates of ticket splitting as are reported in this book (Burden and Kimball 2001).[14]

AN APPLICATION TO THE 1988 ELECTIONS

To provide a better sense of King's method of ecological inference, this section describes the steps in applying King's method to presidential-House voting in the 1988 elections. Voters in 1988 could have split their ballots in one of two ways: by selecting Bush and a congressional Democrat, or by choosing Dukakis and a congressional Republican. "Bush splitters" denotes the fraction of Bush voters who split their ballots by selecting congressional Democrats (β_i^w in table 3.2) and "Dukakis splitters" denotes the fraction of Dukakis voters who choose a congressional Republican ($1 - \beta_i^b$ in table 3.2). In this case, we are more interested in Bush splitters because they mirror the divided government pattern of the 1980s.

We apply King's method in two stages. The first stage estimates ballot roll-off for each party, and the second stage estimates ticket splitting. Since both stages involve similar procedures, and since we are primarily interested in ticket splitting, this section discusses only the ticket-splitting (second stage) estimation.

Before reporting on the estimation, it is helpful to examine the aggregate data being used. We emphasize that the only data that are on hand before estimation begins are aggregate election returns for major party candidates in the 1988 presidential and congressional elections. Simple division transforms these figures into the marginal proportions X (Dukakis's share of the presidential vote) and T (Democratic share of the House vote) represented in table 3.2. Figure 3.1 presents a scatter plot of these two variables for the presidential and House elections of 1988. Each point on the graph represents a congressional district—Maryland's sixth district, the example in table 3.1, is represented by the point where $X = .33$ and $T = .75$). When considering only the districts with contested House races, there is a positive bivariate relationship ($r = .64$) between the share of votes going to Dukakis and the Democratic House candidate, as one would expect. The range of presidential outcomes is smaller than the range of congressional outcomes since the presidential contest was more competitive than most House contests. The relationship between X and T is not quite linear and is heteroskedastic since the spread of data along the vertical axis is greatest near the middle of the horizontal axis. These features of the data create further problems for Goodman's regression.

The first step in applying King's method is to incorporate the deterministic bounds available from election returns for each district. King (1997) produces a new way to visualize the deterministic bounds for each district: a tomography plot. A tomography plot is a two-dimensional graph with each axis representing one of the unknown quantities to be estimated (β_i^w and β_i^b). Each observation in a tomography plot is represented by a line that indicates the deterministic bounds on each of the unknown quantities.

Figure 3.2 shows the tomography plot of the same 1988 data. Each line

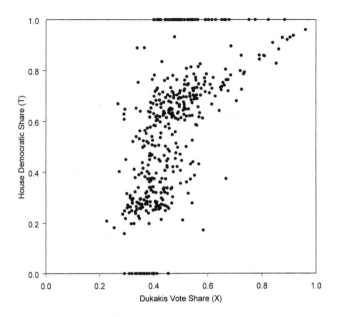

FIG. 3.1.   Relationship between presidential and congressional vote shares, 1988

corresponds to a congressional district and is based on the deterministic identity between β^w and β^b, given the aggregate proportions X and T (equation 3.1). The vertical axis in figure 3.2 represents values of B^w (the proportion of Bush voters who vote for a Democratic House candidate). The horizontal axis represents B^b (the proportion of Dukakis voters who select a Democrat for the House). Each point on the scatter plot (fig. 3.1) becomes a line in the tomography plot (fig. 3.2). Maryland's sixth district is represented by one of the many lines that cuts off the upper right corner of the tomography plot. Applying the method of bounds, we know with certainty that the true values for β_i^w and β_i^b for each district must lie at some point on its tomography line.

The range within the unit square that each of these lines covers indicates the possible values of the quantities of interest based on the method of bounds. Projecting a tomography line to the horizontal axis indicates the range of possible values for β_i^b. Thus, in the case of Maryland's sixth district, β_i^b (the fraction of Dukakis voters who also voted for Byron, the Democratic House candidate) must lie between .24 and 1. Similarly, by

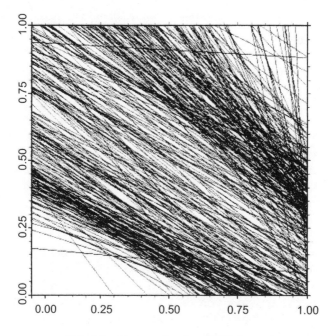

FIG. 3.2.   Tomography plot of 1988 data

projecting the tomography line on the vertical axis, one can determine the range of possible values for β_i^w (which must lie between .63 and 1 in Maryland's sixth district).[15] Thus, the deterministic bounds are narrower for β_i^w than for β_i^b in this particular district.

One important consideration in applying King's method is the amount of information contained in the deterministic bounds. Before applying the method of bounds, the widest possible bounds on any quantities of interest are [0,1]. That is, no less than 0 percent and no more than 100 percent of voters can split their tickets. In many districts, applying the method of bounds substantially narrows the range of possible values of β_i^w and β_i^b. Some tomography lines stretch across smaller portions of the unit square than others. This means that the deterministic bounds are narrower in some districts and wider in others.

King (1997, 129) points out that informative aggregate data often have a wide range of values on the X variable (Dukakis's share of the district-level vote in 1988). Variation in X produces different sloping lines in a tomography plot, increasing the chances that the lines will intersect in a common area (thus locating the mode of the TBVN distribution, as we discuss subsequently).[16] In 1988, Dukakis's share of the vote ranges from .23 to .96, with a standard deviation of .12. As a result, the tomography plot includes some lines that are almost vertical (where Dukakis ran well ahead of Bush), some lines that are close to horizontal (where Dukakis ran far behind Bush), and many diagonal lines (where Dukakis ran close to Bush). Near-vertical lines give maximally informative estimates for the fraction of Bush voters who voted for the Democratic House candidate, whereas near-horizontal lines give maximally informative estimates for the fraction of Dukakis voters who cast their ballots for the Republican House candidate. In addition, lines that cut off the bottom left corner or top right corner (lines that represent many congressional districts) have narrow bounds on both quantities of interest.

We can aggregate the bounds for each district to calculate the deterministic bounds on β^w and β^b at the national level. For 1988 the national bounds on β^w are [.24, .75] and the national bounds on β^b are [.28, .91]. Thus, before any statistics are applied, and without any assumptions, we know that the aggregate bounds can be roughly cut in half in our data. Many of the district bounds are even narrower than the national bounds. We thus eliminate half of the ecological inference problem up front. As King (1997, chaps. 10–12) demonstrates, if the deterministic bounds suitably constrain the estimated quantities of interest, there can be enormous aggregation bias, yet inferences will still be accurate.

Ideally, we would prefer data with even narrower bounds. However, even having data that are not incredibly informative does not render King's method unusable but simply increases the uncertainty (that is, standard errors) of the estimates produced (King 1997, 129). As we will demonstrate, the standard errors of the district-level estimates of ticket splitting reflect the amount of information in the district-level bounds. Districts with wider bounds produce larger standard errors.[17]

The tomography plot can also be used to visualize the mode of the bivariate normal distribution to be estimated by maximum likelihood. The likely mode appears where there is the greatest density of lines. The mode of the estimated bivariate normal distribution represents the clump of points that produce the "emitted" lines of the tomography plot (King 1997, 131). This is how King's method borrows strength from all observations. In the tomography plot of the 1988 data in figure 3.2, the estimated mode should appear near the right edge of the graph, roughly where $\beta_i^b =$ .95 and $\beta_i^w = .45$. The mode of the distribution does not represent the national estimates of β^b and β^w. The national-level estimates are averages of the district-level estimates, weighted by the number of voters in each district. The mode of the distribution is closer to the unweighted mean.

The bivariate normal distribution can be visualized as a bell-shaped hill growing out of the tomography plot, with the peak of the hill occurring at the mode. Figure 3.3 illustrates the same tomography plot of our 1988 data showing where the estimated bivariate normal distribution is located. The thick curves added to the tomography plot in figure 3.3 are contour lines denoting the 50th and 95th percentiles of the estimated bivariate normal distribution. The contour lines indicate where most of the probability mass of the estimated bivariate normal distribution lies.

We also rely on some common sense in interpreting the tomography plot and diagnosing the ticket-splitting estimates produced by King's method. Given the importance of partisanship and the (albeit weakened) presence of presidential coattails in congressional elections, it is safe to assume that the Democratic House candidate's share of the vote in contested races should be higher among Dukakis voters than among Bush voters by a nontrivial amount ($\beta_i^b > \beta_i^w$). Thus, imagining a diagonal line from the lower left corner to the upper right corner of the tomography plot, the truth for each district (and the nation) must fall on the corresponding tomography line but below that diagonal. This cuts the deterministic bounds further and indicates that the mode of the truncated bivariate normal distribution (the area where the lines tend to intersect) should fall toward the lower right-hand corner of the tomography plot (where β_i^b is large and β_i^w is small).[18] In other words, the true levels of ticket splitting in each district (and in the nation) should be considerably closer to the lower bounds than the upper bounds, as studies of actual ballots indicate (Gitelson and Richard 1983). While we do not impose this assumption in our application of King's method, this information is important because it places half of the unit square off-limits for any estimates of ticket splitting and makes King's distributional assumption appear more justifiable. The maximum likelihood estimation in King's method indeed locates a mode above the lower right corner of the unit square (see fig. 3.3). The lines do not literally intersect at a single point, but most cluster in that area (near the edge of the unit square).[19] The procedure estimated more ticket splitting among Bush than Dukakis voters, as we expected, though it was not required to do so. In addition, the 95 percent contour line falls below the main diagonal, thereby confirming our intuition, for almost the entire probability mass for the estimated TBVN distribution falls below the main diagonal.

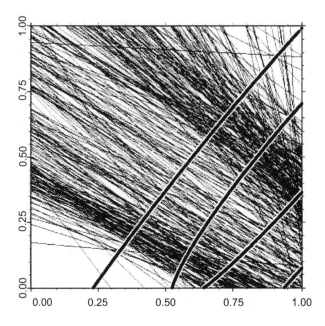

FIG. 3.3.   Tomography plot of 1988 data with likelihood contours

Another part of King's intuition is that the most likely values for β_i^w and β_i^b fall along their respective tomography lines at points closest to the mode of the TBVN, the peak of the bell-shaped distribution. To estimate the quantities of interest for each district, King observes where the tomography line for each district slices through the estimated TBVN distribution. Since each district slices a different cross-section out of the hill, each slice provides a different probability distribution for both unknown quantities of interest (β_i^w and β_i^b). King then uses Monte Carlo simulation to take random samples from these probability distributions to estimate each quantity (by taking the mean of the simulated values) and its standard error (the standard deviation of the simulated values).

Thus, in the current example, King's method generates an estimate of the frequency of ticket-splitting for each congressional district and provides an estimate of uncertainty for each estimate. In the case of Maryland's sixth district, King's method produces an estimate of .658 for β_i^w (the proportion of Bush voters who split their tickets in the House contest), with a standard error of .023. In the same district, we get an estimate of .049 for $1 - \beta_i^b$ (the proportion of Dukakis voters who split their tickets), with a standard error of .046. In this case, note that the estimate of β_i^b, which has wider deterministic bounds than β_i^w, has a larger standard error as well. Thus, the estimated standard errors are a function of the amount of information in the deterministic bounds.

The final step in King's method aggregates all of the district-level simulations of β_i^w and β_i^b (keeping in mind the number of voters in each district) to generate estimates of ticket splitting at the national level. For 1988, we estimate that .336 of Bush voters split their tickets in the House race (with a standard error of .006), while .193 of Dukakis voters split their tickets (with a standard error of .008).[20] As expected, Dukakis voters remained more loyal to their party in House contests than did Bush voters. While most people in 1988 voted straight party tickets in the presidential and House races, the 1988 election produced relatively high levels of ticket splitting compared to other elections.

We use the method described earlier to estimate president-House ticket splitting in other elections from 1952 to 2000, with the exception of years with strong third-party presidential candidates (see chap. 4). In chapter 5, we use the same approach to estimate voter transitions in midterm House elections. In chapter 6, we examine president-Senate ticket splitting, estimates of which come from pooling 350 Senate elections from 1952 to 1996.[21]

REFLECTIONS ON KING'S METHOD

The ecological inference problem is a difficult one, which explains why nearly a century of scholarship has been devoted to it. King's approach is imperfect, of course, but a better technique is not yet available. By combining the insights of two heretofore divergent approaches to ecological inference and by adding modern statistical techniques such as maximum likelihood estimation and simulation, King produces a real advance over the standard techniques used by social scientists from Goodman through the mid-1990s (Achen and Shively 1995). King's method is not without its critics. Unfortunately, the critics have not offered plausible substitutes, and currently available alternatives to King's method impose less realistic assumptions or require external data that often do not exist.[22]

For the electoral data that we examine in this book, we are confident that the ecological estimates we produce improve on individual survey and aggregate election data enough to warrant the use of these estimates. Ultimately, the proof is in the pudding. Do our estimates of ticket splitting correlate with other nonecological measures of ticket splitting? The following section provides evidence that they do.

THE VALIDITY OF OUR ESTIMATES

When discussing our estimates of split-ticket voting, we will often use a two-letter abbreviation to indicate the voting pattern, where the first letter is the party of the presidential candidate chosen and the second letter is the party of the congressional candidate chosen. For example, an RD voter is one who voted for Bush and the Democratic congressional candidate. This terminology is used throughout the book.

Our new ticket-splitting estimates appear valid on several fronts. First, as we will show, the estimated frequencies of ticket splitting are close to estimates derived from other, independent sources. Second, our estimates always conform to expectations that straight-ticket voting is far more common than is ticket splitting in national elections. Third, as studies of actual ballots confirm, our estimates indicate higher levels of ticket splitting than the BCR aggregate difference measure, which generally represents the lowest possible amount of ticket splitting. Fourth, contrary to the assumption of Goodman's regression, we find a great deal of variation in ticket splitting across districts and states. For example, our estimates of president-House ticket splitting in 1988 (ignoring uncontested House races) indicate that the proportion of Bush splitters ranges from .03 to .90, with a standard deviation of .19. This variation is associated with split outcomes at the state and district level in meaningful ways.

Comparisons with Other Aggregate Estimates

We demonstrate the validity of our estimates by comparing them with existing aggregate and individual measures of split-ticket voting rates. As noted previously, the best-known aggregate measure is the aggregate difference calculation (Burnham 1965; Cummings 1966; Rusk 1970), which is simply the difference between the Democratic share of the presidential and congressional vote. We computed this value for each of the contested House districts in 1988. Though the correlation between our estimates of total ticket splitting and the BCR measure is high ($r = .86$), the scatter plot in figure 3.4 reveals that the BCR estimates are lower than our ecological estimates. If the two sets of estimates were identical, the points in the scatter plot should fall on the dotted diagonal line in figure 3.4. The difference between our estimates and the BCR measure is greatest where the BCR measure indicates low levels of ticket splitting. This is exactly the

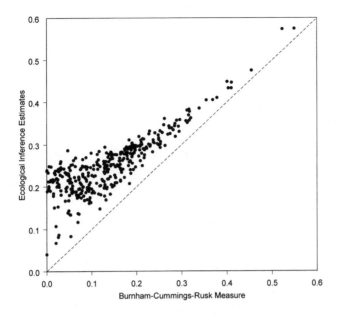

FIG. 3.4.   Old and new ticket-splitting measures compared, 1988

pattern predicted in theory (Cowart 1974), found in studies of actual ballots (Gitelson and Richard 1983), and replicated in all of the election years we analyze in this book. More importantly, it is consistent with Rusk and Burnham's suspicions that the indicator undercounts the number of split ballots.

The data in figure 3.4 are heteroskedastic in the sense that the relationship between the two measures weakens as one moves from right to the left. Many districts have BCR estimates of close to zero (where the presidential and congressional Democratic percentages are similar), yet our estimates put the total amount of ticket splitting in those districts at 10 to 25 percent in many cases. If the two techniques produced identical estimates, we would expect a regression line that goes through the origin and runs upward to the right at a 45 degree angle, as shown in the figure. Instead, regressing our estimates on BCR yields a slope of .62 (not 1.0) and constant of .16 (not zero), indicating that more than 15 percent of voters are splitting their ballots in districts where the BCR aggregate measure predicts none.[23] This discrepancy in measures is consistent with Rusk's critique that the measure understates ticket splitting by missing the extent to which RD and DR ticket splitters cancel out one another.

The BCR measure matches our estimates most closely in uncontested House races, where only one type of ticket splitting (and thus no canceling) can occur. (Uncontested races are excluded from figure 3.4.) As noted earlier, the difference between the two measures is correlated with the BCR measure itself ($r = -.82$), so that the greatest difference is at the low end of the BCR scale. The difference between the two measures is also correlated with ballot roll-off in the House contest ($r = -.58$), with a larger difference in districts where there is little ballot roll-off.[24] These are usually the most competitive House races, where we expect that voters from both sides are crossing party lines. In any case, the difference between our ticket-splitting estimates and the BCR indicator is largest in cases where the BCR measure is expected to exhibit the most bias. This increases our confidence in the validity of our estimates using King's method.

Split-Ticket Voting and Split District Outcomes

One might wonder if ticket splitting really matters if only a minority of the voting public is doing it. Are higher levels of ticket splitting associated with split outcomes when votes are aggregated at the district level? Table 3.3 provides the mean levels of each type of president-House ticket splitting in different types of districts in 1988. The cell entries are the mean proportion of Bush and Dukakis voters who split their tickets, so the figures do not add up to 1.0 within each row or column. Ticket splitting by Bush voters is quite high (57 percent) in districts that chose Bush and a Democratic House candidate but low (11 percent) in districts that supported a Republican for both offices. Ticket splitting certainly helps explain why one district produces a split verdict while another produces a straight party result. Nevertheless, ticket splitting and split outcomes are not entirely synonymous, though they are sometimes treated as such. Substantial numbers of voters split their tickets even in districts where candidates of the same party are elected. For example, ticket splitting among Bush voters is high in districts that chose a Democrat for both offices.

Consider the type of district in which Bush is expected to beat Dukakis. These districts are probably more conservative than average. When a Democratic congressional candidate wins in such a district, it is likely the result of high rates of ticket splitting among Bush voters. If divided outcomes and split-ticket voting were unrelated, one would expect no connection between the fraction of Bush splitters in a district and an RD election result. To test this connection, we examine the statistical relationship between the level of split-ticket voting among Bush voters and the probability of districts having unified Republican electoral outcomes (RR) or split outcomes (RD) in 1988. Our estimation technique is a logit model where the dependent variable is the probability of selecting a Democratic congressional candidate, conditional on the selection of a Republican for president. The results, found in table 3.4, show that the relationship is strong; split-ticket voting is a prime cause of divided outcomes. The classification rate of the one-variable model significantly improves on the naive baseline (54.7 percent), mispredicting less than 2 percent of districts based only on our knowledge of ticket-splitting rates. The logit equation predicts that if more than 29 percent of the Bush voters split their ballots, there is a better than 50 percent chance that the district will elect a Democrat to the House. Thus, both the direction and frequency of ticket splitting shape split district outcomes. The observed relationship between our

TABLE 3.3.   Mean President-House Ticket Splitting by District Outcome, 1988

Ticket Splitting	District Outcome			
Type	RR	RD	DR	DD
Bush splitters	.11	.57	.09	.59
	(.08)	(.24)	(.05)	(.24)
Dukakis splitters	.41	.09	.43	.07
	(.22)	(.06)	(.13)	(.05)
Number of cases	163	135	12	125

Note: Standard deviations of point estimates are in parentheses.

TABLE 3.4.   Logit Equation Predicting Split Outcomes, RD versus RR Districts, 1988

Variable	b
Bush splitters	63.84*
	(16.29)
Constant	−18.71*
	(4.77)
Number of cases	298
Correctly predicted	98.3%
Log likelihood	−11.82

Note: Standard errors are in parentheses.
*$p < .01$, two-tailed t-test

estimates of ticket splitting and split districts provides further evidence for
the validity of our estimates.

Comparisons with Individual-Level Estimates

It is also useful to compare our ecologically based estimates with those
from a more traditional individual-level source. Table 3.5 provides a comparison between our estimates of president-House ticket splitting in 1988
and estimates from the 1988 NES. Using the 1988 NES, the estimated
proportion of Bush voters who chose the House Democrat (Bush splitters)
is .348, compared to our estimate of .336. The corresponding proportion of
Dukakis voters who split for the House Republican (Dukakis splitters) is a
little less than half that, at .149, compared to our ecological estimate of
.193. At the national level, our ecological estimates of ticket splitting are
close to those produced by NES survey data. Overall, NES estimates that
the proportion of presidential voters casting a split president-House ballot
is .254, compared to our estimate of .271. Thus, our estimates of ticket
splitting at the national level in 1988 closely match those generated by
individual-level survey data.

For the 33 1988 Senate races, split-ticket voting was about as common
as in the House contests. Roughly one in three Bush voters chose a Democratic Senate candidate, and about one in five Dukakis voters chose a
Republican for the Senate. To compare the ecological estimates with individual data, we also estimate the frequency of split-ticket voting using the
1988 SES, which drew modest but representative samples from each state.
As table 3.6 indicates, the ecological estimates of president-Senate ticket
splitting are somewhat lower than those produced by the SES. We did not
weight the SES data by state population, which may explain why the SES
estimates are higher. Small states (where ticket splitting was more common in 1988) are overrepresented in the SES sample.

TABLE 3.5. Comparing Estimates of President-House Ticket
Splitting, 1988, Using NES and King's Ecological-Inference
Technique

	Proportion Splitting Ballots	
Source	Bush Voters	Dukakis Voters
Ecological estimate	.336 (.006)	.193 (.008)
NES estimate	.348 (.021)	.149 (.016)

Note: Standard errors are in parentheses.

As a final validity check, we compare estimates of major-party president-House ticket splitting using King's method and quadrennial NES surveys from 1952 to 2000. As figure 3.5 shows, the methods produce similar estimates of ticket splitting each year, with the greatest discrepancy occurring in 1992 (when Ross Perot captured 19 percent of the presidential vote). Accounting for the large Perot vote might have strained King's technique or introduced additional measurement error in this case. In most years, the deviations can be understood in terms of the literature on overreporting for winning and incumbent candidates: landslide elections such as 1964 and 1972 predictably exhibit some of the largest differences. Though the figure does not display information about the certainty of the aggregate estimates, in no year besides 1992 are the differences in estimates statistically significant. More importantly, the ecological and NES estimates reveal the same trends in president-House ticket splitting over the past forty years: a steep increase in the 1960s and early 1970s, a plateau in the 1980s, and a decline in the 1990s.[25]

Conclusion

In summary, our ecological inference estimates hold up quite well when compared to other estimates of ticket splitting. First, our measures provide empirical support for the longtime expectation that the BCR indicator undercounts ticket splitting, and ecological inference allows us to estimate the magnitude of the bias in different districts. Second, our measures are for the most part close to aggregated estimates drawn from mass surveys, which, despite their imperfections, are the current standard for measuring split-ticket voting. Third, our earlier research shows that using ecological inference techniques on data from different units of analysis—precincts rather than districts—also produces similar estimates of ticket splitting (Burden and Kimball 1997). These findings give us confidence in the

TABLE 3.6. Comparing Estimates of President-Senate Ticket Splitting, 1988, Using SES and King's Ecological-Inference Technique

| | Proportion Splitting Ballots | |
Source	Bush Voters	Dukakis Voters
Ecological estimate	.285 (.017)	.187 (.020)
SES estimate	.333 (.020)	.255 (.022)

Note: Standard errors are in parentheses.

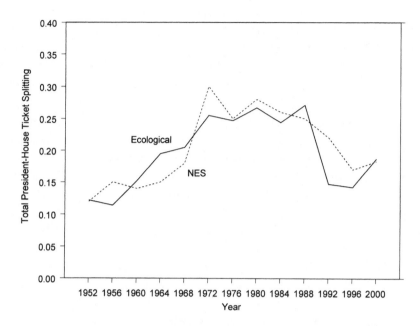

FIG. 3.5.   Ecological and NES estimates of president-House ticket
splitting compared over time

validity and reliability of our ecological inference estimates. We do not
argue that our approach is flawless, but we believe it to be a reasonable way
to study ticket splitting within important political boundaries, given the
data and statistical techniques available. Perhaps better estimates will be
produced by another data set or estimation technique in the future, but for
now we have what we believe to the be most accurate district-level estimates possible. Though we rely heavily on the technique, we buttress some
of our findings in the following chapters with data from other sources,
either individual-level surveys or aggregate-level outcomes.

Since ticket splitting is a strong predictor of split-district outcomes, we
now turn to explaining variation in ticket splitting across voting districts.
We devoted this chapter to explaining how we produced the estimates and
then providing some evidence for their validity. What is more important
than the estimates themselves, however, is what is done with them.

CHAPTER IV

President-House Ticket Splitting
from 1952 to 2000

Ticket splitting is thought to be a new, potentially disruptive, force in American politics. Following more than a century in which few voters cast split tickets—either by choice or as a result of ballot limitations—the past half century has seen ticket splitting become a standard part of the electoral landscape. Many citizens now consider it a reasonable if not desirable way to vote, and it has the potential to make elections both more unpredictable yet more meaningful. At the same time, divided government has gone from occasional appearances in the first 150 years of our nation's existence to the predominant form of governance in the postwar era. In this chapter we explain why ticket splitting increased by examining how it varies both across districts and over time.

First we will review some essential evidence. First, as figure 1.1 shows, split-ticket voting has increased noticeably since the 1950s. According to National Election Study (NES) postelection surveys, major-party president-House ticket splitting rose from about 12 percent of voters in the 1950s to more than a quarter of all voters in the 1980s, although this form of ticket splitting has declined in the 1990s. Consequently, divided government has become the dominant partisan configuration in Washington. Divided government resulted from 16 of the 25 elections from 1952 to 2000, or roughly two-thirds of recent history (see table 1.1).

Though the two phenomena are certainly related, it is important not to equate ticket splitting and divided government. The 1956 election was the first in American history that failed to provide the winning presidential candidate (in a "normal" two-way race) with party majorities in either chamber of Congress (Fiorina 1996), yet ticket splitting in 1956 was still only as frequent as left-handedness. The 1976 elections fell during a period of relatively frequent ticket splitting, yet unified government was the outcome. Finally, the drop in ticket splitting during the 1990s largely coincided with divided government, although the 2000 elections produced a unified government for the first time in eight years. A large majority of voters have and still do cast straight tickets, yet divided government often results. Part of this disjunction, we shall show, results from the process of vote aggregation. Ticket splitting predicts split-district outcomes much better than it does national outcomes precisely because votes are translated into outcomes within these geographic units.

We examine split-ticket voting across presidential and House elections to help understand why the United States has been experiencing divided government. During the postwar period, ticket splitting increased, and divided government is more common now than ever, so a causal link between the two is plausible. We use the ecological estimates of ticket splitting described in the previous chapter to examine varying rates of ticket splitting across House districts throughout this time period.

Our main finding is that much of the variation in ticket splitting across space and time can be explained by the level of competition in congressional elections. Ticket splitting and divided government are largely the by-product of lopsided congressional contests that often feature a well-funded and highly recognizable incumbent versus a lesser-known and underfinanced challenger. In such cases, many voters split their ballots simply by choosing the more appealing candidate. Candidate appeal, of course, depends heavily on the strength of a candidate's message relative to that of the opponent, which in turn is a function of such things as candidate experience, incumbency, and campaign spending.

We also find that incumbents with moderate roll-call voting records attract more ticket splitters than do ideologues in Congress. When candidates occupy the ideological center, it is easier for voters to cross party lines. In contrast, when candidates and parties take clear and opposing positions, ticket splitting is less common. Furthermore, our evidence shows that one result of the growing incumbency advantage of the late 1960s and 1970s was a corresponding increase in ticket splitting. Conversely, the decline in the incumbency advantage during the 1990s coincides with a drop in ticket splitting. Thus, incumbency is an important force in understanding national trends in ticket splitting (Born 2000a). In addition, we find that regional differences in ticket splitting have diminished over the past four decades. In particular, our evidence is consistent with other findings suggesting that an incremental Republican realignment has occurred in the South (Aistrup 1996; Brunell and Grofman

1998). Finally, we find evidence that presidential candidates help induce ticket splitting, although our measures of a presidential effect are often indirect.

VARIATION IN TICKET SPLITTING
ACROSS DISTRICTS

We begin by examining the variation in ticket splitting across congressional districts. We wish to know whether split-ticket voting rates are relatively constant across the country (suggesting that national forces are at work) or differ substantially from one district to the next (suggesting that local forces matter more). Local variation does not rule out a common explanation, of course, but at least it helps narrow our focus in the search for answers. The 1988 national elections serve as a focal point for several studies of divided government (Burden and Kimball 1997; Fiorina 1996; Jacobson 1990b; Sundquist 1993) because these contests seem to provide the clearest signal yet that voters prefer split control of government. George Bush, a Republican, was easily elected president, but Democrats simultaneously gained three seats in the House to increase the size of their majority to a whopping 260 to 175 seats. We estimate that roughly one-third of Bush voters and one-fifth of Dukakis voters split their tickets in 1988 House contests. Bush's negative coattails in 1988 and continuance of divided government beyond the Reagan years suggested that ticket splitting was a phenomenon with which political science needed to reckon.

The histogram in figure 4.1 shows that there was quite a bit of variation in president-House ticket splitting across districts in 1988. The figure shows the distribution of Bush splitters (RD voters) as estimated from aggregate election data. The figure includes uncontested House races and shows three modes of RD ticket splitting. The spike at the right edge of the histogram indicates that Democrats ran unopposed in about 50 districts, and thus, all of the Bush voters who cast votes in those House contests voted for Democrats. Similarly, the bar at the left edge of the histogram denotes 16 districts where Republicans ran unopposed for the House. Thus, much of the variation in ticket splitting can be accounted for by the mere presence or absence of major-party opposition in House contests. Ignoring the bars at each edge of the figure provides the distribution in contested House races. Even after moving beyond the uncontested races, there is still quite a bit of variation in ticket splitting across districts. There is a second clump of observations in the middle of the figure where almost half of the Bush voters split their ballots (and generally where a Democrat

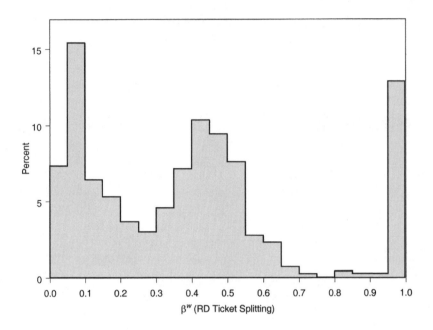

FIG. 4.1.   RD ticket splitting in 1988

won the House race). Finally, there is a third clump of districts near the left edge of the figure where no more than 10 to 15 percent of the Bush voters split their tickets (usually where a Republican won the House seat).

The variation in ticket splitting illustrated in this figure discredits the idea that there was a nationwide preference in 1988 for a Republican president and a Democratic Congress. In almost 150 districts, no more than 10 to 15 percent of the Bush voters split their ballots by selecting a Democratic House candidate. In addition, as the example in chapter 1 shows, the direction and frequency of ticket splitting often varies widely even across neighboring districts with similar sociodemographic characteristics.

While the overall frequency of split-ticket voting increased in the 1960s and 1970s, as is well documented, so did the variation across House districts. For a comparison, figure 4.2 provides the distribution of RD splitting in 1956, the presidential election that ushered in the divided era, producing a Republican president and Democratic Congress. At the time, ticket splitting was less frequent and congressional elections were not as

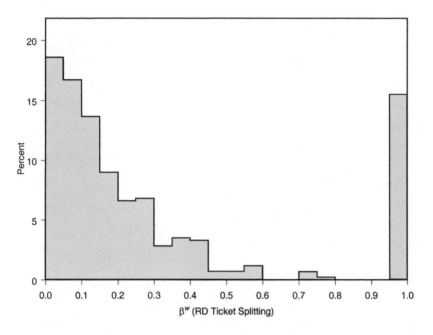

FIG. 4.2.   RD ticket splitting in 1956

dominated by fund-raising, incumbency, and candidates as they are today. Again, a spike appears at the right edge of the figure, representing 68 districts where Democrats ran unopposed. The uncontested seats helped the Democrats maintain their majority in the face of Eisenhower's landslide victory in the presidential contest. Twenty-two of the uncontested Democrats represented districts—almost all in the South—that Eisenhower carried in 1956. After removing these uncontested seats, however, there is considerably less variation in RD splitting than in 1988, even though both elections produced Republican presidents and a Democratic Congresses. Indeed, when examining just the contested House seats in 1956, only a single mode remains (at about .10), compared to the two modes in the 1988 histogram. Thus, divided government was based on a wider foundation of split-ticket voting in 1988 than in 1956.

The most common form of national divided government in the postwar era has featured a Republican president and a Democratic Congress. From 1952 to 2000, 16 of the 25 national elections produced divided government. Until the 1990s, elections producing divided government during this period always resulted in a Republican executive and a Democratic majority in at least one chamber of Congress. Thus, we first examine the frequency and variation in RD splitting across congressional districts for each presidential election from 1952 to 2000 (see table 4.1). For each year, summary statistics are provided for all districts and for the subset of districts with contested House races. As these numbers indicate, the mean and standard deviation of RD splitting are substantially smaller when only the contested races are examined. Thus, a significant amount of RD splitting occurs in districts where a Democratic House candidate faces no Republican opposition. In addition, both the mean and variance in ticket splitting increase in the 1970s and then drop in the 1990s, even after uncontested seats are removed from the analysis. (There is an unusually high level of variance in RD splitting when canvassing all districts in the 1950s because of the large number of unopposed Democrats in those years.)

Furthermore, the shape of the distribution of RD splitting (after dropping uncontested House races) changes from unimodal in the 1950s and 1960s (as in figure 4.2) to bimodal in the 1970s and 1980s (as in figure 4.1). This pattern seems to mirror the changing distribution of the two-party vote in House contests identified by Mayhew (1974) as the "vanishing marginal" seats. The bimodal distribution of RD splitting in contested

TABLE 4.1.   Mean and Variation in Levels of RD Splitting in House Districts

Year	All House Districts		Contested Seats Only	
	Mean	σ	Mean	σ
1952	.29	.36	.14	.15
1956	.29	.33	.17	.14
1960	.33	.33	.20	.16
1964	.26	.26	.18	.11
1968	.28	.27	.21	.15
1972	.36	.27	.30	.19
1976	.37	.25	.31	.17
1980	.34	.24	.30	.16
1984	.36	.28	.30	.18
1988	.38	.29	.31	.19
1992	.19	.18	.17	.11
1996	.14	.14	.13	.08
2000	.23	.25	.19	.14

House races begins to appear in 1972 and remains through the 1988 elections before returning to a unimodal distribution in the 1990s. These changes correspond roughly with trends in the incumbency advantage, which increased sharply in the 1960s and 1970s and then dipped in the early 1990s (Gelman and King 1990; Jacobson 2001).[1] We argue that ticket splitting is driven partly by incumbency and the rise of candidate-centered congressional campaigns. Both of these developments mean that House elections became determined more by candidate quality (and less by district partisanship) than in the past. Thus, the bimodal distribution of RD ticket splitting in many elections separates House districts with high-quality Democratic candidates (often incumbents) from districts where the Republican candidate holds a quality advantage.

Table 4.2 shows a summary of the distribution of DR ticket splitting in each presidential election during the same period. Not surprisingly, given the typical pattern of divided government during the past 50 years, DR splitting is much less common than RD splitting. During the period being examined, 1996 is the only election where DR splitting is more frequent than RD splitting. Since the distribution of DR splitting tends to mass near the low end, there is less variation across districts when compared to RD splitting. Finally, the distribution does not change much after excluding uncontested House races. In most years of this study, few Republican candidates avoid Democratic opposition in House elections. However,

TABLE 4.2. Mean and Variation in Levels of DR Splitting in House Districts

Year	All House Districts		Contested Seats Only	
	Mean	σ	Mean	σ
1952	.07	.11	.07	.05
1956	.03	.09	.03	.03
1960	.08	.10	.09	.07
1964	.17	.14	.19	.12
1968	.19	.17	.20	.13
1972	.15	.14	.15	.08
1976	.17	.15	.18	.13
1980	.23	.20	.23	.16
1984	.16	.16	.15	.10
1988	.21	.22	.20	.14
1992	.11	.13	.10	.07
1996	.18	.14	.17	.12
2000	.22	.25	.17	.14

since Republicans gained majority control of Congress in 1995, the number of unopposed Republican House candidates has increased.

EXPLAINING TICKET SPLITTING

Our next task is to explain why ticket splitting is more common in some
districts than in others. The variation across districts spans the full range
of possible values, so district variables must be identified that can account
for these tremendous differences. Our unit of analysis is accordingly the
congressional district. Since the direction of ticket splitting is important
in determining the outcome of the election, we treat separately the two
types of ballot splitting (RD and DR). Fiorina (1996) and others have
noted that the asymmetry in divided government configurations must be
considered, so we have accordingly estimated models for each type. Total
ticket splitting is a less useful quantity when one wants to understand why
voters act as they do. Given the nature of most divided governments in the
United States since 1952, we focus primarily on RD splitting (the fraction
of Republican presidential voters who select a Democratic House candidate), although we examine DR splitting when it becomes more conse-
quential in the 1990s.

Our analysis provides a direct comparison of two competing theories of
split-ticket voting. As discussed in chapter 2, policy-balancing theories are
based on the idea that some voters prefer divided government and pursue
it at the ballot box. Ideological moderates purposely vote for presidential
and congressional candidates of different parties so that the parties can
check each other by controlling separate branches of government. Surveys
consistently suggest that many people prefer divided government to
unified government, so strategic policy balancing has some immediate
credibility. In its balancing framework, ticket splitting might be a viable
strategy for balancing the extreme positions of opposing parties, thereby
producing moderate policies favorable to the median voter.

Conversely, accidental theories of divided government posit that ticket
splitting is a by-product of other forces, such as the level of competition in
congressional contests (Burden and Kimball 1998; Jacobson 1990b), weak
partisan attachments in the electorate (Petrocik and Doherty 1996), candidate positioning (Frymer 1994; Grofman et al. 2000), and ballot devices
(Beck 1997; A. Campbell et al. 1960; A. Campbell and Miller 1957;
McAlister and Darcy 1992; Rusk 1970). We are careful to note that the
lack of strategic behavior is attributed only to voters: strategic candidates
can play an important purposive role in producing split-ticket voting as we

discuss below. Democratic voters in a district with an unopposed Republican candidate for Congress have little choice but to vote for the Republican or abstain. Furthermore, as party attachments in the electorate have weakened, campaigns have become more candidate centered (Wattenberg 1991b), making it more likely that voters will choose candidates from different parties for different offices, even if not motivated by a principled desire for divided government. Jacobson (1997) demonstrates that well-funded candidates with previous political experience are most adept at attracting voters from the opposite party. Voters often select the most visible and/or appealing candidate for each office. Given the low level of competition in many congressional contests, this decision can often lead to ticket splitting. In fact, most president-House ticket splitters defect from their identified party in the congressional contest (Brody, Brady, and Heitshusen 1994; Kimball 1997).

In the following sections, we test the policy-balancing and accidental theories of divided government by estimating a multivariate model of ticket splitting that seeks to account for variation across House districts. Since divided government has usually featured a Republican president with a Democratic Congress, we focus more attention on RD splitting. Thus, the dependent variable is usually our estimate of the proportion of Republican presidential voters who choose a Democratic House candidate within each district. We examine DR splitting as well. The coupling of a Democrat (Clinton) in the White House and a Republican majority in Congress for six years in the 1990s makes the DR pattern more salient, but we also believe that any explanation of divided control ought to be able to explain its existence in both directions.

Now we turn to the development of an explanatory model. We wish to keep the baseline model parsimonious without excluding the most important variables. Our theory suggests that the variables that shape congressional elections also drive much of the variance in split-ticket voting, so we begin by including three explanatory variables in the model to account for the nature of the congressional campaign and the advantages enjoyed by particular candidates. Two are dummy variables indicating the party of the incumbent, who often develops a personal bond of trust with constituents that crosses partisan and ideological lines (Bianco 1994; Cain, Ferejohn, and Fiorina 1987; Fenno 1978; Fiorina 1978; Mayhew 1974). We expect that RD ticket splitting will be higher in contests with a Democratic incumbent and lower in districts represented by a Republican incumbent. Conversely, DR splitting should be more common when a

Republican is the House incumbent and less common when a Democratic incumbent is running for reelection.

The other campaign variable is a measure of the Democratic candidate's spending as a fraction of total spending in the House contest. Campaigns are contests of competing messages crafted to attract voters, and the spending variable measures the extent to which the Democrat's campaign message dominates that of the Republican. By calculating Democratic spending in relation to overall expenditures, this measure allows us to control for the fact that campaign costs vary from one district to another. Since campaign costs have increased tremendously over the past 25 years, this measure also allows us to compare the effects of spending in different elections without having to adjust for inflation.

Evaluating the relative impacts of challenger and incumbent expenditures in congressional elections has been the subject of several methodological debates (Gerber 1998; Green and Krasno 1988, 1990; Jacobson 1990a). These debates turn on the problem of endogeneity. Campaign expenditures are both causes and effects of election results in the sense that candidates (especially challengers) are able to raise and spend a lot of money on their campaigns only if potential donors believe the candidates have a decent chance of winning (Westlye 1991). For example, potential donors often respond to polling data that substantiate a candidate's claims of viability (Herrnson 2000). In addition, incumbents who anticipate tough elections tend to redouble their efforts to raise campaign money, producing a paradoxical negative bivariate association between incumbent spending and incumbent vote share.

We chose not to account for endogeneity statistically because (1) there is no consensus on how to solve the problem, (2) we are not interested in estimating the effects of spending for incumbents versus challengers, and (3) we are primarily interested in assessing how voters respond to the alternative candidates presented. In addition, our spending measure still is a good indicator of the quality of the competing candidates. Campaign spending (especially candidate spending in proportion to opponent spending) is a powerful factor because it is the primary vehicle for transmitting a candidate's message to the voters. Candidates spend most of their campaign funds on advertising (Herrnson 1998; Jacobson 1997). To the extent that congressional candidates can dominate campaign advertising and frame campaign issues, the candidates will attract more votes from the opposite party. Though our spending measure is correlated with the party of the incumbent, the former is not a simply proxy for the latter, as we will show. We expect that our campaign spending measure will be positively associated with RD ticket splitting and negatively associated with DR splitting.

We also include a dichotomous variable for districts in the South.[2] In the post–World War II era, the South has supported Republican presidential candidates and Democratic congressional candidates more often than the rest of the country. Some argue that RD ticket splitting has been more common in the South because Democratic candidates for Congress have been able to position themselves toward the conservative end of the ideological spectrum, thus capturing the support of many Republican presidential voters (Frymer 1994; Frymer, Kim, and Bimes 1997; Grofman et al. 2000). We likewise expect RD ticket splitting to be more common in the South.

As the authors of The American Voter note, "any attempt to explain why the voter marks a straight or split ballot must take account of the physical characteristics of the election ballot" (A. Campbell et al. 1960, 275). They find that during the 1950s, split-ticket voting was about 8 percentage points higher in states without a straight party option on the ballot.[3] Other studies have reached similar conclusions (Beck 1997; A. Campbell and Miller 1957; McAllister and Darcy 1992). Thus, we include a dummy variable for states with a straight party ballot mechanism, and we expect it to be negatively associated with both types of ticket splitting.[4]

Policy-balancing theories of ticket splitting offer a clear hypothesis that we also test. Based on a simple spatial voting model in which moderate voters are located between a conservative Republican Party and a liberal Democratic Party, Fiorina (1996) argues that classic proximity voting is not rational when all candidates are far from a voter's ideal point. Instead, moderate voters may choose candidates from opposite parties so they will be required to compromise and produce moderate policies after taking office.

Thus, policy-balancing theory predicts that ticket splitting is more common when there is greater ideological distance between the two political parties and their candidates. On the surface, it may seem illogical for moderate voters to prefer extreme candidates of opposite parties, but the balancing intuition makes it plausible. This prediction fits well with some anecdotal evidence (Fiorina 1996). For example, national polarization between a conservative Republican president and leftist Democratic majorities in the House in the 1980s coincided with high levels of ticket splitting and divided government.

There are other ideological motivations for divided government beyond balancing. Some argue that ticket splitting is actually the product of ideological consistency (or classic proximity voting) in which voters select the candidates whose positions most agree with their own. Grofman and colleagues (2000) develop a spatial model of voter and candidate positions based on the crucial observation that candidates of the same party running in different districts often have different policy positions because of distinct constituency preferences. As a result, the median voter in a particular district might be closer to the policy positions of one party's congressional candidate but closer to the opposing party's presidential candidate. A sincere decision rule of choosing the closest candidate in each race would then produce a split ballot. Frymer (1994) and colleagues (1997) make a similar argument in explaining why ticket splitting has been more common in the South, where some conservative Democratic House incumbents have managed to survive while their constituents elected Republican presidents. In contrast to policy-balancing theories, the main thrust of these ideological-consistency theories is that ticket splitting is more common when candidates adopt moderate rather than extreme positions.

We test these contrasting hypotheses in this chapter using data on the ideological positions of House incumbents. Given a Republican presidential candidate located somewhere near the conservative end of the ideological spectrum, policy-balancing theories might predict that RD ticket splitting should be more common in districts where the Democratic House candidate is more liberal, creating greater polarization between the two parties. In contrast, simple candidate proximity theories posit that RD splitting should be more common in districts where the Democratic House candidates are conservative, positioning themselves closer to the ideal points of Republican voters. As proximity theories of voting predict, we find that RD splitting is more common where the Democratic House candidate leans toward the conservative end of the ideological spectrum. Similarly, DR splitting is most common in districts where the Republican candidate has a moderate to liberal voting record.

RD TICKET SPLITTING

First, we examine RD splitting in contested House districts. Table 4.3 provides estimates of the predictors of RD ticket splitting in each election since 1972, when congressional campaign spending data were first available nationwide. The linear regression analysis presented in table 4.3

TABLE 4.3. Explaining RD Splitting in Contested House Races, 1972–2000

Independent Variable	1972	1976	1980	1984	1988	1992	1996	2000
Campaign spending (Democratic share)	.244*** (.023)	.279*** (.021)	.299*** (.017)	.293*** (.020)	.311*** (.023)	.224*** (.021)	.161*** (.013)	.226*** (.021)
Democratic incumbent	.126*** (.015)	.046*** (.014)	.057*** (.013)	.066*** (.016)	.085*** (.017)	.023** (.011)	.047*** (.008)	.018 (.017)
Republican incumbent	-.103*** (.016)	-.129*** (.016)	-.063*** (.014)	-.077*** (.016)	-.050*** (.017)	.020 (.014)	.006 (.008)	-.049*** (.014)
Partisan ballot device	.020* (.010)	-.022** (.010)	-.020*** (.007)	-.012 (.008)	-.027*** (.008)	-.007 (.008)	.002 (.005)	.015* (.008)
South	.072*** (.012)	.007 (.011)	.007 (.009)	.024** (.010)	.038*** (.009)	.019** (.009)	.016*** (.005)	.013 (.009)
Constant	.126*** (.018)	.184*** (.019)	.145*** (.014)	.132*** (.018)	.119*** (.019)	.023 (.016)	.025** (.010)	.075*** (.015)
Standard error	.095	.089	.071	.073	.071	.078	.045	.073
Number of cases	379	378	379	367	355	405	414	370
Adjusted R^2	.741	.718	.806	.831	.859	.498	.699	.709

Note: Analysis excludes districts with uncontested House races. Cell entries are OLS coefficients. Standard errors are in parentheses.

*p < .1, two-tailed *t*-test; **p < .05, two-tailed *t*-test; ***p < .01, two-tailed *t*-test

serves as a baseline model that will be used and modified throughout this chapter.[5] To examine as many electoral districts as possible, the statistical model presented here does not yet include a measure of the incumbent's ideological position. Even though table 4.3 uses a rather parsimonious model with a handful of explanatory variables, we account for a substantial amount of variation in ticket splitting across districts (as indicated by the adjusted R^2 values).

The most robust finding in the evidence presented here is that candidate quality in House contests (as measured by spending and incumbency) has a tremendous effect on split-ticket voting. The greatest influence on ticket splitting, by far, is campaign spending, with a positive and statistically significant coefficient that hovers around .25 in almost every year studied. This suggests that a Democratic House candidate who matches the Republican opponent dollar for dollar can increase RD ticket splitting by a whopping 12.5 percentage points over a Democrat who spends no money on the campaign.

Though money is an important factor in congressional campaigns, its power to induce ticket splitting has been largely unexplored (cf. Kimball 1997). Because expenditures affect congressional elections and congressional elections are central to understanding divided government, money ought to be considered in studies of both. It is not spending per se that induces straight or split tickets, however. We suggest that campaign spending increases voter defection by drowning out the opposing candidate's message. For example, as the spending proportion of the Democrat nears 1, the Republican's self-promotion is scarcely noticed by voters. Lopsided spending patterns suggest one-sided messages in a campaign. As Zaller (1992) has shown, a political campaign can have a substantial effect on public opinion when countervailing messages are absent. The dominant campaign's repeated advertising raises the number of favorable "considerations" associated with that candidate in voters' minds. On Election Day, voters have little evidence to support the unknown candidate for sincere or strategic reasons.

Incumbency and spending exert independent influences on ticket splitting, thereby supporting our theoretical justification for including both types of variables in the analysis. We find that the two types of variables cannot easily be summarized in a single measure. Incumbents attract voters from the other party because of name recognition, constituent service, and the trust they have accrued generally from cultivating districts. Spending is a rough indicator of the relative strengths of candidates' messages. It need not reinforce the incumbency advantage, though it probably does in many districts. In addition, we know that some incumbents coast to easy reelection, while others are pushed to the limit (and occasionally defeated) by serious challengers. Figure 4.3 shows how closely related our measure of campaign strength, based as it is on spending patterns, is related to ticket splitting in 1988. The scatter plot looks like one a student might find in an introductory statistics textbook: RD ticket splitting clearly rises as the Democrat's share of campaign spending increases. This same relationship appears in each year of our study. As we will discuss, we find the same relationship when comparing DR ticket splitting and Republican campaign spending.

Nevertheless, the results also demonstrate the power of incumbency. As expected, the Democratic incumbency coefficient is positive and statistically significant every year but one (although the size of the coefficient varies). The results suggest that the presence of a Democratic incumbent boosted RD voting by as little as 1.8 percent and as much as 12.6 percent. Similarly, the Republican incumbency coefficient is negative and statistically significant in all but the last two elections, indicating that a Republican incumbent reduces the fraction of Republican presidential voters who cross over and choose a Democrat for the House. It appears that incumbency's contribution to RD splitting is weaker in the last three presidential elections, just as the incumbency advantage in House elections has declined at the same time. Estimates produced by Gelman and King (1990) and Jacobson (1997) suggest that the incumbency advantage in House elections peaked in the 1980s at roughly 10 percent, then dropped to about 5 or 7 points by the 1996 election (Jacobson 1997; J. Campbell 1996). G. Cox and Katz (1996) attribute much of the growth of incumbency's power to changes in the quality of challengers. Setting aside the origins of incumbency for the moment, these changes bear a remarkable resemblance to the observed shifts in coefficients for incumbency seen in table 4.3. This supports the idea that the incumbency advantage helps shape ticket splitting and divided government in the United States.

RD splitting is more common in the South in several elections, although this regional effect has almost disappeared. Recent Republican gains in subpresidential elections in the South have probably nationalized party politics enough to diminish the region's distinctiveness. Finally, the partisan ballot variable yields mixed results. In all but two years its coefficient is negative, as expected, though it reaches traditional statistical significance levels in just three of those cases. Even when the ballot vari-

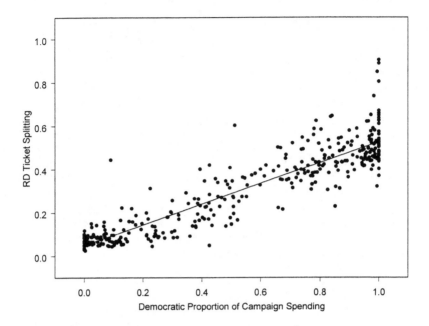

FIG. 4.3. House RD ticket splitting by Democratic campaign spending, 1988

able is significant, the results suggest that RD splitting is no more than 2.7 percent lower in states with a straight party ballot device.

We can see how well our empirical model accounts for variation in ticket splitting across geographic units by returning to the four neighboring congressional districts in Illinois introduced in chapter 2 (see table 4.4). These districts have similar demographic profiles, and all supported Republican presidential candidates in the 1980s. Nevertheless, the amount of ticket splitting by Bush voters in 1988 varied dramatically across these four districts. As table 4.4 indicates, our parsimonious model of RD splitting predicts the amount of ticket splitting among Bush voters with near precision, with one exception. In the 18th district, represented by Republican Bob Michel, our multivariate model predicts that .11 of Bush voters would split their ballots, while the calculated level of RD splitting is .21. In 1988, Michel was House minority leader, nearing the end of a long career in Congress, and he probably devoted less time and energy to his reelection campaign than did a typical incumbent. These factors may explain why Michel lost more Bush voters than our empirical model pre-dicted.[6]

While we have not tested directly for presidential effects, the evidence in table 4.3 suggests that presidential candidates also influence ticket split-ting. One might interpret RD splitting as evidence of defection among Democrats in the presidential contest. Thus, RD splitting should decline when a Democrat wins the presidential election. Democratic defections in presidential elections have been common in the South, where Democrats long dominated electoral politics. As early as 1964, however, Republican presidential candidates carried several southern states by appealing to con-servative Democrats, especially in elections when the Democratic nomi-nee is a northern liberal. Democrats have been more successful at main-taining the support of southern party members when they nominate a southerner for president. Thus, one would expect the effect of the South on RD splitting to be muted in elections when the Democratic presiden-tial nominee is from the South. The coefficient for the South variable in table 4.3 is larger in the three elections when the Democratic presidential nominee was from outside the South (average coefficient of .045) than in the five elections when the Democrats nominated a southerner for presi-dent (average coefficient of .012).

In addition, one implication of the incumbency advantage is that it might insulate congressional candidates from electoral tides that favor the opposite party in presidential elections. Thus, one might expect that incumbency's impact on ticket splitting is asymmetrical, depending on which party wins the White House (Born 2000a). Incumbents from the losing presidential party generate more ticket splitting since there are more opposite-party presidential voters available to support the incum-bents. In contrast, incumbents of the winning presidential party generate

TABLE 4.4.   Variation in RD Splitting, 1988, across Four Illinois Districts

Illinois District	Ticket Splitting Among Bush Voters (estimate)	Predicted Ticket Splitting Among Bush Voters
15	8%	8%
18	21%	11%
19	44%	47%
20	46%	43%

Note: The original estimates of RD splitting (middle column) are calculated using King's (1997) ecological-inference method. The predicted ticket-splitting figures (third column) are generated from the OLS equation in table 4.3.

less ticket splitting because the rising electoral tide limits the number of opposite-party presidential voters who might support the incumbents. Thus, the effect of Democratic incumbents on RD splitting is expected to be weaker in years when Democrats were elected president. As expected, the coefficient for the Democratic incumbent variable in table 4.3 is smaller in the three elections when the Democrats won the White House (average coefficient of .039) than in the five elections when the Democrats lost the presidential contest (average coefficient of .070).[7]

We now examine these presidential effects on ticket splitting in a more rigorous fashion by pooling the data from contested House races for all seven presidential elections from 1972 to 2000. We expand on the model in table 4.3 by adding dummy variables indicating whether the Democrats nominate a southerner for president and whether the Democrat wins the presidential election. We also include two interaction variables to capture the expected effects described earlier. First, we interact the southern Democrat variable with the South indicator to test whether there is less RD splitting in the South when the Democrats nominate a presidential candidate from that region. Second, we interact the Democratic victory variable with the Democratic incumbent indicator to test whether incumbency has a weaker effect on ticket splitting when the incumbent's party wins the presidential election. Both interaction terms should have negative coefficients.

The results of the pooled analysis are presented in table 4.5, and they provide further support for a presidential effect on ticket splitting.[8] Coefficients for the added variables are statistically significant and in the expected directions. First, we see that RD splitting is roughly 1.0 percent smaller in each district when a Democrat is elected president. When the Democratic candidate for president is more appealing, fewer Democratic voters defect to the Republican presidential candidate. Second, the effect of incumbency is indeed weaker when the Democrats win the presidential contest. In years when the Democrats lost the presidential race, RD splitting is roughly 11 percent higher in districts with Democratic incumbents. In years when a Democrat was elected president, RD splitting is only 3.4 percent higher in districts with Democratic incumbents running for reelection (.111 − .077 = .034).

Third, the presence of a southern candidate heading the Democratic ticket almost eliminates any regional effect on RD splitting. In years when the Democrats nominate a nonsoutherner for president, RD splitting is roughly 4.5 percent higher in southern congressional districts. In years when the Democratic nominee for president is a native of the South, RD splitting is basically no more frequent in the South than in the rest of the country (.045 – .042 = .003). In sum, presidential candidates can influence the direction and frequency of ticket splitting as well as its determinants.

The Effects of Incumbent Positioning

The dominant view in political science might leave little room for ideology to affect congressional elections. As we demonstrate in chapter 2, studies of House elections in particular find that voters tend to choose candidates on the basis of party identification and incumbency and that candidacy decisions are undertaken with regard to national tides and the

TABLE 4.5. Pooled Analysis of RD Splitting in Contested House Races, 1972–2000

Independent Variable	OLS Coefficient
Campaign spending (Democratic proportion)	.204***
	(.010)
Democratic incumbent	.111***
	(.007)
Democrat elected president	−.010**
	(.004)
Democratic incumbent × Democrat elected president	−.077***
	(.008)
Republican incumbent	−.065***
	(.006)
Partisan ballot device	.003
	(.004)
South	.045***
	(.007)
Southern democrat for president	−.042***
	(.005)
South × southern Democrat for president	−.042***
	(.009)
Constant	.149***
	(.007)
Standard error	.098
Number of cases	3,076
Adjusted R^2	.693

Note: The dependent variable is the fraction of Republican presidential voters splitting their ballots in the House contest. Analysis excludes uncontested seats. Cell entries are OLS coefficients with robust Huber/White standard errors in parentheses.

$*p < .1$, two-tailed t-test; $**p < .05$, two-tailed test; $***p < .01$, two-tailed test.

career patterns of incumbents. Some researchers question whether ideological positions are an important determinant in either voter or candidate
choices in congressional elections (Jacobson 1997; Mann and Wolfinger
1980; Miller and Stokes 1963; Stokes and Miller 1962). Researchers'
default position might well be the null hypothesis of no relationship (cf.
Abramowitz 1995). It is possible to infer that we too are taking this position. But although we argue that ticket splitting is often locally driven by
the strength of candidate messages, the content of these messages is also
important, especially the incumbent's legislative record.

The Downsian spatial model assumes that ideology matters in a
straightforward way. At least at the margins, voters ought to choose candidates nearest the voters' ideal points. Thus, centrist candidates win more
votes than do extremists. The balancing argument turns this view on its
head. Because ticket splitting rises with polarization, extremism might win
rather than lose votes if presidential and congressional candidates are all
relatively distant from the median voter.

Having demonstrated that candidate quality in House elections is an
important factor in explaining split-ticket voting, our next task is to test
policy-balancing theories of divided government. From a practical stand-
point, this means adding variables to our baseline model. Do ticket splitters attempt to balance two ideologically extreme parties by electing a liberal Democratic House candidate with a Republican president, as
policy-balancing theories might predict? Or do voters tend to pair a Democratic legislator with a Republican executive in districts where the Democratic House candidate is more conservative, as ideological consistency or
simple proximity theories might predict? There is also a third alternative,
suggested earlier. Ideology (as defined in chapter 2) might play no role in
congressional elections, reaffirming the view that subpresidential elections
are largely devoid of issues.

We first address these questions by examining RD ticket splitting in
relation to the ideological positions of Democratic House incumbents.
Our ideology measure is Poole and Rosenthal's (1997) W-NOMINATE
score, a commonly used indicator based on statistical analyses of roll-call
votes in Congress.[9] Since roll-call voting scores are not available for challengers, this limits our analysis to races with Democratic incumbents. We
use first-dimension W-NOMINATE scores for the Congress preceding
each presidential election to measure the ideological position of the
incumbent candidates. Values range from –1 (most liberal) to +1 (most
conservative). If voters are more likely to split their ballots when the par-

ties are polarized, then the ideological position coefficient ought to be negative. In other words, if motivated to balance extreme parties and candidates, Republican presidential voters should be more likely to split their tickets for a liberal Democratic House candidate than a conservative one.

We acknowledge that using the ideological position of only one of the House candidates is potentially problematic. If anything, it probably understates the importance of ideology. However, voters are much more likely to be aware of incumbents' policy positions because roll-call votes force them to take public positions on hundreds of issues. In contrast, challengers, many of whom have never held elective office, present more of a blank slate. Voters are frequently forced to infer challengers' policy positions from their party affiliation, personal characteristics, and campaign propaganda. Finally, congressional elections are often framed as a referendum on the incumbent's performance. Thus, we find it reasonable to proceed by examining solely the incumbent's ideological position at this point.

We included the ideology measure for the Democrat in a regression equation similar to the one in table 4.3, except that the incumbent dummies have been removed by necessity. The number of observations is smaller in this analysis because we have an ideology measure only for incumbents. Table 4.6 provides the results for presidential election years from 1972 to 2000. While campaign spending remains a powerful influence on RD ticket splitting, the ideological position of the Democratic incumbent plays an important part as well. In each year the coefficient for the ideological position variable is positive, and it is statistically significant in all but one year. This indicates that the proportion of RD voters in a district increases in response to the conservatism of the Democratic incumbent. This relationship remains remarkably stable from year to year despite great changes in how elections were conducted over this period. Since Republican presidential candidates adopt a right-of-center position, RD voting is more common if the ideological position of the Democratic House candidate is closer to the conservative end of the spectrum. This suggests that voters seek ideological consistency rather than balance, as Frymer (1994), Grofman and colleagues (2000), and Petrocik and Doherty (1996) have argued. More generally, these results also indicate the importance of ideology and issues in congressional elections. Although some scholars have concluded that congressional elections often are not based on issues and ideology, we find clear evidence consistent with proximity voting.[10]

TABLE 4.6. Explaining RD Splitting in House Races with Democratic Incumbents, 1972–2000

Independent Variable	1972	1976	1980	1984	1988	1992	1996	2000
Campaign spending (Democratic share)	.252***	.327***	.317***	.347***	.317***	.337***	.243***	.453***
	(.037)	(.029)	(.016)	(.029)	(.039)	(.046)	(.026)	(.043)
Democrat's ideology (W-NOMINATE)	.193***	.125***	.140***	.152***	.140***	.047	.165***	.200***
	(.048)	(.040)	(.034)	(.027)	(.038)	(.031)	(.019)	(.031)
Partisan ballot device	–.013	–.049***	–.050**	–.036***	–.060***	–.028*	–.014	–.002
	(.017)	(.014)	(.011)	(.012)	(.012)	(.015)	(.009)	(.015)
South	.038	–.009	–.011	–.021	.026*	.033*	.016	.005
	(.026)	(.012)	(.014)	(.016)	(.015)	(.017)	(.011)	(.017)
Constant	.323***	.244***	.239***	.245***	.252***	–.020	.086***	–.020
	(.032)	(.024)	(.021)	(.025)	(.036)	(.035)	(.023)	(.036)
Standard error	.108	.093	.076	.079	.080	.101	.054	.084
Number of cases	177	208	210	199	186	203	157	170
Adjusted R^2	.317	.398	.516	.430	.348	.250	.481	.427

Note: Analysis includes only districts with a challenged Democratic incumbent. Cell entries are OLS coefficients. Standard errors are in parentheses.

*p < .1, two-tailed *t*-test; **p < .05, two-tailed *t*-test; ***p < .01, two-tailed *t*-test

The magnitude of the ideology coefficient in table 4.6 lingers around .14 in most years. Substantively, this means that RD ticket splitting increases by 14 percent if a Democrat were to (hypothetically) move one unit in the conservative direction on the [–1,1] W-NOMINATE interval. This is not a trivial effect. For example, of the 250 Democratic incumbents running in 1984, roughly 20 percent had W-NOMINATE scores lower than –.7, while more than 25 percent had scores higher than –.2. Our results suggest that RD voting was about 7 percent higher in districts held by the latter type of moderate to conservative Democrat.

An example comparing two Democratic incumbents from New Jersey in the 1988 elections illustrates this point. William Hughes, who represented the second district, in the southern part of the state, had a centrist voting record (W-NOMINATE score of –.061) that put him well to the right of most Democrats. This helped Hughes survive in a Republican-leaning district: our estimates indicate that half of the Bush voters supported Hughes in the 1988 House elections. About an hour's drive to the north, New Jersey's sixth congressional district was represented by Bernard Dwyer, whose roll call record (–.419) was about average for House Democrats but well to the left of Hughes. As a result, Dwyer appealed to fewer Bush voters (39 percent by our estimates) than Hughes, even though Dwyer's 1988 opponent was poorly financed.

Including the ideology variable in our ticket-splitting equation also reduces the magnitude of the coefficient for the South variable: in table 4.6, the southern effect is significant in only two years, whereas it was significant in five of the seven years in table 4.3. In the 1970s and 1980s, southern Democrats had mean W-NOMINATE scores roughly .3 higher than the mean scores for nonsouthern Democrats. Thus, RD ticket splitting has been more common in the South, where Democratic incumbents position themselves closer to the conservative end of the spectrum. Controlling for ideological positioning removes much of the South's uniqueness, especially in earlier elections.

In recent years, the number of conservative Democrats in Congress has waned (Poole and Rosenthal 1997; Rohde 1991). Furthermore, the drop in conservative Democrats has occurred mostly in the South. The mean DW-NOMINATE score for southern Democrats in 2000 was –.31 (compared to –.12 in 1984), only .11 higher than the mean score of –.42 for nonsouthern Democratic incumbents. The declining number of conservative Democrats helps explain why RD ticket splitting has dropped substantially in recent elections, especially in the South.

Explaining the Rise and Fall in RD Splitting

Based on our ecological estimates and those from NES surveys presented in chapter 3, RD ticket splitting increased sharply during the 1970s and then declined a bit in the 1990s (see figs. 1.1 and 3.5). In this section, we explore these changes by examining the determinants of RD voting from 1952 to 2000. However, because we do not have data on campaign spending prior to 1972, we estimate a model of RD ticket splitting for each election year that includes just four explanatory variables: dichotomous measures indicating the presence of a Democratic incumbent, a Republican incumbent, a southern district, and a straight party ballot device. As indicated earlier, the ballot variable has a fairly weak effect on ticket splitting. In the 1950s, RD splitting was 4 or 5 percent higher in states without a straight party mechanism on the ballot, but the effect is weaker (even nonexistent) in recent elections. In contrast, regional differences and the effect of incumbency have changed quite a bit over the years.

Rather than report a table with each estimated coefficient for each year, we present a graph showing how the determinants of RD splitting change over time. Figure 4.4 traces the effects of incumbency and the South on RD splitting in each election from 1952 to 2000 for districts with contested House races. The figure reports the OLS coefficient for the South variable and the difference between the OLS coefficients for the Democratic and Republican incumbent variables. Thus, the incumbency effect measures the expected difference in RD splitting between a district with a Democratic incumbent and a district with a Republican incumbent. Our results demonstrate one consequence of the growing incumbency advantage in House elections: the effect of incumbency on ticket splitting increases sharply in the late 1960s and early 1970s and remains at a high level through the 1980s. As the lines show, in contested districts in the 1950s and early 1960s, RD ticket splitting was roughly 15 percent higher in races with Democratic incumbents running. By the 1970s, however, RD voting was roughly 30 percent higher in districts with Democratic incumbents (reaching an apex of 35 percent in 1988). Whether measured by the "sophomore surge" or "retirement slump" (Jacobson 1997), the Gelman-King index (Gelman and King 1990), or recent estimates provided by G. Cox and Katz (1996), the incumbency advantage in House elections grew at the same time that incumbency's contribution to ticket splitting has increased. Similarly, as the incumbency advantage receded in 1992 and 1996 (Jacobson 2001), so did the effect of incumbency on ticket splitting.

In contrast to the growing contribution of incumbency, regional differ-

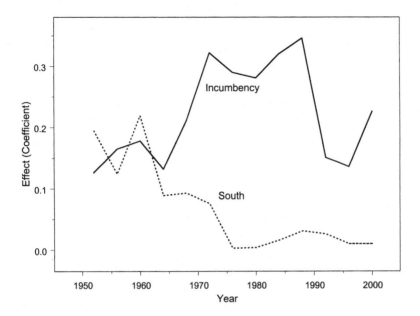

FIG. 4.4.   Effects of region and incumbency on RD ticket splitting

ences in ticket splitting gradually disappear during the period of our analysis. As figure 4.4 shows, RD voting was roughly 15 to 20 percent higher in
the South than in other contested districts from 1952 to 1960. This
regional difference rivals the effect of incumbency in these three elections.
The southern effect drops to 10 percent during the 1964–72 period and
then almost vanishes after 1972. The southern effect on RD splitting does
not rise above 3 percent from 1976 to 2000. As we have shown, the presence of a southern candidate leading the Democratic ticket in several
recent elections (1976, 1980, 1992, 1996) might partly explain the declining regional disparity in RD splitting. However, the difference between
the South and the rest of the country is small even in recent elections
when the Democrats have nominated nonsoutherners for president.[11]
   Our evidence of a steadily declining regional effect on ticket splitting is
consistent with theories of a "glacial, top-down" Republican realignment
in the South (Aistrup 1996; Brunell and Grofman 1998; Bullock 1988).
While Republican presidential candidates have generally fared well in the

South during the past forty years, the GOP has only gradually recruited more high-quality candidates for many of the House contests in southern districts (Jacobson 1990b). The Republican Party has slowly turned the tide in its favor in terms of two important measures of candidate quality in House contests: fielding candidates and spending money. In the 1950s, the GOP failed to run candidates in more than half of the House contests in the South. By the 1970s, roughly 25 percent of the Democratic seats were uncontested by Republican candidates, and in 1996, only two Democrats ran unopposed in the South (1.5 percent of the southern contests). Similarly, in 1996 and 2000, Republican House candidates outspent their Democratic opponents in 59 percent of the contests in the South, compared to only 41 percent of the contests in 1980. As the GOP has closed the gap in candidate quality in the South, the regional disparity in RD ticket splitting has just about vanished.

DR SPLITTING

To this point our model emphasizing candidate quality and incumbent positioning in House contests has performed well in accounting for variation in RD splitting. But that is only part of the story. Ticket splitting occurs in two directions. While RD splitting has generally been more common than DR splitting (the 1996 election being the only exception in our sample), a nontrivial number of voters split their ballots by voting for a Democratic presidential candidate and Republican House candidate. We find that the same explanatory variables (except the South) account for DR ticket splitting. Table 4.7 provides the results of a regression analysis in which the dependent variable is the fraction of Democratic presidential voters who chose a Republican House candidate in each election from 1972 to 2000. The independent variables are the same ones used to explain RD splitting.

Once again, a handful of predictors accounts for a large amount of variation in DR splitting across congressional districts. The results again point to the importance of candidates in the House races. In particular, campaign spending remains a critical factor. The higher the Democrat's share of spending in House races, the lower the levels of DR splitting. The regression coefficient for spending is negative and statistically significant for every year in table 4.7. The mean of the spending coefficients across all eight elections is −.18. This means that as the Democratic candidate's expenditures increase from zero to 100 percent of all spending, DR ticket splitting decreases by roughly 18 percent, even after controlling for incum-

TABLE 4.7. Explaining DR Splitting in Contested House Races, 1972–2000

Independent Variable	1972	1976	1980	1984	1988	1992	1996	2000
Campaign spending (Democratic share)	-.103***	-.168***	-.260***	-.141***	-.222***	-.092***	-.262***	-.230***
	(.011)	(.015)	(.017)	(.012)	(.017)	(.014)	(.017)	(.018)
Democratic incumbent	-.037***	-.032***	-.040***	-.023**	-.036***	.001	-.004	-.058***
	(.007)	(.010)	(.013)	(.009)	(.012)	(.007)	(.010)	(.015)
Republican incumbent	.065***	.130***	.110***	.072***	.067***	.036***	.025**	.033***
	(.007)	(.012)	(.014)	(.010)	(.013)	(.010)	(.011)	(.012)
Partisan ballot device	-.016***	.003	-.012	-.001	.006	.002	-.017***	-.021***
	(.005)	(.007)	(.008)	(.005)	(.006)	(.006)	(.006)	(.007)
South	-.013**	.005	.005	-.009	-.001	-.001	.0004	-.018**
	(.006)	(.008)	(.009)	(.006)	(.007)	(.006)	(.007)	(.007)
Constant	.209***	.251***	.351***	.219***	.316***	.041***	.291***	.314***
	(.009)	(.013)	(.015)	(.011)	(.014)	(.008)	(.013)	(.013)
Standard error	.045	.063	.072	.043	.052	.078	.061	.061
Number of cases	379	378	379	367	355	405	414	370
Adjusted R²	.704	.752	.803	.812	.856	.497	.725	.812

Note: Analysis excludes districts with uncontested House races. Cell entries are OLS coefficients. Standard errors are in parentheses.

*p < .1, two-tailed *t*-test; **p < .05, two-tailed *t*-test; ***p < .01, two-tailed *t*-test

bency. Thus, the fraction of DR ticket splitters may shift by almost 20 percent based on spending patterns in House contests. Campaign spending certainly is a proxy for other factors, such as the candidates' relative experience and abilities, but the results still suggest that the quality of House candidates accounts for a lot of president-House ticket splitting.

As in the previous analyses, table 4.7 suggests that incumbency exerts a strong effect on ticket splitting. Other things being equal, DR voting is less common when a Democratic incumbent is running and more common when a Republican incumbent is running. Finally, DR splitting is largely unaffected by straight party ballot mechanisms and is not associated with any regional differences between the South and the rest of the country.

We also examine DR ticket splitting in races with Republican incumbents to assess the impact of the incumbent's ideological position. We conduct the same analysis as in table 4.6, except that the dependent variable is DR splitting and the W-NOMINATE variable represents the Republican incumbent's score.

When examining races with Republican incumbents, the evidence again shows that the ideological position of the incumbent is important (see table 4.8). The coefficient for the W-NOMINATE variable is negative and statistically significant in every election examined, indicating that the proportion of DR voters is higher in districts where the Republican incumbent has a moderate to liberal record (rather than a pure conservative record). Across all eight elections, the mean value of the ideology coefficient is –.19, which indicates that DR splitting increases by 19 percent as one moves from a district where the Republican incumbent has a very conservative voting record (W-NOMINATE score of .9) to a district where the Republican incumbent has a left-of-center voting record (W-NOMINATE score of –.1).

An example from the 1996 election illustrates the effect of the incumbent's ideological position on ticket splitting. Connie Morella, the most liberal-leaning Republican incumbent running in 1996 (W-NOMINATE score of .226) and Roscoe Bartlett, solidly entrenched in the right wing of the Republican House membership (W-NOMINATE score of .776), represented neighboring districts in Maryland (the sixth and eighth, respectively). According to our estimates, 38 percent of Clinton voters in 1996 split their ballots to vote for Morella in the sixth district, while only 17 percent of Clinton supporters voted for Bartlett in the eighth. Although Bartlett faced a tougher opponent than did Morella, Morella's more mod-

TABLE 4.8. Explaining DR Splitting in House Races with Republican Incumbents, 1972–2000

Independent Variable	1972	1976	1980	1984	1988	1992	1996	2000
Campaign spending (Democratic share)	-.180***	-.177***	-.454***	-.240***	-.293***	-.166***	-.413***	-.362***
	(.022)	(.045)	(.041)	(.031)	(.031)	(.048)	(.029)	(.029)
Republican's ideology (W-NOMINATE)	-.172***	-.237***	-.247***	-.093***	-.179***	-.132***	-.210***	-.219***
	(.028)	(.043)	(.042)	(.021)	(.028)	(.035)	(.031)	(.032)
Partisan ballot device	-.029***	-.022	-.056***	-.012	-.005	.007	-.015	-.032***
	(.009)	(.013)	(.014)	(.010)	(.010)	(.016)	(.010)	(.011)
South	.021*	.046***	.076***	-.015	.011	-.011	.017	-.012
	(.012)	(.017)	(.020)	(.013)	(.013)	(.018)	(.011)	(.012)
Constant	.337***	.434***	.565***	.354***	.472***	.247***	.481***	.522***
	(.011)	(.017)	(.016)	(.013)	(.011)	(.020)	(.022)	(.023)
Standard error	.051	.071	.078	.055	.058	.085	.069	.067
Number of cases	143	119	129	140	143	122	202	166
Adjusted R^2	.448	.291	.554	.341	.482	.137	.526	.579

Note: Analysis includes only districts with challenged Republican incumbents. Cell entries are OLS coefficients. Standard errors are in parentheses.

*p < .1, two-tailed t-test; **p < .05, two-tailed t-test; ***p < .01, two-tailed t-test erate record surely helped her appeal to more Democratic-leaning voters than did Bartlett.

Next we consider the degree to which ticket-splitting levels change within the same district from one election to the next. So far, our multivariate model has performed well in accounting for variation in ticket splitting across congressional districts. Can it explain changing levels of split-ticket voting over time, or do some moderate districts produce steady rates of ticket splitting regardless of the level of competition in the House contest?

In the absence of measures of voters' preferences within each House district, comparisons over time are a good way to control for such variation. As long as district boundaries remain fixed and population movements are modest, we expect that district ideology will stay nearly constant. We cannot examine every interelection shift with our data because a new round of redistricting alters district boundaries every ten years. Consequently, we chose two election cycles in which House district lines remained constant: the 1972 and 1976 elections and the 1984 and 1988 elections.[12] Although the nationwide frequency of ticket splitting was quite stable from 1972 to 1988, ticket splitting within congressional districts varied greatly from one election to the next. The over-time correlation for our district-level estimates of RD splitting is .58 for 1972–76 and .63 for 1984–88, both well below 1.0. It is unlikely that the desire to balance comes and goes so quickly within a given district. It is also unlikely that voters' preferences shift markedly between elections. Instead, the candidates shape ticket splitting, since the level of competition within the same district can change dramatically from one election to the next while most other factors remain constant.

For the analysis presented here, we simply calculated the change in RD splitting from one presidential election to the next (for example, RD voting in 1988 minus RD voting in 1984). This measure of changing levels of ticket splitting serves as our dependent variable. Since regional boundaries do not change and ballot format rarely changes from one election to the next, we do not use these variables to explain changing levels of ticket splitting.

To account for changes in RD splitting, we create three measures that tap into the level of competition in the House contests. The first measure indicates whether there has been a change in the contested status of the seat (–1 = uncontested in 1972/contested in 1976; 0 = no change in the contested status; +1 = contested in 1972/uncontested in 1976). We are thus explaining change with change. We expect ticket splitting to increase when a candidate runs unopposed after the seat had attracted candidates from both parties in the previous election. In contrast, we expect ticket splitting to decrease if a seat was uncontested in the previous election but is now contested by both parties. As a result, this variable should have a positive regression coefficient.

Our second independent variable is a five-point scale that measures the extent of any change in the party of the incumbent. This variable takes on the following values: −2 (Republican incumbent in 1976, Democratic incumbent in 1972), −1 (Republican incumbent in 1976/open seat in 1972 or open seat in 1976/Democratic incumbent in 1972), 0 (no change in incumbency), +1 (Democratic incumbent in 1976/open seat in 1972 or open seat in 1976/Republican incumbent in 1972), +2 (Democratic incumbent in 1976/Republican incumbent in 1972). Because of the power of incumbency, RD voting should increase when a seat has switched into the hands of a Democrat but should decrease when a seat has fallen into the hands of a Republican incumbent. Thus, we should see a positive regression coefficient associated with this variable.

The third independent variable measures the extent to which the Democrat's share of House campaign spending has changed from one election to the next. We simply take the arithmetic difference (for example, Democratic proportion of spending in 1976 minus Democratic proportion of spending in 1972). Again, this variable should have a positive regression coefficient. RD splitting should rise if the Democratic candidate's share of campaign spending increases and drop if Democratic spending declines. Finally, because each independent variable takes on a value of zero when there is no change from the previous election, the constant term in the regression model estimates the expected direction and magnitude of change in ticket splitting when the competitive context of the House race remains fixed.

The results, presented in table 4.9, suggest that the nature of the House campaign goes a long way toward explaining any changes in the frequency of RD ticket splitting in congressional districts. In both cases, all three of the independent variables have regression coefficients that are statistically significant and in the expected positive direction. When the competitive context of the House race shifts in favor of the Democratic Party, RD ticket splitting increases. When the level of competition changes in favor of the GOP, RD ticket splitting declines.

Furthermore, the constant term is statistically indistinguishable from zero in both cases, suggesting that ticket-splitting levels remain constant when the level of competition in the House contest stays the same. Thus, it seems that the nature of the congressional campaign can explain the direction and magnitude of changes in the frequency of ticket splitting as well as its stability over time. Some caution might be required when generalizing from these findings, since we only examine pairs of elections during a period when president-House ticket splitting (and RD splitting in particular) reached high levels. But given that other evidence in this chapter dovetails with these findings, we are more confident about their general meaning.

ANALYSES ESCHEWING ECOLOGICAL INFERENCES

Given some of the controversy surrounding King's (1997) method of ecological inference, some readers will be skeptical about our measures of ticket splitting and our analyses in this chapter. To allay some of these concerns, we will discuss and present analyses that do not rely on ecological estimates of ticket splitting. These findings buttress our conclusions that president-House ticket splitting is influenced primarily by the level of competition in House contests.

TABLE 4.9.   Explaining Changing Levels of RD Ticket Splitting across Elections

Independent Variable	1972 to 1976	1984 to 1988
Change in contested status	.335*	.358*
	(.018)	(.015)
Change in incumbency	.078*	.044*
	(.008)	(.012)
Change in spending	.349*	.415*
(Democratic share)	(.024)	(.033)
Constant	−.007	.005
	(.006)	(.007)
Standard error	.129	.132
Number of cases	412	418
Adjusted R^2	.714	.704

Note: Analysis excludes districts where spending data or vote totals were unavailable. Cell entries are OLS coefficients. Standard errors in parentheses.

*p < .01, two-tailed test.

One alternative to our ecological estimates of ticket splitting is the Burnham-Cummings-Rusk (BCR) measure. This aggregate difference measure—the difference between the Democratic Party's share of the House vote and presidential vote within a constituency—essentially measures the extent to which a House candidate runs ahead of (or behind) his party's presidential nominee. The aggregate difference measure is the combined result of two processes that differ in the degree to which they reflect disloyalty to a party: (1) ballot roll-off (a weak form of disloyalty), and (2) ticket splitting (a strong form of disloyalty). Although crude, this measure of ticket splitting still provides a rough indicator of the extent to which voters deviate from casting straight party ballots.

For each of the analyses presented in this chapter, we reach the same substantive conclusions about the determinants of ticket splitting and divided government when using the BCR measure.[13] This should not be a surprise since the correlation between our measure and the BCR measure is quite strong (see chap. 3).

ANALYSIS OF INDIVIDUAL-LEVEL DATA

We also examine individual-level data from a 1988 NES survey to test theories of ticket splitting. We use a multinomial logit model to estimate the effects of 11 explanatory variables on vote choice. The dependent variable indicates the four possible major-party president-House voting combinations (DD, DR, RD, and RR), and thus allows us to examine separately the predictors of both forms of ticket splitting. The odds of a voter choosing a particular combination of candidates rather than another are expressed as a linear function of several explanatory variables and estimated coefficients (Greene 1993). The constraint that all four probabilities must sum to 1 for each voter allows one of the categories to be designated the reference category, leaving three equations to be estimated. We chose DD voters as the reference category, so that each equation estimates the probability of a voter choosing one of the other candidate combinations.[14]

We selected several predictors to test competing theories of voting. Table 4.10 provides summary statistics for each explanatory variable in our model as well as its expected effect in each equation. We include the standard seven-point measure of party identification to control for psychological attachment to a party as a predictor of voting. We include two measures of a voter's ideological position to test different theories of issue-based voting. A seven-point ideological self-placement measure tests whether voting is influenced by sincere ideological considerations. Thus, other things being equal, conservatives should be more likely to vote Republican than liberals.

Conversely, moderate voters might have an incentive to balance the two parties and split tickets. Thus, our model includes a dichotomous variable identifying voters who place themselves at one of the three most moderate locations on the seven-point ideology scale (as roughly one in five voters did in 1988). If these centrist voters are more likely than ideologues to cast either type of split ballot, we would have evidence consistent with policy-balancing theories.[15]

In chapter 2, we hypothesized that voters who see no policy differences between the parties are more likely to cast split ballots. To test our theory that ticket splitting is partly a function of the size of the ideological gulf between the parties, we include a variable indicating whether voters per-

TABLE 4.10.   Summary of Explanatory Variables for President-House Voting, 1988

		Expected MNL Coefficient		
Independent Variable	Mean (s.d.) [min,max]	P_{DR}/P_{DD}	P_{RD}/P_{DD}	P_{RR}/P_{DD}
Party identification	4.0 (2.2) [1,7]	−	−	−
Ideology	4.5 (1.4) [1,7]	+	+	+
Ideological moderate	.26 (.44) [0,1]	+	+	0
Presidential candidate affect differential	.2 (2.6) [−5,5]	0	+	+
Recall Democratic House candidate	.37 (.48) [0,1]	−	0	−
Recall Republican House candidate	.27 (.44) [0,1]	+	0	+
Democratic incumbent	.59 (.49) [0,1]	−	0	−
Republican incumbent	.33 (.47) [0,1]	+	0	+
South	.20 (.40) [0,1]	0	+	0
Partisan ballot device	.43 (.49) [0,1]	−	−	0
Important differences between parties	.72 (.45) [0,1]	−	−	0

ceive important differences between the two parties. Thus, we expect this variable to be negatively associated with either form of ticket splitting.

Individual-level data allow a more direct test of the effect of presidential candidates on ticket splitting. We mimic Sigelman, Wahlbeck, and Buell (1997) in counting the number of "likes" a voter mentions about each presidential candidate to produce a presidential candidate affect differential (the difference between the two numbers). Such a measure should distinguish between Bush and Dukakis voters, regardless of whether they split their ballots.

We also include four measures to capture the competitive context of House elections. We conceptualize elections as a test of competing messages. To the extent that candidates can dominate the battle of campaign advertising and reach more voters, the candidates will increase their chances of winning. Thus, we measure whether voters accurately recall the names of the competing House candidates. These measures provide more direct indication than does campaign spending of the extent to which a candidate has penetrated the voter's consciousness. In addition, these measures avoid the controversy over using campaign spending as an exogenous variable. Given our view of congressional campaigns, we expect that people are more likely to vote for the candidate with whom they are familiar. We also include measures of incumbency to test whether incumbents enjoy other campaign advantages beyond superior name recognition. Finally, our model includes indicators for southern voters and citizens in states with a straight party punch on the ballot. We expect to find the same association between these variables and ticket splitting as presented earlier. A summary of our expectations can be found in table 4.10, which presents the hypothesized significance and direction of each coefficient in the model.

The estimated coefficients and standard errors in table 4.11 indicate the effect of each explanatory variable on voting DR, RD, or RR. We include respondents only in districts where both major parties fielded House candidates as these are the only voters who have a choice between voting a straight ticket and a split ticket. The fit of our model, as indicated by the summary statistics at the bottom of the table, is quite good. The predictors in the model have some success in accounting for each combination of president-House voting.

For the most part, partisanship, evaluations of the presidential candidates, and the nature of the congressional contest are the strongest influences on voting in 1988 national elections. Not surprisingly, party attachments predict the degree to which voters support the same party in more than one contest. Whether incumbency and name recognition favor one party more than the other influences voting in the House contest but not in the presidential contest. Similarly, affinity for the two presidential candidates has a strong impact on voting in the presidential contest.

At first blush, the fact that affect for the presidential candidates also helps distinguish between DR and DD voters might be seen as evidence for some form of balancing. It suggests that Dukakis voters who did not especially like Dukakis were more likely to cast a Republican vote in the House

TABLE 4.11.   Multinomial Logit Regression Coefficients for President-House Voting, 1988

Independent Variable	P_{DR}/P_{DD}	P_{RD}/P_{DD}	P_{RR}/P_{DD}
Party identification	−.31**	−.84***	−1.07***
	(.13)	(.11)	(.12)
Ideology	.02	.09	.48***
	(.17)	(.14)	(.16)
Ideological moderate	.37	.34	.08
	(.45)	(.37)	(.40)
Presidential candidate affect differential	.37***	.83***	1.04***
	(.11)	(.11)	(.11)
Recall Democratic House candidate	−1.13**	−.49	−.78*
	(.55)	(.38)	(.43)
Recall Republican House candidate	1.83***	1.21**	1.89***
	(.53)	(.53)	(.52)
Democratic incumbent	−2.33***	1.44*	−.40
	(.82)	(.84)	(.81)
Republican incumbent	1.73**	.11	2.01**
	(.67)	(.96)	(.82)
South	−.28	1.39***	.49
	(.57)	(.44)	(.47)
Partisan ballot device	−.58	−.60	.22
	(.45)	(.37)	(.38)
Important differences between parties	−1.68***	−1.30***	−.95**
	(.46)	(.35)	(.39)
Constant	1.57	2.45**	2.06*
	(1.30)	(1.21)	(1.25)

Number of cases	755
Log likelihood	−388.3
Model χ^2 (33 df)	1036.5***
Pseudo R^2	.57

Note: Analysis excludes respondents in districts with uncontested House races.
Cell entries are multinomial logit coefficients. DD is the reference category.
Standard errors in parentheses.
*$p < .1$; **$p < .05$; ***$p < .01$, two-tailed test.

contest (perhaps to offset their less-than-enthusiastic vote for the top of the Democratic ticket). However, the substantive impact of affect for the presidential candidates on DR voting is quite small. In addition, the presidential affect variable does not help distinguish RD voters from RR voters, and the RD voters matched the divided-government alignment produced by the 1988 elections. Furthermore, candidate evaluations are simply not the same as their ideological locations.

The results also point to some other important factors in explaining voting in 1988. Even in 1988, voters in the South are more likely to cast a split RD ballot than vote a straight Democratic ticket. Ballot format, however, appears unrelated to ticket splitting. The coefficients associated with the partisan ballot device carry the expected signs but fall short of conventional levels of statistical significance.

In addition, ideology seems only to help separate the staunch Republican (RR) voters from the die-hard Democratic (DD) voters. Furthermore, ideological moderates are no more likely to cast a split ballot than are liberals and conservatives, a finding that is clearly inconsistent with policy balancing. One might argue that this is not a fair test of policy balancing. Although moderates might have an incentive to balance the two parties, perhaps only a subset of moderates have the knowledge and interest in politics needed to employ a balancing-decision rule instead of an alternative voting calculus. To capture this possibility, we created a separate dichotomous variable identifying moderates who are above the NES sample mean in political knowledge, external efficacy, and interest in politics. This measure fares no better when used in place of the ideological-moderate variable in the multinomial logit model

In contrast, the blurring of ideological differences between the parties helps explain ticket splitting, even after controlling for several other factors. Seeing important differences between the political parties (a necessary condition for policy balancing) reduces the probability of casting either type of split ballot in 1988. Thus, a perception of indistinguishable rather than ideologically extreme parties is the more common route to ticket splitting. This is consistent with our earlier findings, based on somewhat different data sources and levels of analysis, that moderate candidates encourage ticket splitting.

SUMMARY

We have examined president-House ticket splitting from several vantage points, and each perspective suggests that split outcomes are largely a by-product of lopsided congressional campaigns that feature well-funded, high-quality candidates versus unknown, poorly financed opponents. In addition, the ideological positions of congressional incumbents can induce splitting in a manner that is consistent with sincere proximity voting. The cross-sectional component of this chapter shows that ticket splitting is more common in districts where one candidate enjoys a tremendous financial advantage over the opponent and where incumbents are running. These are separate meaningful effects rather than simple statistical controls. In addition, we find that incumbency's contribution to ticket splitting rises and falls at the same time that the incumbency advantage in House elections, as measured by other scholars, rises and falls. And as the caliber of GOP House candidates in the South has gradually improved over time, regional differences in ticket splitting have disappeared. Finally, we find that changing levels of competition in House contests can account for changing levels of president-House ticket splitting over time.

All of these results point to the conclusion that president-House ticket splitting is driven primarily by characteristics of the congressional campaign in each district. This is not to say that the presidential contest does not matter at all. We find evidence that the appeal of presidential candidates shapes ticket splitting and modifies the effects of other predictors in systematic ways. Some voters surely split their ballots by defecting from their identified party in the presidential race. However, the large majority of ticket splitters defects in the congressional contest (Brody, Brady, and Heitshusen 1994; Burden and Kimball 1998; Kimball 1997). As a result, the level of competition in congressional contests and the ability of candidates to position themselves near voters from the opposing party go a long way toward explaining the presence of divided-party government in the United States.

CHAPTER V

Midterm Elections and Divided Government

Midterm congressional elections have puzzled political scientists for decades. Midterm elections exhibit systematic patterns, such as the well-documented loss of seats by the president's party, but the reasons for these regularities are not entirely clear (Erikson 1988). Both local and national forces are simultaneously at work, sometimes conflicting but often reinforcing one another. Understanding how these forces interact to produce the observed voting behaviors and election outcomes is an important endeavor for scholars because it touches on larger issues of strategic candidate behavior, mandate theories, retrospective voting, and voter mobilization. To improve our understanding of these issues, we will now consider midterm elections in the context of divided government.

While divided government has recently occurred after presidential elections, it historically has been delivered at the midterm (Fiorina 1996). Our constitutional system of staggered terms for different national offices creates the need for midterm congressional elections without a presidential contest on the ballot. National conditions and campaign issues during midterm elections can differ dramatically from the issues and conditions present during the previous presidential election. In addition, a president's public approval ratings at midterm are usually substantially lower than during the honeymoon period when he first took office (Kernell 1977). As a result, it is no surprise that the president's party usually loses seats in the House during midterm elections and subsequently often faces an opposition Congress.

In this chapter, we argue that midterm elections can be understood within the divided voting framework developed in earlier chapters, with the main difference being that votes are considered across elections rather than on just one ballot. We examine the sources of electoral change in three recent midterm elections by using King's (1997) ecological inference technique to estimate voter transitions from on-year to off-year House elections. We argue that surge-and-decline theories (A. Campbell 1960; J. Campbell 1993) overstate the importance of voter abstention and understate the importance of party defection in midterm elections. Voters who switch parties make up a sizable portion of the midterm electorate, and the net direction of party defection is always away from the president's party in the elections we examine. In addition, the number of seats the president's party loses is associated with the magnitude of the partisan disparity in voter defections. We find that party defection among midterm voters is determined by the level of competition in the House contest, the baseline level of support for the president's party in the district, and the incumbent's voting record in Congress. In particular, incumbents of the president's party who hold marginal seats yet strongly support the chief executive's legislative agenda risk provoking voter defections in midterm elections.

ELECTORAL CHANGE IN MIDTERM ELECTIONS

The modern era (since World War II) has witnessed more than the usual share of divided government. It has also seen the president's party lose seats in nearly every midterm House election. Divided government has ensued after 10 of the 14 midterm elections held since 1946. In addition, divided government has become more persistent in the modern era. Figure 5.1 shows the size of the loss (or gain, in the case of 1998) for each postwar midterm election. The figure also indicates which of these elections created or continued divided government using hatched lines within the bars. Before the 1950s, when midterm elections produced divided national governments, single-party control was usually returned in the following presidential election. From 1826 to 1946, 16 midterm elections produced divided government, but unified government returned after the following presidential election in 13 of those 16 cases (Silbey 1996). By comparison, of the nine midterm elections that produced divided government from 1954 to 1998, the subsequent presidential election produced unified government in only four cases.

Aside from the 1998 results, the rather consistent finding that the president's party loses seats in Congress in midterm elections is often cited in support of a policy-balancing theory of divided government (Alesina and Rosenthal 1989; Erikson 1988). The argument is that on-year voters for the president's party defect in midterm elections to help elect an opposition Congress that can moderate the president's agenda. In particular, vot-

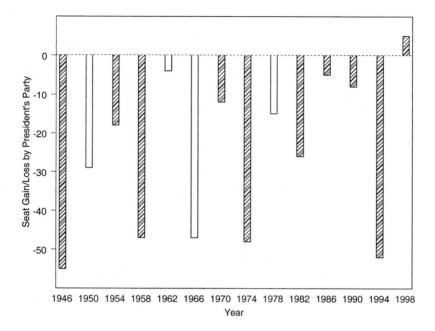

FIG. 5.1. Performance of the president's party in midterm House elections

ers punish incumbents with a legislative record of robust support for the president's agenda. However, our view is that midterm losses might instead reflect simple proximity voting if the electoral punishment is concentrated on incumbents holding marginal seats. In these cases a legislator usually must deviate from constituent preferences to support the president's policies, thus making the incumbent even more vulnerable.

Other nonbalancing explanations (such as the increased motivation of voters with negative evaluations of the president) can account for midterm losses (Erikson 1988, 1014). In fact, alternative explanations for midterm losses abound. The original surge-and-decline theory (A. Campbell 1960) fingers the decline in voter turnout as the primary culprit. In addition, midterm elections are a referendum on the president's performance and the state of the national economy (Tufte 1978), and midterm losses reflect inevitable negative evaluations of the president after two years in office (Kernell 1977). In addition, the more seats the majority party holds (the more exposed it is), the more susceptible it is to midterm losses (Marra and Ostrom 1989; Oppenheimer, Stimson, and Waterman 1986). Finally, strategic politicians are thought to magnify referendum effects if potential challengers wait to run for Congress until national conditions are most favorable (Kernell and Jacobson 1983). A revised surge-and-decline theory (J. Campbell 1993, 1997) combines several of these elements but also argues for the importance of voter turnout. In any case, there is substantial controversy as to which of these explanations (including the balancing model) best accounts for midterm losses (Niemi and Weisberg 1993).

We focus on the surge-and-decline explanation in particular because it makes the clearest predictions about the nature and influence of abstention and party defection in midterm elections. The following section discusses surge-and-decline theories in more detail. We then explain our use of the ecological inference procedure to estimate party differences in midterm abstention and voter defection. After discussing our estimates of both sources of electoral change, we conclude by explaining why voters defect from the president's party in midterm elections.

SURGE-AND-DECLINE THEORIES
OF MIDTERM ELECTIONS

The most prominent explanations of electoral change in congressional elections focus on turnout as the primary source of change. The theory of surge and decline posits that the surge of turnout in a presidential election helps congressional candidates from the winning presidential candidate's party, while the decline in turnout in the ensuing midterm then hurts candidates from the president's party. The name implies an elegant tidal metaphor in which congressional candidates of the president's party are represented by the ocean debris carried into shore (election to Congress) at high tide and then washed out to sea (electoral defeat) at low tide. The theory divides the electorate into "peripheral" voters who participate only in presidential elections and "core" voters who participate in presidential and midterm elections (A. Campbell 1960). Thus, independent or peripheral voters are responsible for the surge and decline in turnout and thus for the president's midterm losses in Congress (cf. J. Campbell 1993).

Efforts to find empirical support for the original surge-and-decline theory have been rather unsuccessful (Born 1990; J. Campbell 1993). For example, the surge-and-decline theory predicts that the midterm electorate should be more partisan, more interested in politics, and more knowledgeable than the presidential electorate. However, differences in the demographic composition of midterm and presidential electorates are small (A. Campbell 1960; Kernell 1977; Wolfinger, Rosenstone, and McIntosh 1981; see J. Campbell 1993 for an overview of these studies), although midterm voters are generally older and thus perhaps more strongly partisan than presidential voters (J. Campbell 1993; Wolfinger, Rosenstone, and McIntosh 1981).

A revised surge-and-decline theory (J. Campbell 1993) posits that partisans are more likely to abstain from voting when they are "cross-pressured"—that is, when current events, issues, economic performance, or other national conditions tilt against their party. For example, the revised surge-and-decline theory would predict that relatively more Republicans than Democrats were discouraged from voting in 1996 because of Bob Dole's lackluster candidacy, public perceptions of a strong economy, and salient issues (such as Medicare, education, and the minimum wage) that favored Democratic candidates. Thus, the peripheral voters who produce the surge in turnout in a presidential election should tilt more toward the winning presidential party than the core voters who participated in the previous midterm.

However, the catch for the president's party is that turnout then favors the opposition party in the subsequent midterm congressional elections. The drop-off in turnout from on-year to off-year congressional elections should fall disproportionately on the president's party. Also, midterm political conditions could tilt against the president, especially considering that the president's approval rating usually declines from the honeymoon period to the midterm election (Brody 1991; Kernell 1978). Thus, the revised surge-and-decline theory predicts that "the disadvantaged partisans' midterm decline in turnout should be less precipitous because cross-pressures of the presidential year had reduced their turnout in the last election" (J. Campbell 1993, 99). In other words, voters who supported the president's party in on-year congressional elections should be more likely to abstain in the following off-year elections.

One piece of evidence cited in favor of the revised theory is that the fraction of Democratic identifiers in the electorate in a given presidential election is proportional to the Democratic share of the presidential vote (J. Campbell 1993). From this, one might conclude that the short-term forces that influence presidential vote choice also influence partisan turnout. So, for example, Democratic identifiers made up a smaller-than-usual share of the electorate in 1984, a relatively bad year for Democrats. Many Democrats might have stayed home in 1984 because the Mondale campaign failed to mobilize them. The problem with this reasoning, however, is that the changing partisan composition of the electorate could also be the result of voters switching parties, in addition to (or rather than) different turnout rates between the two major parties. This presents another ecological inference problem, where two individual-level processes (differential turnout and partisan defection) could account for the same aggregate-level observation (changing partisan composition of the electorate).

Though party identification is surely more stable than voting behavior, recent evidence indicates that citizen party identification shifts in response to current political events (Brody and Rothenberg 1988; MacKuen, Erikson, and Stimson 1989; Weisberg and Smith 1991). Thus, the changing partisan composition of the electorate may result in part from voters changing their party identification. Table 5.1 provides evidence from National Election Study (NES) panel surveys indicating that people who switch parties in their voting behavior are more likely than others to change their party identification as well.[1] For example, the 1992–94 NES panel study indicates that 21.3 percent of House voters who switched parties in 1994 also changed their party identification in 1994, while only 12.5 percent of those who voted for the same party in the 1992 and 1994 House contests changed their partisanship. Table 5.1 indicates similar and even stronger patterns in the 1990–92 and 1972–74 House election cycles.

TABLE 5.1.   Changing Party Identification and Votes in Consecutive House Elections

	Party Identification		Total
	Changed	No Change	
1992–94 House Voting Behavior			
Switched parties	21.3%	78.7%	100%
Same party in both elections	12.5%	87.5%	100%
Total ($n = 358$)	$\chi^2 = 3.3$, df = 1, $p < .1$		
1990–92 House Voting Behavior			
Switched parties	26.5%	73.5%	100%
Same party in both elections	11.8%	88.2%	100%
Total ($n = 461$)	$\chi^2 = 13.1$, df = 1, $p < .001$		
1972–74 House Voting Behavior			
Switched parties	26.1%	73.9%	100%
Same party in both elections	11.6%	88.4%	100%
Total ($n = 696$)	$\chi^2 = 18.6$, df = 1, $p < .001$		

Source: 1992–94, 1990–92, and 1972–74 NES Panel Studies
Note: Independent "leaners" are coded as party identifiers.

Not surprisingly, voters tend to shift their party identification in the same direction as their voting behavior. For example, those voters who changed their party identification in 1974 tended to move away from the Republican Party, the same direction in which people moved in their vote choices. Consequently, comparing the partisan composition of the electorate in different elections cannot ultimately determine whether turnout or partisan defection is the source of electoral change, and such an approach usually overstates the effect of turnout.[2]

Since Angus Campbell's original work on the topic, few tests of the surge-and-decline theory have attempted to follow individuals from one election to the next to see which ones vote, which abstain, and which ones switch parties (for an exception, see Born 1990, which finds no evidence for a midterm turnout decline for the president's party). The following section does just that by testing the midterm turnout predictions of surge and decline in three recent elections. Contrary to surge-and-decline theories, we find that the midterm turnout decline tends to fall slightly harder on the Democrats, regardless of which party holds the White House. In addition, in the elections we examine, voter defection is the main source of seat losses for the president's party.

TURNOUT DECLINE IN MIDTERM ELECTIONS

To estimate party differences in midterm abstention and party defection, we use an ecological inference procedure similar to the one described in chapter 3 to estimate ticket splitting. Table 5.2 illustrates the ecological inference problem, using election results from Indiana's ninth congressional district as an example. Somewhat emblematic of the difficulties faced by Democrats in 1994, incumbent Lee Hamilton saw his share of the vote drop from 70 percent in 1992 to 52 percent in 1994. Our primary data set consists of the number of votes received by the major party House candidates in each congressional district in on-year and off-year elections.[3] As the table suggests, on-year House voters have three options as the midterm election approaches: (1) vote for the Democrat; (2) vote for the Republican, or (3) abstain.[4] As the question marks in the cells of table 5.2 indicate, we do not know how many voters from each party abstained in 1994, and we do not know how many voters who chose Hamilton in 1992 crossed over to support Jean Leising, the Republican challenger, in 1994. Applying the method of bounds, the number of voters who switched from the Democratic to the Republican candidate could be as low as 14,258 or as high as 84,315.

Our ecological inference estimation proceeds in two stages and divides table 5.2 into two parts. The first stage estimates the proportion of each party's on-year House voters who turn out for the following off-year election (that is, the proportions that do not appear in the "Abstain" column).[5] We then combine these estimates with the other known aggregate information in the second stage to estimate the fraction of voters who switch parties in the midterm election. It is crucial to first estimate voter abstention before estimating party defection. In the first place, the turnout decline from on-year to off-year congressional elections is quite large. Voter turnout in on-year House elections is roughly 10 to 15 percent higher (on average) than turnout in off-year House elections. Estimates of party defection that fail to account for abstention are likely to be biased, especially if there is any partisan disparity in abstention. More importantly, surge-and-decline theories make predictions about the nature of abstention and party defection as sources of change in congressional elections. By estimating party differences in both processes, we can test theories of electoral change.

The turnout component of the surge-and-decline perspective also seeks to explain the typical losses suffered by the president's party in midterm House elections. In particular, the theory predicts that the midterm decline in turnout falls disproportionately on the president's party. However, as table 5.3 indicates, Democrats (as measured by previous voting behavior) are somewhat more likely than Republicans to abstain in recent midterm elections, regardless of the party of the president.[6] For example, we estimate that 23 percent of Republican House voters and 27 percent of Democratic House voters in 1992 abstained from the 1994 contest. Our ecological estimates for the 1992–94 cycle compare favorably to those from the 1992–94 NES panel survey, the only case in which we have comparable data from a panel survey of voters.[7] The Democratic disadvantage in turnout may partly explain why Democrats are less successful than

TABLE 5.2.   Election Results for Indiana's Ninth District in 1992 and 1994

| House Vote in 1992 | House Vote in 1994 | | | Total |
	Hamilton (D)	Leising (R)	Abstain	
Hamilton (D)	?	?	?	160,980
Bailey (R)	?	?	?	70,057
Total	91,459	84,315	55,263	231,037

Republicans in protecting House seats in midterm elections (Coleman 1997).

Of the three midterms we examine, the 1994 case is the only one consistent with the surge-and-decline prediction. However, after applying our abstention estimates to the 1992 House electorate, remaining Democratic voters still outnumbered Republicans by more than two million nationwide. Thus, while turnout appears to have contributed to the Republican gains in the 1994 elections, turnout alone cannot account for the new GOP majority. We turn next to the role of party defection as a source of midterm electoral change, especially in 1994.

PARTY SWITCHING IN MIDTERM ELECTIONS

The second stage of our ecological inference estimation provides the fraction of House voters (after removing those who abstain from the midterm) who switch parties from on-year to off-year elections. King's method, which borrows strength by assuming that all observations share something in common, is particularly suited to estimating voter transitions because of the presence of national tides that are often observed in midterm elections. A national tide was especially evident in 1994, when the Democratic share of House votes and seats declined in all regions of the country, although the decline was most dramatic in the South and West (Brady et al. 1996).

Table 5.4 presents our estimates of party defection in three recent midterm elections. Again, our ecological estimates for the 1992–94 cycle closely resemble estimates of party defection from the NES panel survey. In all three midterm elections, party defection occurred more frequently for voters who had supported the president's party in on-year elections. In

TABLE 5.3. Partisan Differences in Voter Drop-Off

Year	On-Year House Vote	Fraction Abstaining at Following Midterm	
		Ecological Estimate	NES Panel Estimate
1992	Republican	.23 (.02)	.25
	Democrat	.27 (.01)	.27
1988	Republican	.23 (.02)	
	Democrat	.30 (.01)	
1984	Republican	.26 (.02)	
	Democrat	.31 (.01)	

Note: Standard errors are in parentheses

1994, the defection rate for Democrats was almost twice as large as for Republicans. The party disparity in voter defections was large enough in 1994 to transform a comfortable Democratic majority in 1992 into a narrow Republican majority in 1994, even if abstention rates had been the same for both parties.

In 1986 and 1990, when Republicans held the White House, the defection rate was higher for Republican voters. However, Democratic gains from party defection in 1986 and 1990 were partially offset by a higher abstention rate among Democratic voters in each year, producing relatively few Democratic seat gains. In contrast, the 1994 midterm, in which abstention and party defection reinforced each other, produced an unusually large number of lost seats for the Democrats and gave Republicans control of the House for the first time in 40 years.

Contrary to the prediction of surge-and-decline theories, observed patterns of midterm seat changes in recent elections appear to be more closely related to party defection than to abstention. At least two analysts (Born 1990; Tufte 1975) have suggested that an improved surge-and-decline theory should place more emphasis on voter defection and less emphasis on turnout effects. Scholars of congressional elections would do well to heed this advice. Since the percentage of voters who defect from their identified party in congressional elections has increased substantially, from about 10 percent in the 1950s to more than 20 percent in the 1990s (Stanley and Niemi 1994), it seems likely that swing voters have become a greater source of electoral instability at the congressional level.

Interestingly, studies of electoral change in recent American presidential elections have placed more emphasis on swing voters and less empha-

TABLE 5.4.   Party Switching from On-Year to Off-Year House Elections

Year	On-Year House Vote	Fraction Switching Parties at Following Midterm	
		Ecological Estimate	NES Panel Estimate
1992	Republican	.11 (.01)	.12
	Democrat	.21 (.01)	.21
1988	Republican	.20 (.01)	
	Democrat	.15 (.01)	
1984	Republican	.22 (.01)	
	Democrat	.13 (.01)	

Note: Calculations exclude voters who abstained from the midterm election. Standard errors are in parentheses.

sis on differential turnout effects (Boyd 1985; Shively 1992). This is not surprising, given that overall turnout often does not change dramatically from one presidential election to the next, as in congressional elections. Thus, one might not instinctively rely on turnout to explain shifting vote totals from one presidential election to the next. Since the 1950s, electoral change in presidential elections is mostly explained by voters switching parties rather than by partisan disparities in turnout (Boyd 1985; Shively 1982, 1992). In particular, Shively (1992) hypothesizes that this change occurred because of the increasing role of television in presidential campaigns, allowing candidates to bypass the party apparatus and appeal directly to voters. By making such personal appeals to voters, candidates are better equipped to attract voters from the opposite party. The same changes in campaign technology surely have taken place in congressional campaigns, where spending has increased dramatically, mostly to pay for more television advertising (Herrnson 1995; Jacobson 1997). The rise of candidate-centered campaigns and incumbents' efforts to cultivate personal followings in their districts (Cain, Ferejohn, and Fiorina 1987; Fenno 1978) should increase the likelihood of voter defection in congressional elections as well.

There is also a theoretical reason why we should pay special attention to voter defections. Each voter who switches parties creates a two-vote swing—one party loses a vote and another party gains a vote. By comparison, an abstaining voter costs a party only one vote, and other parties gain nothing. Thus, a net shift from one party to the other among swing voters has twice the impact on the overall election outcome than does a partisan turnout disparity of the same magnitude. At a minimum, it is necessary to pay closer attention to swing voters as a source of electoral change in American politics. The next section begins to do so by examining the forces that lead voters to switch parties.

EXPLAINING PARTY SWITCHING
IN MIDTERM ELECTIONS

The national figures on party defection in table 5.4 mask considerable variance in party defection across districts. For example, after eliminating uncontested House contests in 1992 and 1994, the fraction of Democratic defectors in 1994 ranges from .02 to .57, with a mean of .19 and a standard deviation of .11. Party defection even varies considerably within states. For example, Pete Peterson, a Democrat representing Florida's second congressional district, suffered a Democratic defection rate of .22 in 1994, while the Democratic incumbent in the neighboring fifth district, Karen Thurman, had a defection rate of only .09.

We now seek to explain why defection is more common in some districts than in others. While we examine both types of party defection, we focus primarily on defection from the president's party, which is most closely associated with midterm seat losses in Congress. We use our district-level estimates of party defection (summarized in the aggregate in table 5.4) as dependent variables in multivariate analyses.

To account for variation in party defection across districts, we examine three explanatory variables to control for the nature of competition in the House contests. We include two dummy variables that indicate the party of the incumbent (if there is an incumbent running). There is voluminous literature on incumbents' ability to withstand the effects of partisan tides in congressional elections (Cain, Ferejohn, and Fiorina 1987; Jacobson 1997). In particular, there is considerable evidence of a "retirement slump" in congressional elections: in open-seat races, the incumbent party's share of the vote declines from the levels enjoyed by the outgoing incumbent (Cover and Mayhew 1981; Erikson 1972). Thus, incumbents of the president's party are expected to be more successful at minimizing voter defection in midterm elections than are candidates in open-seat races. By the same token, incumbents of the opposition party are in the best position to ride electoral tides in midterm elections. Based on their record of opposing the president's legislative agenda, incumbents of the opposition party are poised to run against the president (as well as their opponents) in midterm elections. Thus, voter defection from the president's party in midterm elections should be more frequent in districts represented by incumbents of the opposition party.

Our third explanatory variable indicates the change in the Democrat's share of campaign spending from the on-year election to the midterm. We take the difference between the Democratic share of midterm campaign spending and on-year campaign spending. Negative values indicate that the Republican share of spending has increased in the midterm election, and positive values indicate that the Democratic share has increased. Campaign spending is a fairly good indicator of the relative strength of the competing candidates, and our measure of changes in spending indicate the extent to which the level of competition in House contests changes in midterm elections. Campaign spending also appears to be distinct from mere incumbency, judging from our results in chapter 4. We expect our spending measure to be negatively associated with defection from the

Democratic Party and positively associated with defection from the Republican Party.

Our fourth explanatory variable indicates the president's level of support in each district, as measured by his share of the vote in the previous presidential election. Midterm elections are partially a referendum on the president's record and performance. In addition, it is probably more common for candidates of the opposition party to campaign against the president in districts where the president ran poorly. Thus, we expect that voter defection from the president's party will be heaviest in districts where the president ran poorly.

Our final control variable is a dummy variable for southern districts. There has been a gradual long-term shift away from the Democratic Party in the southern electorate (Stanley and Niemi 1999). In addition, as the previous chapter demonstrates, southern ticket splitting in favor of Democratic House candidates slowly evaporated by the 1990s. In light of these trends, we include the South variable to test whether voter defection from the Democratic Party has been more pronounced in the South in recent midterm elections.

We examine party defection in two rather different midterm elections, one taking place with a Republican in the White House and few incumbent defeats (1990) and one with a Democratic president and many upset incumbents (1994). The results of our multivariate analyses of Democratic defections are reported in table 5.5, and our analyses of Republican defections are found in table 5.6. The columns present OLS coefficients (and their standard errors) for each election.

The results indicate that the congressional campaign and local support for the president are related to voter defections in midterm elections. When the Democrat's share of campaign spending increases in the midterm elections, fewer Democratic voters switch to the Republican Party. The coefficient for 1994 predicts that when the Democrat's share of spending drops 15 percent (as happened in more than 30 percent of contested districts in 1994), Democratic defection increases by 3 percent. The effect of campaign spending on Democratic defection is significant but substantively weaker in 1990, when the president was a Republican and Democratic defections were smaller in magnitude. By comparison, spending's effect on Republican defection (as indicated in table 5.6) is stronger in 1990 than in 1994. The 1990 election also was one of the best ever for House incumbents (Stanley and Niemi 1999), so the second equation simply has less variance to explain.

The results also indicate that incumbency was more closely associated with voter defection in 1994 than in 1990. On average, Democratic defection in 1994 was 5 percent higher in districts represented by Republican incumbents and almost 5 percent lower in districts represented by Democratic incumbents (compared to open-seat races). However, while Republican incumbents were able to withstand Republican defection in 1994 (see table 5.6), Democratic incumbents failed to capitalize on Republican defection in 1994. These results help confirm that 1994 was a relatively bad year for Democratic congressional candidates. The 1990 equations, however, do not support our hypothesis about incumbency. In 1990, incumbency has almost no impact on party defection, although the results in table 5.5 suggest that Democratic defection was slightly less common in contests with Republican incumbents.

The multivariate analyses also demonstrate that both types of party defection are influenced by the president's level of support in the district. In addition, the effect of presidential support is stronger in 1994 (especially on Democratic defection), possibly reflecting Republicans' impressive efforts to nationalize the 1994 elections and draw attention to Presi-

TABLE 5.5.   Explaining Democratic House Voter Defections in Midterm Elections

Independent Variable	1990	1994
Democratic incumbent in midterm	−.013	−.047***
	(.011)	(.013)
Republican incumbent in midterm	−.020*	.050***
	(.011)	(.014)
Change in spending (Democratic proportion)	−.137***	−.214***
	(.022)	(.018)
District support for president	.136***	−.268***
(1992=Clinton; 1988 = Bush)	(.027)	(.027)
South	−.016**	.013
	(.007)	(.009)
Constant	.061***	.300***
	(.017)	(.016)
Standard error	.049	.068
Number of cases	301	371
Adjusted R^2	.235	.616

Note: The dependent variable is the fraction of on-year Democratic House voters who switched to the Republican Party in the following midterm election. Analysis excludes uncontested seats in on-year and off-year elections. Cell entries are OLS coefficients with robust Huber/White standard errors in parentheses.
*$p < .1$; **$p < .05$, ***$p < .01$, two-tailed t-test

dent Clinton's record. Not surprisingly, Democratic seat losses occurred primarily in districts where Clinton had run poorly in 1992 (Brady et al. 1996). The 1994 presidential-support coefficient in table 5.4 predicts that the difference between the mean district (giving Clinton 44 percent of the vote in 1992) and a strong Democratic district (where Clinton received 60 percent in 1992) is an additional 4 percent in Democratic defection (other things being equal). We will later return to the importance of the president's record in midterm elections.

Finally, our findings indicate that, after controlling for incumbency, campaign spending, and presidential popularity, the Republican Party has yet to gain from midterm voter defection in the South. Our results for 1994 indicate that there was nothing unique about party defection in the South relative to the rest of the country. In 1990, however, Democratic defection was lower and Republican defection was higher in the South, even after controlling for other factors. The 1990 midterms might have been a last gasp of Democratic strength in the South.

Our final analysis examines the fate of incumbents of the president's party in midterm elections. In 1994, 35 Democratic incumbents but no

TABLE 5.6. Explaining Republican House Voter Defections in Midterm Elections

Independent Variable	1990	1994
Democratic incumbent in midterm	−.006	−.007
	(.022)	(.012)
Republican incumbent in midterm	−.027	−.053***
	(.023)	(.010)
Change in campaign spending	.283***	.135***
(Democratic proportion)	(.039)	(.018)
District support for president	−.118	.191***
(1988 = Bush, 1992 = Clinton)	(.080)	(.035)
South	.040**	.003
	(.019)	(.007)
Constant	.261***	.062***
	(.047)	(.015)
Standard error	.097	.061
Number of cases	301	371
Adjusted R^2	.270	.404

Note: The dependent variable is the fraction of on-year Republican House voters who switched to the Democratic Party in the following midterm election. Analysis excludes uncontested seats in on-year and off-year elections. Cell entries are OLS coefficients with robust Huber/White standard errors in parentheses.
*$p < .1$; **$p < .05$; ***$p < .01$, two-tailed t-test

Republican incumbents lost their seats. In 1990, 9 Republican incumbents and 6 Democratic incumbents lost their seats (Stanley and Niemi 2000). Why do some incumbents succeed while others fail? Given the importance of district-level support for the president, do incumbents of the president's party face electoral danger if they associate too closely with the president? More specifically, do incumbents suffer higher levels of midterm voter defection the more they support the president's legislative agenda?

To answer these questions, we estimate a final multivariate analysis of voter defection from the president's party in districts represented by legislators of the president's party. Our sample includes only districts with an incumbent of the president's party running. Thus, we reestimate the regression models for Democratic defection in 1994 (table 5.5) and Republican defection in 1990 (table 5.6), including measures of the incumbent's roll-call record in Congress and dropping the incumbency variables.[8] One such measure is the incumbent's presidential-support score, the fraction of roll-call votes in which the incumbent voted for the president's position during the year before the midterm election. We expect that incumbents who most closely support the president's program will lose the most midterm voters.

Finally, we hypothesize that strongly supporting the president's agenda may be most hazardous for incumbents holding marginal seats. In contrast, incumbents holding safe seats are expected to support their president vigorously and face no penalty for doing so; in fact, such legislators might risk losing votes by failing to support the president. Thus, we estimate a second equation that includes an interaction term created by multiplying the president's electoral support in the district by the incumbent's presidential support score. The interaction term should have a negative regression coefficient, consistent with our expectation that the penalty for backing the president declines for safer seats.

Table 5.7 presents our analysis of voter defection from incumbents of the president's party. The results suggest that incumbents assume some electoral risk when they strongly support their president's agenda. In 1990 and in 1994, the stronger the legislator's support for the president's program, the more voters defected to the opposition party in the midterm election. This effect holds up even after controlling for campaign spending and the president's support in the district. While others have attributed Democratic losses in 1994 to incumbents who paid with their jobs by supporting the Clinton agenda (Brady et al. 1996), the surprise here may be that the same process worked against Republicans in 1990.

The last column of table 5.7 indicates that the penalty for vigorously supporting President Clinton's legislative record was imposed primarily on Democratic incumbents in swing districts (note the statistically significant interaction term). This suggests that simple proximity voting, rather than policy balancing, accounts for the presidential penalty applied by disgruntled former Democratic voters in 1994. Heavy multicollinearity unfortunately hampers an investigation into the same type of conditional effect of presidential support on voter defection in the 1990 election.[9] However, a closer inspection suggests that the 1990 results are also more consistent with a proximity model of voting.[10] In 1990, 22 Republican incumbents in marginal districts (where Bush received less than 55 percent of the vote in 1988), had a positive and significant bivariate relationship between presidential support and midterm voter defection ($r = .37$, $p = .09$). For 87 Republican incumbents running in safe seats in 1990, there is no relationship between presidential support scores and midterm voter defection ($r = .09$, $p = .41$).[11]

However, the substantive impact of an incumbent's support for the presidential agenda is somewhat modest. Table 5.8 provides predicted levels of voter defection suffered by Democratic incumbents in 1994 under varying

TABLE 5.7. Explaining House Vote Defections in Midterm Elections

Independent Variable	1990		1994	
Change in campaign spending	.285***	.285***	−.172***	−.172***
(Democratic proportion)	(.032)	(.032)	(.025)	(.025)
District support for president	−.214*	−.211	−.245***	.648***
(1988 = Bush, 1992 = Clinton)	(.108)	(.299)	(.025)	(.322)
Incumbent presidential support	.156***	.158	.081**	.573***
(roll-call votes)	(.058)	(.282)	(.040)	(.174)
District support for president	—	−.004	—	−1.14***
× incumbent presidential support		(.484)		(.460)
Constant	.197***	.196	.182***	−.202
	(.049)	(.162)	(.032)	(.133)
Standard error	.065	.065	.055	.054
Number of cases	109	109	201	201
Adjusted R^2	.424	.418	.394	.410

Note: The dependent variable is the fraction of on-year House voters for incumbents of the president's party who switched parties in the following midterm election (Democratic defectors in 1994, Republican defectors in 1990). Analysis excludes uncontested seats in on-year and off-year elections. Cell entries are OLS coefficients. White (1980) robust standard errors are in parentheses.

*p < .1, two-tailed t-test; **p < .05, two-tailed t-test; ***p < .01, two-tailed t-test scenarios. We simulate these predicted values from the regression estimates in the last column of table 5.7 using a method created by King, Tomz, and Wittenberg (2000). The difference between a Democratic incumbent in a marginal district who strongly supported Clinton's legislative program and one who weakly supported Clinton's program is an extra 3 percent of voters defecting to the Republican challenger. By comparison, equivalent changes in the partisan leaning of the district and campaign spending have stronger effects on voter defections in the 1994 elections.

We also find evidence of strategic behavior on the part of Republican challengers in 1994. Vulnerable Democratic incumbents (i.e., those holding seats in competitive districts) who strongly supported the Clinton agenda tended to face more vigorous Republican challengers. For the 39 Democratic incumbents running in districts that Bush had carried in 1992, the spending measure is negatively correlated with the incumbent's presidential support score ($r = -.32$, $p < .05$). Supporting the Clinton agenda brought vulnerable Democrats a tougher reelection battle (as measured by

TABLE 5.8.   Predicted Levels of Democratic House Voter Defections in 1994 Midterm Election

	Marginal District	Safe Democratic District
Incumbent strongly supports Clinton agenda	.18	.07
	(.009)	(.014)
Incumbent weakly supports Clinton agenda	.15	.11
	(.006)	(.014)
Incumbent faces a substantially weaker challenger in 1994	.13	.05
	(.007)	(.006)
Incumbent faces a substantially stronger challenger in 1994	.20	.12
	(.008)	(.009)

Note: Cell entries are the predicted fraction of 1992 House voters for Democratic incumbents who switched to the Republican Party in the 1994 election (standard errors in parentheses). Estimates were generated from the regression estimates in the last column of table 5.7 using the Clarify software with Stata version 6.0 (King, Tomz, and Wittenberg 2000; Tomz, Wittenberg, and King 1999). Other independent variables were held constant at median values. Analysis excludes uncontested seats in on-year and off-year elections. A safe Democratic district is one where Clinton received 68% of the presidential votes in 1992 (the 90th percentile case). A marginal district is one where Clinton received 37% of the vote in 1992 (the 10th percentile case). A strong supporter of the Clinton agenda has a presidential support score of .90 (90th percentile case). A weak supporter of the Clinton agenda has a presidential support score of .69 (10th percentile case). An incumbent facing a substantially weaker challenger represents the 90th percentile in the campaign spending measure (an 18 percent increase in the incumbent's share of spending compared to the 1992 election). An incumbent facing a substantially stronger challenger represents the 10th percentile case (a 24 percent drop in the incumbent's share of campaign spending since 1992).

campaign spending) in 1994. For 162 Democratic incumbents running in districts that Clinton carried, there is no relationship between the spending measure and the incumbent's presidential support score. Safe Democratic incumbents did not face a stronger challenger as a result of vigorously supporting the Clinton agenda.

In comparison, there is little evidence of strategic behavior by Democrats in 1990, primarily because there were very few opportunities for the party to gain House seats. In the 1990 House elections, only seven Republican incumbents ran in marginal districts (that is, districts that Dukakis had carried in 1988). However, none of those seven Republicans faced a substantially stronger Democratic challenger in 1990, and all seven were reelected.

A few examples from the 1994 elections illustrate the dangers of close association with the president's agenda for Democrats holding marginal seats. The most vivid examples come from Georgia, where incumbent Democrats Nathan Deal, Don Johnson, and Buddy Darden had all been elected on pledges to serve as moderate to conservative Democrats. In addition, all three men represented districts where Clinton carried less than 40 percent of the vote in 1992. However, the three incumbents varied tremendously in their support for Clinton's legislative program. Darden's support score was a robust .92, Johnson's was .79 (the mean for all incumbent Democrats), and Deal's was a low .59. Darden and Johnson suffered heavy voter defection (.27 for Darden, .43 for Johnson) and lost their seats to Republican challengers who hammered the incumbents for supporting the Clinton agenda (Duncan 1997). In contrast, Deal faced a weaker challenger and suffered only modest voter defection (.09) in the 1994 election. Less than a year after the election, Deal switched his affiliation to the GOP.

As another example, Democratic incumbents Lewis Payne and Norman Sisisky represented neighboring districts in southern Virginia. Clinton received 41 percent of the vote in Payne's fifth district and 40 percent in Sisisky's fourth district. Payne had a slightly higher presidential support score than Sisisky (.86 to .78). While both incumbents faced stronger challengers in 1994, Payne had more voters defect than Sisisky (.28 to .17), although both won reelection. Finally, Florida incumbents Peterson and Thurman represented neighboring districts in which Clinton received 42 percent of the vote in 1992. Peterson had a high presidential support score of .91, while Thurman's was below the Democratic average (.74). Interestingly, Thurman was first elected in 1992 by a slim margin, while

Peterson had won reelection easily in 1992. In 1994, Peterson faced a slightly stronger challenger than in 1992, and Peterson saw more voters defect than Thurman (.22 to .09), although both won reelection. Our multivariate results and these cases demonstrate that incumbents enthusiastically support the president's program at some risk if they represent districts where the president failed to win a majority of the vote. In this sense, waning coattail effects and mass partisanship do not necessarily imply that presidential and congressional elections have become disaggregated.

SUMMARY

Midterm elections are often an important source of change in Congress, yet much remains unknown about the causes of electoral change in midterms. We believe that previous attempts to explain midterm congressional losses for the president's party have focused too much on voter turnout and not enough on party defection. Our findings suggest that party defection is the more reliable source of midterm losses for the president's party, though turnout and partisanship are of course related. Future studies of midterm elections should pay closer attention to the forces that lead voters to switch parties.

One of the difficulties in studying party defection involves generating reliable measures of the phenomenon. This chapter uses King's ecological inference method to estimate party defection from aggregate vote totals. Where possible, we compare our ecological estimates of party defection to estimates from NES panel surveys, and the methods produce similar estimates. Our estimates also reveal several important observations that are consistent with our examination of ticket splitting in the previous chapter. First, midterm party-defection rates vary considerably from one district to the next. Second, these defection rates are best explained by levels of competition in the House contests and the districts' levels of electoral support for the president. Third, incumbents of the party occupying the White House who represent competitive districts and zealously support the president's program with their roll-call votes risk losing voters to challengers in midterm elections. Even after controlling for other factors, incumbents' voting records in Congress are significantly related to their electoral success.

An incumbent's record in Congress can lead to electoral reward or punishment. In the previous chapter we show that incumbents with moderate ideological records (likely near the median voter in their constituency) tend to gain votes from the opposite party in on-year elections. This chapter suggests that the converse holds as well. Incumbents who support the president more than their constituents would prefer tend to lose votes to the opposite party in off-year elections. The fact that the penalty for supporting the president is largely confined to incumbents representing marginal districts suggests that the midterm loss phenomenon is driven by sincere proximity voting, at least to the extent that ideological positions matter. Incumbents representing marginal districts might have to deviate from constituent preferences to support the president's legislative program, thus incurring the wrath of voters. If policy balancing accounts for the presidential penalty of voter defection in midterm elections, we would expect to see the penalty applied in more than just the marginal districts. However, the evidence in this chapter could be construed as being consistent with policy-balancing theory if balancing voters are believed to be concentrated in marginal congressional districts. If that is the case, the likelihood of continued divided government depends on whether district lines are drawn to produce many competitive districts or few of them.

After research indicating a dearth of knowledge about candidates and issues among congressional voters (Mann and Wolfinger 1980; Stokes and Miller 1966), most studies of congressional elections have paid little attention to the incumbent's record in Congress. This seems to be contradicted by the fact that members of Congress spend a lot of time worrying about how their actions in Congress (especially their votes) will be received by their constituents (Arnold 1990; Burden 1998; Fenno 1978; Mayhew 1974; Miller and Stokes 1963). For example, as the 1996 elections approached, some Republicans anticipating close races repeatedly voted against approving the House minutes from the previous day just to lower their party support scores (Koszczuk 1996). A smaller and more recent literature emphasizes the Election Day importance of an incumbent's roll-call record (Box-Steffensmeier and Franklin 1996; Burden and Kimball 1998; Franklin 1991) and general competence in Congress (Mondak, McCurley, and Millman 1999). Our findings that consistent support for the president can lead to lost votes in midterm elections are in line with this more recent literature.

CHAPTER VI

Splitting the Senate

The previous two chapters have shown that the degree to which voters choose presidential and congressional candidates from different parties depends heavily on the nature of the local House race. Lopsided congressional campaigns encourage voters who would otherwise vote straight tickets to pick candidates from opposing parties for different offices. In particular, two of the strongest influences on ticket splitting are candidates' relative abilities to disseminate their messages (largely via campaign spending) and the quality of incumbents' challengers. These findings reinforce the theory of "strategic politicians" (Jacobson and Kernell 1983), which stresses the importance of local candidate decisions on congressional election outcomes. To alter a common phrase, the short story is again that "most politics is local."

Our argument might end there. To do so would be a mistake since conclusions based only on House results would be incomplete. Though most research on congressional elections focuses exclusively on House contests, this practice is not adequate for our purposes. The patterns of divided government and normative questions about representation that the Senate raises compel us to consider how voters make decisions in senatorial elections.

We argue here that the Senate—designed to be more insulated from public influence than is the House—has paradoxically been more influenced by elections than has the House. Senate elections are more competitive because of the greater importance of each seat and the fact that high-quality candidates are more attracted to run for Senate seats. This makes the Senate more prone to changes in party control, as evidenced by the 1981–86 period and the historic 50–50 split following the 2000 elections. The triumph of Reagan and his fellow Republicans in 1980 was clearer in presidential and Senate races than in the House, where the insulated Democratic majority remained in control. This is remarkable because it runs against the Framers' intentions and stands in contrast with much of the research on congressional elections, which relies mostly on House elections to draw conclusions about voters' intentions.

The Framers of the American Constitution intended for the House to be more representative of the public will. Representatives are elected from smaller, more intimate districts than are senators. They must face public scrutiny "every second year" by constitutional decree. Senators of course represent larger constituencies in most cases and face reelection at longer, six-year intervals. Their terms are staggered so that only about a third of the chamber may be replaced in any one election. These electoral rules were designed to make the Senate less responsive to changes in citizens' preferences. In fact, until the adoption of the 17th Amendment to the Constitution in 1913, senators were not even popularly elected.[1] So, for a majority of our country's history, the Senate has been resistant to public control. Though times have changed, the Senate still clings to its republican heritage. Among other features, its smaller size and longer terms make it more attractive than the House to most politicians. Because the Senate has only 100 seats and each member represents an entire state, senators enjoy more national attention than do representatives. Senators are seen as more responsible for national policy because of their greater visibility, fueled in part by the fact they are often considered potential presidential candidates.

What do these interchamber differences have to do with split-ticket voting and divided government? We argue that levels of ticket splitting are driven largely by what is happening in the congressional campaigns. To the extent that the House and Senate differ institutionally, elections to the two chambers will do so as well. Senate campaigns are not as parochial, are less influenced by incumbency advantages, and probably depend more on issues and ideology because they are more competitive. Ticket splitting should vary across the races, in frequency, and perhaps in purpose too. To develop hypotheses about the levels and causes of ticket splitting in presidential and senatorial elections, we must briefly review what is known about Senate elections.

HOUSE AND SENATE ELECTIONS COMPARED

The literature on Senate elections has grown tremendously over the past several years, in part because of the availability of the Senate Election Study (SES), a state-based survey conducted during the 1988, 1990, and

1992 cycles (Abramowitz and Segal 1992; Gronke 2000; Kahn and Kenney 1999; Krasno 1994; Lee and Oppenheimer 1999; Westlye 1991). The changes in party control of the Senate in 1980 and 1986 also interested researchers because of its contrast with Democratic control of the House, which lasted from 1953 until 1995. We would like to continue this new movement beyond House elections as the sole source of information on subpresidential elections. House contests have some special features that do not necessarily generalize to other kinds of elections. The most dominant characteristic of House elections is what has come to be known as the incumbency advantage.

A central feature of House elections is that incumbents are astonishingly successful at getting reelected. Over the past several decades, about 9 out of 10 running representatives have been reelected. Turnover in the House is relatively low because most incumbents—on average nearly 400—seek reelection in a typical election year. Less than 15 percent of congressional districts typically are open seats in any given election year.[2] In fact, a larger percentage of seats are uncontested because many incumbents face no major-party challengers. Though representatives might not feel safe (Fenno 1978), barring scandal or health problems, most members of the House can expect to be reelected every two years. Members of the Senate have less reason to feel safe. Senators' reelection rates vary more from year to year and hover around 80 percent in recent years. Between 1946 and 1992, 93 percent of running representatives were reelected, compared to just 81 percent of senators (Krasno 1994). Between 1946 and 1996, only 75.2 percent of running senators were reelected.[3]

Why are senators more vulnerable than representatives to defeat? Indeed, why are members of the House more likely to be reelected than nearly all other U.S. officeholders? The answers to these questions have to do with competition (Gronke 2000; Kahn and Kenney 1999; Krasno 1994). House incumbents do not regularly face credible challengers. This might be because House members raise campaign money early enough to scare off potentially strong candidates (Box-Steffensmeier 1996). House incumbents now outspend their challengers by an average margin of three to one. High-quality challengers are strategic and wait until conditions are right to run, as when an incumbent retires or a promising midterm election year is looming (Jacobson and Kernell 1983). Because they represent relatively small, homogeneous districts, representatives may develop personal bonds with their constituents in ways that may be impractical for senators.[4] A representative's "personal vote" (Cain, Ferejohn, and Fiorina

1987) results from constituent casework (Fiorina 1989), a particular repre-sentational style (Fenno 1978), and generally advertising their names through pork-barrel projects and other perquisites of office (Mayhew 1974). Most representatives deemphasize their policy positions and take credit for noncontroversial accomplishments. As a result, constituents tend to view their representatives quite favorably, even if they dislike Congress as an institution (Fenno 1978).

Incumbents probably also benefit from the drawing of district lines. Every 10 years the 435 House districts are reapportioned to states based on census population data. State legislatures or commissions then redraw the district lines within their jurisdictions. Senators, in contrast, run in fixed districts defined by state boundaries. The typical House district contains more than 600,000 people and is more politically homogeneous than larger states. Congressional incumbents often have a hand in drawing their district lines, with the goal of protecting their reelection chances (Butler and Cain 1992). Thus, the redistricting process often produces a large number of safe House seats. Some congressional districts, such as the third in Nebraska, are conservative and likely to elect Republicans. Qualified Democrats are unlikely to run there, at least while a Republican is the incumbent. Similarly, for example, Democrats are heavily favored in several districts in and around Cleveland, Ohio, where registered Demo-crats are a large majority and Republicans rarely win. Though the evidence is mixed on whether gerrymandered districts purposely benefit incumbents (see, for example, Butler and Cain 1992), it seems clear that smaller dis-tricts are, ceteris paribus, more predictable and politically homogeneous.

Without entering into arguments about exactly what mix of factors causes interchamber differences, our point is merely that House elections are largely noncompetitive. Partly as a result, voter turnout in House races is usually low, around 35–40 percent in midterm elections where congres-sional races are often at the top of the ticket. The House experienced lit-tle turnover in individual post–World War II elections, and Democrats controlled the chamber for 42 consecutive years. Because Republicans tended to win the presidency during that era, the national government was divided more than it was unified. During the 1980s, Presidents Ronald Reagan and George Bush easily won the White House, while Democrats maintained their hold on the House. In 1988, Democrats gained three House seats even though Bush defeated Michael Dukakis—an example of negative coattails. The Senate did not follow this pattern. Republicans gained control of the Senate in 1980 and held power through the 1986 elections. Some observers have suggested that a Republican tide that swept the country in the early 1980s was blocked only in the House because the incumbency advantage limited citizen control of the chamber. Incumbents are able to insulate themselves and dampen voter impact on Congress (Fiorina 1989).

This is surprising given the Framers' intentions. The House, with its local districts and short terms, was supposed to be most representative of the people. The Senate, with larger constituencies and longer, staggered terms, would resist the popular will and provide some stability in an otherwise changeable government. The Senate's image as a more deliberate and prestigious chamber, where members wield more individual influence and have longer terms than representatives, tends to attract more capable candidates. Senate elections have become more competitive than House races in part because of better challengers. Qualified, experienced people might avoid running against a House incumbent who is well known and highly regarded. But Senate challengers are often politicians who have held another office, such as representative, mayor, governor, or state legislator. As a result, they possess campaign experience, credibility with the media and potential donors, and name recognition with voters. The result is that Senate campaigns are often more competitive than are House campaigns (Westlye 1991; Kahn and Kenney 1999). For example, Krasno (1994) finds that only 12 percent of House races could be classified as "hard-fought" in 1988 and 1990, while 44 percent of Senate campaigns met this definition.

In summary, Senate elections are more competitive because they more often feature two high-quality candidates. These races attract more media attention and campaign contributions, in turn raising voter interest and turnout. This allows voters to exert more control over the Senate than the House because genuine electoral choices are available. Senators are more vulnerable than representatives are, so turnover is more frequent. Party control changes more often as well, as recent history demonstrates.

These facts have clear consequences for divided government and ticket splitting. Since constituents exert more control over Senate membership, mandates for bipartisanship should be most visible there. If divided government is the will of the American electorate, then, conditional on who is elected president, the Senate ought to reflect these preferences. Of course, the fact that only a third of Senate seats are up in any election year

limits popular control, yet an exclusive focus on House elections is likely
to underestimate the degree to which voters apply their preferences for
party control on Election Day.

STATES AS THE UNITS OF ANALYSIS

When moving from House to Senate outcomes, the unit of analysis
switches from the congressional district to the state. This has some real
benefits for drawing inferences about causal relationships. Because states
are fixed geographical units, they have more political integrity than do districts, which are small, sometimes irregularly shaped, and often exist for
just 10 years. Those who draw district lines also anticipate election outcomes in a way that state borders cannot, thus making district composition
endogenous to many of the outcomes of interest. States also have distinct
political cultures and electoral histories that continue to affect contemporary politics (see Erikson, Wright, and McIver 1993).

As a practical matter, this continuity allows analysts to develop measures of state characteristics. Some of these are based on histories of election outcomes, patterns of state offices held by the parties, and other electoral patterns, such as turnout levels, frequency of split outcomes, and
tenure of office. Though these variables are probably not constant over
time, the fact that senators may represent the same geographic constituency for decades eliminates the redistricting effects that are often used
as explanations for features of House elections, particularly the incumbency advantage.

We will use several measures drawn from state surveys. Some of these
will come from the SES, a national state-based survey conducted in 1988,
1990, and 1992. Sizable numbers of respondents in each state were asked,
among other things, to place themselves and both parties' senatorial candidates on a traditional seven-point ideological scale. Erikson (1990) and
Bradford Jones and Norrander (1996) have shown these responses to be
reliable and valid when aggregated to the state level. We also have self-
reports of voting behavior and other opinions relevant to Senate elections.
The other major sources of state variables are the ideological measures
developed by Erikson, Wright, and McIver (for example, 1993), who
assembled a series of state exit polls conducted by CBS/*New York Times* to
create summary indicators of each state's partisan and ideological tendencies. The authors have demonstrated that these indicators are reasonably
valid and reliable measures of state political culture. Alternative measures
of state opinion that allow for temporal variation were introduced by Berry

and colleagues (1998) using congressional roll-call and election data. The utility of these measures will become clearer as they are employed in this chapter.

METHOD

Our method for estimating rates of ticket splitting parallels that used for House races in previous chapters. The main data sets consist only of aggregate election returns. For each state for each year, we have the number of people voting for each Senate and presidential candidate. We use these aggregate data to estimate the direction and frequency of president-Senate ticket splitting in each state. The main limitation of Senate election data is the small number of cases. There are on average 33 Senate races every two years, and some of these races are uncontested, effectively further reducing the number of interesting elections. This makes estimation difficult. Maximum likelihood techniques, including King's ecological inference method, require a large number of observations to invoke the attractive properties of the estimators.[5] Because King's ecological inference technique uses maximum likelihood to estimate the parameters of interest, we have chosen to pool Senate elections from all of the years to achieve a reasonable sample size. Since we have data from 1952 to 1996, this adds up to 350 observations.[6]

EXISTING RESEARCH ON
PRESIDENT-SENATE TICKET SPLITTING

As noted earlier, research on Senate elections generally has blossomed in the last decade. The renewed interest in Senate contests derives from new data sources as well as a desire to move beyond incumbent-dominated House races to learn about congressional elections. The competitiveness of Senate elections also provides more differences in a key variable. Despite interest in Senate elections, research on split-ticket voting remains restricted to the president-House dyads. Studies of ticket splitting at the Senate level have focused almost exclusively on divided Senate delegations (cf. Brody, Brady, and Heitshusen 1994; Soss and Cannon 1995). A number of observers have noted that the rise of ticket splitting and divided national government has been accompanied by an increase in the number of states represented by senators of different parties. Less than a third of state electorates chose senators from different parties in the 1950s, whereas nearly half of states were doing so regularly in the 1980s and early 1990s. Figure 6.1 plots the percentage of states with split

delegations. The overall trend in split delegations (increasing in frequency in the 1970s, decreasing in frequency in the 1990s) resembles the
rise and fall of president-House ticket splitting seen in figures 1.1 and 3.5.
It is clear that states became more likely to elect senators of different parties through much of the 1960s and 1970s, reaching a maximum above 50
percent in the 96th Senate (1979–80). This upturn has generated more
interest than the decline that followed it (cf. Brunell and Grofman 1998).
From 1980 onward, state delegations are more and more likely to be
unified, in part because Republicans took control of a number of previously mixed delegations by replacing Democrats in the Senate. Though
our goal is not just to explain the rise and fall of divided Senate delegations, the graph indicates that a surprising amount of variation in party
control occurs.[7] We seek to locate the forces that lead to these outcomes
at the state level.

These trends become less clear when one examines "split states" rather
than split delegations. A split state is akin to a split district for the House.
Here, the measure is the percentage of states that elect a senator of one
party while giving a plurality of votes to a presidential candidate from the
other party. Figure 6.2 displays the percentage of split states since the
advent of direction election in the early 1900s. To assist in identifying the
aggregate trend, the variability resulting from the small number of elections each year is smoothed using a three-period moving average as well.
We believe this to be the first time split president-Senate results have been
examined. Such an analysis is enlightening because it is contrary to trends
found in other data. While the rise in divided voting in the postwar era
apparent in other figures also appears here, the recent abatement in such
patterns does not. Indeed, the maximum number of split-state outcomes
actually occurs in the 1990s, although it drops sharply in 2000.

While interinstitutional divisions at the national level are not the same
as intrainstitutional divisions at the state level, there are reasons to believe
that they are produced by many of the same forces (Fiorina 1996; Soss and
Cannon 1995). The decline in mass party attachments and rise of candidate-oriented campaigns clearly facilitates ticket splitting and divided
Senate delegations (Wattenberg 1991b). However, divided Senate delegations raise a number of additional theoretical questions about voter motivation. Do the same voters choose senators of different parties across elections, or do the electorates differ substantially? What sorts of state
electorates are more likely to choose split delegations, and why? And how
do split delegations relate to president-Senate ticket splitting and divided

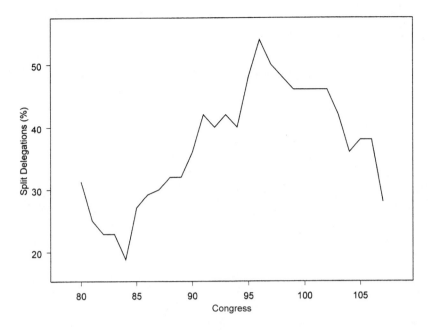

FIG. 6.1.   Split Senate delegations by Congress

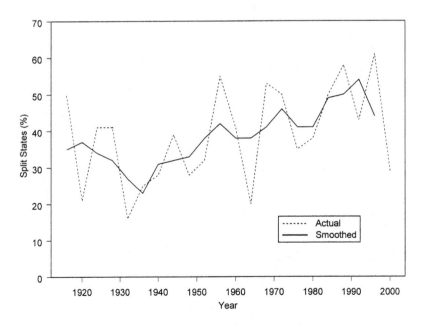

FIG. 6.2.   Split state outcomes in presidential and Senate elections by year

voting more generally? While we cannot provide authoritative answers to all of these questions, we will address each of them. Some will be examined by reviewing the recent literature on divided Senate delegations. Our analysis then focuses on president-Senate ticket splitting from 1952 to 1996.

What causes voters within a state to elect a Democrat and a Republican to represent them simultaneously in the U.S. Senate? This question is complicated because Senate elections are staggered rather than concurrent within states. Fiorina (1996) considers the possibility that voters choose a Senate candidate who will balance the incumbent senator who is not up for election. Voters could act this way because the midpoint of the Democratic and Republican senators' policy positions is sometimes closer to the median voter's ideal point than would a pair of same-party senators. Alesina, Fiorina, and Rosenthal (1994) and Alesina and Rosenthal (1995) formalized this logic in models that demonstrate the possibility of an "opposite party advantage" whereby a Senate candidate benefits if the nonrunning incumbent senator is from the other party. Much like the policy-balancing model advanced to explain national divided government, voters elect divided delegations in an effort to seek moderate policies. Empirical analysis in an article on a related topic by Schmidt, Kenny, and Morton (1996) finds support for the opposite party advantage, though the examination is limited to races where an incumbent is running for reelection.

Studying elections in which Senate seats transition from one party to another, Segura and Nicholson (1995) compare two models that could explain such transitions. They find that candidate-specific variables explain most of the differences in partisan transitions, in accord with Jacobson's (1990b) general depiction of "electoral disintegration." This finding is also consistent with candidate-centered politics, where voters are more concerned with individuals' characteristics than with party labels (Wattenberg 1991b); dealignment of voters from the party system (Beck 1997; Wattenberg 1998); the two-constituencies thesis that senators must respond to inter- and intraparty electorates (Bullock and Brady 1983; Fiorina 1974; Huntington 1950; Shapiro et al. 1990), and other general explanations. More importantly, Segura and Nicholson find no support for the opposite party advantage that might be produced by voters wanting to balance the ideology of the senator whose term has not expired with a senator from the other end of the spectrum.

There are a variety of more general explanations for the presence of split Senate delegations. Bullock and Brady (1983) show that, perhaps in accord with the differing "reelection constituencies" (Fenno 1978) of senators from the same states, politically heterogeneous states are most likely to elect split delegations. Brunell and Grofman (1998) adeptly point out that the percentage of divided delegations follows a cyclical pattern in which they are most common in periods of partisan realignment. The cycle peaked in 1930, well before the modern rise in ticket splitting, declined just after a realigning election, and slowly rose thereafter.

Split Senate delegations are clearly an interesting part of the larger relationship between split-ticket voting and divided government. We will try to unravel their mystery further to get a handle on the nature of voter motivation. We devote considerably more attention, however, to ticket splitting across rather than within institutions. As with the House in previous chapters, we wish to understand why voters vote for presidential and congressional candidates of different parties. For conflicting reasons discussed at the outset of this chapter, the Senate may be more or less responsive to voter sentiment than is the House. The fact that the Senate is less than a quarter the size of the House means that each Senate seat is more important to outcomes there. Voters in a state such as Wyoming, for example, elected a member of each chamber to represent them in 1996. Though each voter carries the same weight in both elections, one might surmise that as far as national policy configurations are concerned, the Senate race is the more important of the two. Without taking this pivotal-seat argument to its logical extreme, we suggest that Senate-president ticket splitting is an important phenomenon to understand in its own right.

THE FREQUENCY OF PRESIDENT-
SENATE TICKET SPLITTING

We begin our analysis by estimating the frequency of ticket splitting across presidential and senatorial races from 1952 to 1996. As with the House analysis in the previous chapter, we use an ecological inference technique to estimate the proportions of RD and DR voters within each state for each presidential election year. We then validate the estimates with survey data. Figure 6.3 presents the mean proportions of RD and DR voters over the entire postwar period. The same data from the House are overlaid for comparison. Senate races do not exhibit a change that parallels ticket splitting in House elections, which increased almost monotonically from the 1950s to the 1980s. The changes in ticket splitting have been much

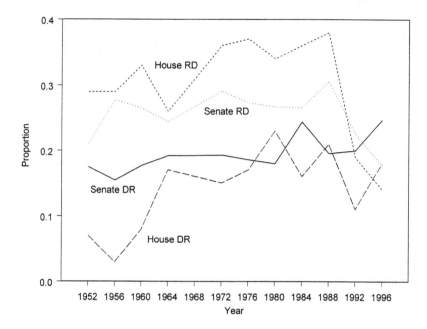

FIG. 6.3.   Senate RD and DR ticket splitting by year

less dramatic in the Senate than in the House, a finding that makes sense given the emphasis we have placed on changes in competition and the incumbency advantage as sources of president-House ticket splitting. Also fitting our theory is the finding that House ticket splitting has been decidedly asymmetric, with RD splitters outnumbering DR splitters by wide margins until the 1990s brought them together. It seems clear that the Democratic dominance in Congress over much of the postwar era lies behind these differences in both the House and Senate. Neither of the RD lines shows a strong pattern over time aside from the drop at the end, though both DR lines are positively (and significantly) correlated with time. Both increases began before the Clinton era and thus cannot be attributed entirely to presidential politics. Much of the change results from action in the states.

A MODEL OF SENATE TICKET SPLITTING

We now develop and estimate a model of ticket splitting across presidential and senatorial elections. To what degree are voters choosing presidential candidates of one party but senatorial candidates from the other? The variables that ought to influence levels of Senate ticket splitting resemble those used in the House analyses in previous chapters. Because we argue that split-ticket voting is driven largely by the local race, most of the variables capture features of the Senate election. Since Senate elections are not quite as "local" as House races because of the larger electorate involved, we expect the effects of these variables to be smaller in the Senate. As before, we include measures of (relative) campaign spending, whether a Democratic or Republican incumbent is running for reelection, whether the state is located in the South, and whether the ballot format allows voters easily to cast a straight party ticket.

Because our unit of analysis is now the state rather than the district, we can also incorporate indicators of state electorate preferences that have already been developed. An indicator that we considered uses the percentage of the vote won by a recent Democratic presidential candidate as a measure of a state's liberalism. While election returns are a promising measure of constituent ideology if the proper elections are used (LeoGrande and Jeydel 1997), their use here would be problematic, explaining election outcomes with election outcomes and almost certainly leading to overestimation of constituent influence. While no indicator is ideal, it is more important to measure concepts in the best way possible—and in multiple ways if feasible—rather than omit important explanatory variables. Consequently, we rely on two alternate measures of state ideology.

We first employ macroideology as defined and assembled by Erikson, Wright, and McIver (1993). They used state exit polls to estimate state voters' ideological tendencies, operationalized as the percentage of voters who identify themselves as liberal minus the percentage who label themselves conservative. This creates an index that theoretically runs from −100 to +100, though we find in practice that it is always negative since self-identified conservatives outnumber liberals in every state. Because the distribution is lopsided, one can interpret higher values, which are closer to ideological parity, as more moderate and lower values (that is, those that are more negative) as more ideologically extreme in the conservative direction. If voters are acting on their ideological tendencies and voting sincerely and independently in each election, moderate electorates should be expected to do more ticket splitting.

Imperfections in Erikson, Wright, and McIver's measures lead to an alternative measure of ideology to ensure that results are robust. A potential concern with their indicator is the temporal limitation of the exit poll data. If state electorates change their ideological preferences over time, then data drawn from a particular period, in this case 1976–88, are misleading indicators in other time periods. Because we are studying all congressional elections from 1952 to 1996, Erikson, Wright, and McIver's measure might be unsuitable (cf. Wright et al. 2000). To give state ideology the best chance of showing itself in the regression analyses that follow, we also employ an alternative measure by Berry and colleagues (1998). Their measure is produced by computing weighted averages of congressional candidates' positions within each district for each year. While this procedure also is not ideal and might in fact be tautological to some degree, it has the advantage of different values for each state each year. Berry and colleagues' measures are dynamic rather than static. Their main limitation is that they exist only for years between 1960 and 1993, inclusive. So we use them in 9 of our 12 presidential election years. The Berry measure runs from 0 (most conservative) to 100 (most liberal), so we fold the measure at 50 so that smaller values indicate more moderate state electorates.

Our estimation strategy is to regress the five variables of interest on levels of ticket splitting estimated within each state. Since campaign spending data are available only after the early 1970s, we estimate models with and without the spending variable to incorporate all of the elections from 1952 to 1996. Spending affects only those elections beginning in 1972. Likewise, Berry and colleagues' measures are only available for elections from 1960 to 1992. As before, we estimate levels of RD and DR ticket splitting separately because several variables may operate in different directions for each type. These combinations require us to run a total of eight models to establish the robustness of the results.

The results from a series of regressions for each of these scenarios are presented in table 6.1. An important point to take from these results is that two local candidate variables—relative campaign spending and incumbency—have the largest and most consistent effect on ticket splitting in every model. As competing campaigns' spending levels change from dollar-for-dollar outlays (a value of .5) to a situation in which the Democrat spends all of the campaign money in the district (a value of 1), RD ticket splitting increases by an average of 15 percent. The same change in the spending ratio would decrease DR ticket splitting by 10 percent. Given that Senate campaigns are often highly competitive and candidates do everything possible to boost their vote percentages by just a point or

two, changes of this magnitude, resulting solely from variations in spending, are substantial. While the coefficients are a bit smaller than those
from the House equations, as expected, the importance of the relative
strengths of the congressional candidates' messages remains. Incumbency
also has a real effect that is separate from our measure of message strength.
A Democratic senator on the ballot increases RD ticket splitting by 5 to 10
points depending on the model specification. A Republican incumbent
increases DR voting by a similar amount.

While incumbency per se might not motivate many voters, the name
recognition and credibility that comes with the Senate seat surely make it
easier for voters without strong preferences to again vote for the senator,
even if those voters selected the other party's presidential candidate. The
bottom line is that voters are selecting candidates based on reasonable criteria: experience, credibility, recognizability, and strength of message.
Most voters are not acting on their desire for divided government; many
are not even thinking of party labels before these other candidate-specific
factors.

The effects of other variables on president-Senate vote splitting are
more fleeting. In accord with the House results, southern electorates are
somewhat more likely to vote simultaneously for Republican presidential
candidates and Democratic senatorial candidates. This tendency was
probably more noticeable in the 1950s and 1960s, when conservative
Democrats dominated southern politics and Congress, which might
explain why the variable is not statistically significant in the equations
limited to elections since 1972. Southern Democrats' positions possibly
are (or were) more attractive to southern voters than to their northern
counterparts. We shall subsequently return to this issue of ideology. While
ballot formats do not have a consistent effect on ticket splitting, in the two
models where the results are statistically significant, the evidence suggests
what we have suspected: the availability of a straight party mechanism on
the ballot seems only modestly to discourage RD split-ticket voting.

The ideology of state electorates, as least as measured by Erikson,
Wright, and McIver, has no effect on ticket splitting. This null result may
be real or potentially an artifact of a time-bound measure since the positive coefficient on Berry and colleagues' measure in two equations indicates that ideologically extreme electorates were surprisingly more likely
to cast split tickets than ideologically moderate electorates. Even in these
couple of cases, however, the size of the effect is trivial. In later models,

TABLE 6.1. A General Model of President-Senate Ticket Splitting

Variable	RD Ticket Splitting				DR Ticket Splitting			
	1972–96	1972–92	1952–96	1960–92	1972–96	1972–92	1952–96	1960–92
Spending ratio	.306**	.335**	—	—	-.202**	-.178**	—	—
	(.059)	(.062)			(.043)	(.042)		
Democratic incumbent	.067**	.048*	.105**	.094**	-.00001	.004	-.033**	-.028**
	(.024)	(.027)	(.019)	(.020)	(.014)	(.015)	(.009)	(.010)
Republican incumbent	-.002	-.015	-.046**	-.075**	.046**	.060**	.066**	.099**
	(.019)	(.021)	(.015)	(.018)	(.016)	(.018)	(.014)	(.019)
South	.016	.019	.067**	.057**	.015	.003	-.002	-.008
	(.018)	(.020)	(.020)	(.022)	(.018)	(.018)	(.013)	(.015)
State ideology (Erickson, Wright, and McIver)	-.001	—	-.0001	—	.001	—	-.0001	—
	(.001)		(.001)		(.001)		(.0006)	
State Ideology (Berry et al.)	—	.002*	—	.002**	—	.0002	—	-.0003
		(.001)		(.001)		(.001)		(.001)
Partisan ballot device	-.014	-.023	-.030*	-.035*	.000007	.008	-.007	.003
	(.016)	(.017)	(.014)	(.016)	(.013)	(.013)	(.009)	(.011)
Constant	.069*	.072*	.223**	.218**	.298**	.258**	.184**	.177**
	(.037)	(.037)	(.018)	(.022)	(.027)	(.020)	(.013)	(.013)
Number of cases	219	195	338	259	219	195	338	259
Adjusted R²	.475	.514	.296	.331	.344	.349	.208	.291
Standard error	.106	.109	.123	.128	.090	.091	.088	.091

Note: Entries are OLS coefficients with robust Huber/White standard errors
Campaign-spending data available only from 1972 onward; Berry et al. data, available from 1960 to 1992.
*p < .05; **p < .01, one-tailed tests

both measures of state ideology are thus omitted to improve the tables' readability. These measures are included here merely to demonstrate the other variables' effects under suitable controls. The state-ideology variables are rarely significant in other models, and the substantive results never change if these variables are included.

As with the House, the overwhelming factor in determining how many voters split tickets is the relative amounts of spending by the Democratic and Republican Senate candidates. In other words, as the share of Senate campaign outlays spent by the Democrat grows, the proportion of Republican presidential voters who defect by voting for the Senate Democrat increases in a significant and linear fashion. To make the centrality of this relationship clear, figure 6.4 presents a simple scatter plot of the spending ratio variable by RD ticket-splitting rates in each state. The OLS regression line has been superimposed on the data. The relationship between campaign spending and RD ticket splitting is quite clear: increased campaign spending means increased ticket splitting. In addition, the variance of points around the regression line increases as spending increases, suggesting that a big spending advantage is a necessary but not a sufficient condition for high levels of ticket splitting. This same pattern is evident in DR splitting and president-House ticket splitting (see, for example, figure 4.3).

This does not necessarily imply, of course, that money buys votes. Rather, spending on advertising, literature, travel, and so on is how candidates communicate their messages to voters. Some campaigns are of course more adept than others at taking advantage of a spending advantage, of converting campaign advertising into votes. For all of the public complaints about the ills of heavy campaign spending, voters react to it positively. Candidates who substantially outspend their opponents greatly increase the likelihood that voters will receive their messages rather than their opponents'. These messages raise the number of considerations in the voters' minds that favor the financially advantaged candidate. Spending on advertising is also a good cue about candidate credibility. Candidates with money have probably earned it by convincing donors of the candidacies' viability. These candidates might be credible because of their experience in office, previously successful campaigns, strong name recognition in the state, or advantages in state party identification. The media tend to cover and value Senate candidates in proportion to their resources (Westlye 1991). Thus, campaign spending is a proxy for a host of variables that affect election outcomes but that voters simplify to a choice between two

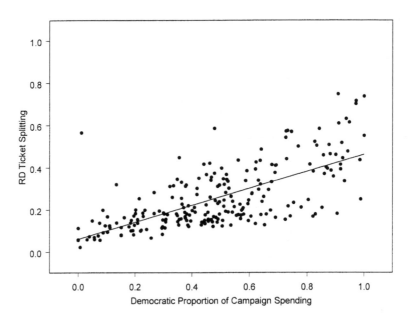

FIG. 6.4. Senate RD ticket splitting by Democratic campaign spending, 1972–96

candidates of different quality. Naturally, when party identification or other personal allegiances are not overwhelming, voters reasonably choose the "best" candidate in this loose sense.

To make the House and Senate results as comparable as possible and to rule out some alternative hypotheses related to such things as coattail effects, we offer a pooled model (from 1972 onward) that includes additional presidential variables. As table 4.5 did for the House, table 6.2 includes dummies for when the Democrats nominate a southerner for president, when a Democrat wins the White House, and interactions of these variables with South and Democratic incumbency. The model is run twice, once using ordinary least squares with robust standard errors and once using a fixed- and random-effects model to account, however crudely, for the panel-like nature of the data set. As in the House, the model indicates that campaign spending has a consistently important effect in president-Senate ticket splitting. Incumbency and presidential effects appear to matter less in the Senate however, as might be expected. Region remains important, as RD ticket splitting is higher in the South, though it is reduced when a southern Democrat runs for president.

TESTING FOR INTENTIONAL POLICY BALANCING

We believe that our model, particularly the spending and incumbency variables, captures the important state-level influences that determine levels of split-ticket voting. One factor to which we have alluded but that we have not yet explicitly measured is candidate ideology. This is a serious omission given that several theories about the causes of ticket splitting and divided government rest on assumptions about the role of ideology in the voting calculus. As we have already discussed, the most notable appearance of ideological positions is in Fiorina's (1996) model of policy balancing. We do not deny that many voters are ideological moderates, that the

TABLE 6.2. Pooled Analysis of RD Splitting in Senate Races, 1972–96

Variable	OLS with Robust Standard Errors	Fixed- and Random- Effects Model
Spending ratio	.334**	.392**
	(.053)	(.069)
Democratic incumbent	.071**	−.019
	(.025)	(.047)
Democrat elected president	−.027	−.039
	(.030)	(.030)
Democratic incumbent × Democrat elected president	−.027	.067
	(.030)	(.055)
Republican incumbent	−.003	−.076*
	(.017)	(.044)
Partisan ballot device	−.014	−.011
	(.014)	(.013)
South	.068**	.126**
	(.023)	(.051)
Southern Democrat for president	−.028	.003
	(.017)	(.044)
South × southern Democrat for president	−.096**	−.217**
	(.029)	(.089)
Constant	.096**	.107*
	(.027)	(.054)
R^2	.580	.507
Standard error	.100	.041

Note: Campaign spending data available only from 1972 onward. Sample size is 228 Senate elections.
*$p < .05$, **$p < .01$, one-tailed tests

median voter can be a pivotal actor, or that moderate policies are desired by many citizens. In fact, we take these assumptions largely as given. However, voters who prefer moderate outcomes are a necessary but far from sufficient condition for policy balancing to hold. More importantly, sincere proximity voting rather than strategic balancing behavior can just as easily flow from these conditions.

To recap briefly, the balancing notion holds that a small but noticeable portion of the electorate splits its ballots strategically to create a divided government involving highly polarized parties. The sole motivation for such behavior is these voters' moderate preferences. Voters intend for presidents and congresses to be controlled by different parties to create centrist policies that lie near their preferred positions. One of the balancing theory's main predictions is that ticket splitting will increase as both parties and their candidates become more extreme. This is a reasonable hypothesis since one might expect that a divided government would produce outcomes closer to moderate voters' ideal points than would a unified government of extreme positions.[8]

The data simply do not support that prediction. Our analysis of House-president ticket splitting already found the opposite relationship: ticket splitting decreases as candidates polarize. This fits with much of the existing empirical literature (Born 1994; Burden and Kimball 1998; Frymer 1994; Frymer, Kim, and Bimes 1997; Garand and Lichtl 2000; Kimball 1997; Petrocik and Doherty 1996; Soss and Cannon 1995). To provide more confidence in the generalizability of this finding, we augment our Senate model with several measures of candidate ideology and the policy distance between candidates.

As with the House, we assess incumbents' positions with roll call scores, here Poole and Rosenthal's (1997) DW-NOMINATE estimates.[9] Table 6.3 reports regression results based on Senate races with an incumbent running for reelection. Incumbency has been removed since it no longer varies within each equation. Once again, the campaign spending ratio is of central importance. The only other variable with a clear effect is the incumbent's position. The coefficients are positive for Democrats, meaning that more conservative DW-NOMINATE scores leads to higher levels of RD ticket splitting. Likewise, as Republicans move to the left (earning lower DW-NOMINATE scores), DR ticket splitting again increases in frequency. In general, as candidates' positions moderate, or converge toward the center of the ideological spectrum, split-ticket voting becomes more common.

As with the House analysis, these results suffer from data limitations. Roll call measures of ideology exist only for incumbents, so open seats were omitted from the previous regression equations. Though we doubt that this change jeopardizes the central finding that candidate moderation increases ticket splitting, it is possible that some important dynamics are missed by ignoring challengers' positions. Credible measures of challengers' ideologies are difficult to find. If theories of retrospective voting (Downs 1957; Fiorina 1981; Key 1966) are accurate, the incumbent's position should be more important to voters. Furthermore, the higher visibility of incumbents should make their ideological locations more salient to voters. Nonetheless, it is necessary to include challengers as much as possible to verify that results based only on incumbents are trustworthy.

Fortunately, a unique survey allows us to produce estimates of both incumbent and challenger ideologies for two election years. The SES, conducted as part of the biennial National Election Studies between 1988 and 1992, uses state-based surveys of constituents living in states with Senate elections. The SES asked these voters to place the presidential and senatorial candidates on a seven-point ideological scale.[10] Taking the mean placements of the four candidates in each state, we computed the distances

TABLE 6.3. Effects of Incumbent Positioning on President-Senate Ticket Splitting

Variable	RD Ticket Splitting		DR Ticket Splitting	
	1972–96	1952–96	1972–92	1952–96
Spending ratio	.402**	—	–.432**	—
	(.119)		(.096)	
South	–.054	.054	.037	.059
	(.037)	(.038)	(.045)	(.044)
Incumbent position	.168**	.136**	–.118**	–.121**
	(.060)	(.054)	(.040)	(.026)
Partisan ballot device	–.021	–.055*	–.0001	–.010
	(.033)	(.027)	(.028)	(.022)
Constant	.199**	.420**	.434**	.297**
	(.086)	(.040)	(.039)	(.018)
Number of cases	88	141	81	132
R^2	.315	.180	.333	.103
Standard error	.134	.154	.129	.129

Note: The analysis of RD splitting is limited to Democratic incumbents and the analysis of DR splitting is limited to Republican incumbents. Entries are OLS coefficients with robust Huber/White standard errors. Campaign-spending data available only from 1972 onward.

*$p < .05$, **$p < .01$, one-tailed tests

between the candidates in two ways to allow the balancing process maximum opportunity to show itself. First, we assessed the absolute difference
between competing Senate candidates (Senate candidate distance). Second, we measured the absolute difference between presidential and senatorial candidates from different parties (president-Senate candidate difference) for the relevant type of ticket splitting. For example, in 1992, it is
measured as the difference between Bill Clinton and the Republican Senate candidate in each state in the DR ticket-splitting equation (see Burden
and Kimball 1998).

If balancing occurs with any regularity, the coefficients on these variables should be positive and statistically significant. That is, as distance
between candidates grows, so should ticket splitting, because voters wish
to balance polarized candidacies. Table 6.4 presents the results of our
regression analyses testing the balancing hypotheses. We find no support
for balancing under either measure of candidate distance. If anything,
ticket splitting seems to decrease as candidates move apart. This fits nicely
with our earlier findings that used measures of incumbent ideology alone.

TABLE 6.4.   Balancing and President-Senate Ticket Splitting, 1988 and 1992

Variable	RD Ticket Splitting		DR Ticket Splitting	
Senate candidate distance	−.061*	—	−.006	—
	(.020)		(.029)	
President–Senate candidate distance	—	−.051*	—	−.005
		(.019)		(.023)
Spending ratio	.368**	.377**	−.184**	−.181**
	(.079)	(.083)	(.075)	(.061)
South	−.021	−.009	−.011	−.007
	(.033)	(.034)	(.025)	(.013)
Democratic incumbent	.028	.033	−.012	−.009
	(.042)	(.042)	(.025)	(.022)
Republican incumbent	.040	.044	.050	.050
	(.032)	(.032)	(.039)	(.038)
Partisan ballot device	−.048*	−.055**	.018	.019
	(.021)	(.022)	(.020)	(.021)
Constant	.126**	.125**	.288**	.270**
	(.050)	(.050)	(.090)	(.070)
R^2	.644	.638	.485	.485
Standard error	.093	.094	.081	.081

Note: Sample size is 66 elections. Entries are OLS coefficients with robust Huber/White standard errors.
*$p < .05$; **$p < .01$, one-tailed tests

When the ideological differences between candidates blur as a result of similarity of positions, voters are more willing to vote for candidates from different parties without consequence. Polarization makes party differences clearer and straight party voting more common. As before, we find that campaign spending has the most important influence on ticket splitting. Though the small number of cases used in these models makes inferences less certain, the results also suggest that ticket splitting was more common outside of the South, when the ballot did not provide a straight party voting mechanism, and when the incumbent senator was not from the presidential candidate's party. State ideology again seems to have a negligible effect on ticket splitting.

Returning to incumbent measures, we can also determine the consistency of the relationship between candidate polarization and ticket splitting by computing simple correlations between candidates' positions and ticket splitting for each election year. Positions are again measured as incumbents' DW-NOMINATE scores where higher scores are more conservative. As we explained earlier, balancing theories might predict that Democrats' positions are negatively associated with RD ticket splitting, and Republicans' positions should be positively correlated with DR ticket splitting.[11] Table 6.5 indicates that this is not the case. For all of the years in which the number of cases is large enough to produce statistically significant relationships, the relationship between incumbent ideology and ticket splitting is positive for Democrats and negative for Republicans. Of the 22 correlations, only 2 are of the wrong sign, and they do not differ significantly from 0. Democrats with higher, more conservative DW-NOMINATE scores and Republicans with lower, more liberal scores attract more ticket splitters on Election Day. These results underscore the point that candidates with moderate positions in a Downsian fashion are more likely to attract votes, particularly from individuals who voted for the presidential candidate from the other party. To the degree that ideological positions shape election outcomes, convergence rather than divergence boosts ticket splitting in the states.

These tests of policy balancing may be considered inappropriate for staggered Senate elections. What reference point do policy-balancing voters use when choosing a Senate candidate? If they are looking at the presidential candidate, it seems clear that voters are not opting to counter extremes with extremes. As the literature review earlier in this chapter indicated, however, there is another way in which voters might use Senate elections to produce moderate outcomes. Balancers might value the state delegation more than the national partisan configuration. Such voters would refer to the incumbent senator who is not running for reelection rather than to the president when making a Senate vote choice. Voters might seek split delegations—those with senators from different parties—in an effort to offset the ideological tendencies of the "anchor" senators in their states. For example, Iowans might have chosen liberal Democrat Tom Harkin (with a DW-NOMINATE score of −.851 in the 105th Congress) in 1996 to balance conservative anchor Charles Grassley (DW-NOMINATE score of .604). This is much like the balancing that is thought to occur in midterm House elections, when the presidency is not up for grabs. Though many states elect senators of the same party, enough choose split delegations to make such an idea intriguing. Since successful incumbents like Harkin and Grassley alternate running for reelection, vot-

TABLE 6.5.   Incumbent Positions and President-Senate Ticket Splitting by Year

Year	Democratic Incumbent and RD Ticket Splitting	Republican Incumbent and DR Ticket Splitting
1952	.771**	−.250
	(7)	(17)
1956	.346	−.198
	(10)	(16)
1960	.489*	−.133
	(14)	(10)
1964	.687**	−.156
	(22)	(8)
1972	.764**	−.537**
	(10)	(15)
1976	−.154	−.039
	(15)	(7)
1980	.152	−.656*
	(17)	(6)
1984	.437*	−.203
	(11)	(17)
1988	.352*	−.515**
	(11)	(12)
1992	.177	−.083
	(14)	(11)
1996	−.066	−.632**
	(6)	(13)

Note: Cell entries are correlation coefficients with sample sizes in parentheses.
$*p < .10; **p < .05$, one-tailed tests

ers may keep returning them to office to maintain the proper mix of ideologies in Iowa's Senate delegation.

A formal depiction of this logic can be found in figure 6.5, which assumes a common unidimensional spatial voting model. The voter (V) is a moderate and is flanked by an extremely liberal Democratic candidate (DC) on the left and an extremely conservative Republican candidate (RC) on the right. If the decision were to be made between these two Senate candidates based on sincere voting or proximity alone, the Democrat would win because the spatial distance to the Democratic candidate (1) is less than that to the Republican (2). A delegation-minded voter would also consider the ideology of the anchor, in this case a moderately liberal Democratic anchor (DA). If the voter chose the Democratic candidate (DC), the mean delegation ideology would lie at the arrow between the two Democrats, an unpleasant situation for a moderate. However, if the voter were to break the candidate-proximity rule and help elect the Republican (RC), the mean delegation ideology would be closer to the voter's ideal point, the right arrow. That is, because distance 4 is less than distance 3, balancing is the rational strategy.

The SES offers a unique opportunity to test this hypothesis. Whereas earlier studies relied only on incumbent ideology, measured by such things as roll call scores or crude dichotomous indicators of party affiliation as cues to ideological position, the SES provides respondents' direct placements of all Senate candidates and anchor senators on a seven-point scale. To allow for different mechanisms underlying delegation balancing, we measure ideological distance in two ways, as we did with president-Senate distance. Our dependent variables will now be the Democratic and Republican Senate candidates' shares of the vote, so both measures involve their positions. First, we compute the absolute difference between the candidate's position and the anchor senator's position. If voters are trying to balance against the anchor, the candidate's share of the vote should increase as this distance grows. Second, we assess the relative distance of candidates from the anchor senator. Like the Downsian proximity model, which predicts that voters will choose the nearest candidates, the balancing model predicts that voters will chose the candidates farthest from the anchor. Thus, we assess the relative distances of the Senate candidates from the anchor senator by computing

| Democratic position – anchor position | – | Republican position – anchor position |

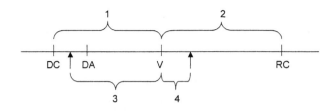

FIG. 6.5.   Proximity and balancing models of Senate delegations

for each Senate contest. Positive values indicate that the Democratic candidate is farther from the anchor senator than the Republican candidate,
suggesting that the Democratic is more appealing to balancing voters. As
a candidate's relative distance from the anchor grows, balancing voters
should be more likely to vote for the candidate. When examining the
Republican share of the vote, we multiply the relative distance measure by
−1. Thus, our measure of distance from the anchor senator should be positively associated with the candidate's share of the vote, regardless of party.
In keeping with our theory of congressional elections, we also control for
candidate spending, region of the country, and incumbency.[12] We also
include the presidential vote as an independent variable to control for any
possible coattail effects that might work against balancing.

  Table 6.6 displays the results of our multivariate analyses. The dependent variable is now the share of the vote received by the Senate candidate, so no ecological estimates are needed. There are a total of three models: two for the Democratic share of the vote using each of the balancing
variables and one for the Republican share of the vote using only the
absolute distance variable.[13] The results provide no support for the notion
that voters are purposely balancing Senate delegations with candidates
from opposite ends of the ideological spectrum. In these models, campaign
spending is the dominant force behind Senate elections, even to the point
of overwhelming incumbency (with which it is only moderately collinear).
Connections between the positions of Senate candidates and the anchor
senator seem not to matter to most voters whether these concepts are measured in absolute or relative terms. We believe that these results, coupled
with the overwhelming individual survey evidence that follows, make
clear what variables are contributing to split-ticket voting. Before concluding our discussion of Senate elections, however, we must consider
aggregate outcomes as well.

Scholars' and journalists' interest in split-ticket voting initially arose as a result of some puzzling election results. In recent decades, the White House and Congress have been ruled by different parties, states have been electing governors and state legislators from different parties, and Senate delegations have become increasingly split by party. However, as figure 6.1 shows, the number of split Senate delegations has declined substantially over the past 10 years. Until rigorous empirical research addressed the subject, observers often assumed that individual voters must prefer divided control based on the aggregate outcomes that electorates produced. We return to the aggregate evidence on split Senate delegations in the concluding chapter to determine whether "as if" assumptions about intentional voter balancing are tenable.

CONCLUSION

The weakening of mass partisanship and rise of candidate-oriented campaigns contributed to an "electoral disintegration" (Jacobson 1991) in

TABLE 6.6.   Tests of Delegation Balancing, 1988 and 1992

Variable	Democratic Share of Senate Vote		Republican Share of Senate Vote
Candidate's distance from anchor	—	−.009	.021
		(.017)	(.016)
Candidates' relative distance from anchor	.003	—	—
	(.009)		
Spending ratio	.342*	.333*	−.335*
	(.060)	(.064)	(.059)
South	−.017	−.017	.020
	(.018)	(.017)	(.018)
Democratic incumbent	.024	.021	−.027
	(.026)	(.026)	(.025)
Republican incumbent	−.004	−.006	.004
	(.030)	(.032)	(.030)
Democratic share of presidential vote	.111	.103	−.139
	(.133)	(.132)	(.137)
Constant	.280*	.296*	.719*
	(.059)	(.064)	(.057)
R^2	.733	.734	.739
Standard error	.066	.065	.065

Note: Sample size is 64 Senate races. Entries are OLS coefficients with robust Huber/White standard errors.
*$p < .01$, one-tailed tests

American electoral politics that reached its high point in the 1970s. In accord with the general trend, presidential and senatorial elections became increasingly independent of one another. Our analysis suggests that this trend has not been growing slowly over the past half century; rather, there seems to be a clear change in patterns in the late 1960s. Over the entire 1952–96 period of our study, 63 percent of the states gave pluralities of their votes to presidential and senatorial candidates of the same party. This percentage differs significantly from random behavior (50 percent, $p < .01$) and suggests that voting behavior across the two elections is interrelated. However, the average masks the highs and lows. Before 1968, 74 percent of states voted for candidates of the same party, but only 57 percent did so afterward. Though both percentages still differ significantly from mere chance, they suggest, along with declining evidence of coattails (J. Campbell 1993; Ferejohn and Calvert 1984), that voters are thinking about one contest at time. The resurgence in mass partisanship and increasing party polarization since the 1980s has reduced ticket splitting and strengthened the links between elections to different offices, if only indirectly.

The weakening of partisanship as a cue in congressional elections (Ferejohn 1977) provides conditions that are conducive to split-ticket voting and increases tolerance for divided government. However, they are not the immediate causes of these phenomena. Split-ticket voting and divided government are also not synonymous. Table 6.7 presents mean levels of both types of ticket splitting by the outcome in each state. The proportion of Democratic presidential voters who voted for the Republican in the Senate race is low in states with DD and RD outcomes but much higher in other states. Similarly, RD ticket splitting is low in states with DR and RR outcomes. The pattern here is that the proportion of voters who split their ballots depends more on the Senate race than the presidential race. For example, mean RD ticket splitting rates vary more across Senate outcomes than within them; conversely, RD splitting varies more within presidential outcomes than across them. A similar process determines levels of DR ticket splitting.

Another way to portray this relationship is to note that Senate election outcomes are closely tied to split-ticket voting rates, whereas presidential outcomes are not. Thus, ticket splitting is related to local rather than national outcomes, making it difficult to read a national mandate for divided government into election results. We believe that voters have a relatively easy time coming to their choices in presidential elections. The candidates are usually of nearly equal quality and have messages of similar strength. Partisanship is the major deciding factor for most voters, but particular issues or salient candidate qualities also can have a substantial influence. At the Senate level, and even more so in House races, messages and candidates are often of unequal strength. Democratic presidential voters might be willing to vote for the Republican Senate candidate if the Democratic opponent is of poor quality and has little shot at winning. This story is reinforced by the results in table 6.8. Here we use logit analysis to predict senatorial and presidential election outcomes based on the amount of ticket splitting in each state. As we expect, the likelihood of a Democrat winning the Senate race grows as RD voting increases and DR voting decreases in frequency. Remarkably, ticket splitting is unrelated to the outcomes of presidential elections, at least on a state-by-state basis. The leverage ticket splitting provides above a naive prediction of always guessing that the majority party wins is around 25 percent in the Senate but is nonexistent for presidential elections.

TABLE 6.7.   Mean Senate Split-Ticket Voting by Election Outcome, 1952–96

| | Outcome | | | |
Direction of Ticket Splitting	DD	RD	DR	RR
DR	.147	.142	.339	.223
RD	.283	.394	.161	.167
Number of cases	82	94	36	138

TABLE 6.8.   Explaining Election Outcomes with President-Senate Ticket Splitting, 1952–96

	Senate Election Outcome		Presidential Election Outcome	
RD voting	21.00**	—	–.66	—
	(2.40)		(.79)	
DR voting	—	–34.06**	—	1.33
		(4.79)		(1.05)
Constant	–4.70**	5.86**	–.51*	–.94**
	(.52)	(.78)	(.23)	(.24)
Prediction improvement over naive baseline	27.7%	25.7%	0.0%	–0.6%
Log likelihood	–144.16	–165.67	–223.34	–222.89

Note: Dependent variable is probability of Democrat winning. Sample size is 350 elections.
*$p < .05$, **$p < .01$, two-tailed test.

Voters, then, are more willing to violate their partisan allegiances in senatorial contests than in presidential elections. What does this mean for representation? On the one hand, the Senate is closer to the people than the presidency because of its smaller constituencies. On the other hand, the Senate has staggered elections to limit popular control, and these elections often feature unbalanced contests where one candidate is the clear favorite. Yet Senate elections are more competitive than House elections, reelection rates are lower, and shifts in partisan control of the upper chamber are more common.

The fact that senators are elected from double-member districts makes Senate elections a natural context in which to find ticket splitters motivated by the desire to produce divided outcomes. Despite the plausibility of balancing arguments, we find no evidence that voters are purposely splitting their tickets to balance ideologically polarized candidates. Voters seem to prefer moderate candidates to extreme candidates whether each race is considered in isolation or when vote decisions are made in a coordinated way. The robustness of this finding provides further evidence for the Downsian view of candidate competition. While issues and ideology are certainly not the most important factors in congressional elections, at least some candidates believe some of the time that they matter (Arnold 1990; Burden 1998; Fenno 1978; Miller and Stokes 1963). Our analyses indicate that voters prefer moderates. There is a consistent positive relationship between candidate proximity to the middle of the ideological spectrum and vote percentage on Election Day. Although some voters might purposely pursue ideological balancing across offices, they are likely few in number and are far less important to election outcomes than is the larger portion of the electorate that seeks reputable, high-quality, moderate candidates for each office.

CHAPTER VII

Conclusion and Implications

Would a straight ticket be simpler? No. Bad idea. Split tickets keep the parties busy the next four years trying to find the overarching rationale behind ticket-splitting. *They fail because there is no rationale but that's not to say there aren't reasons.*
—Dale McFeatters (October 25, 2000, emphasis added)

The unprecedented frequency of divided government in the United States during the past thirty years has fostered a tremendous effort to understand the phenomenon's causes and consequences. Divided voters, who split their ballots or switch parties in midterm elections, are the target of fierce political campaigns and an important source of electoral change in American politics. While various indicators show a decline in ticket splitting in the 1990s, divided voters continue to hold tremendous power, given the remarkable national competitive balance between the parties. As we detail in chapter 1, many observers conclude that voters prefer divided party control of government and consequently split votes in a strategic fashion to produce the moderate policies expected from divided government. As a result, journalists often interpret elections that produce divided government as mandates for bipartisan cooperation in Washington.

It is clear by now that we disagree with this assessment. This final chapter summarizes our major arguments and findings. Ticket splitting and divided government are best understood in terms of the level of competition in congressional elections and the policy positions of the two major political parties and their candidates. We also return to the national trends in ticket splitting presented in chapter 1 and discuss the implications of our findings for American politics.

CONGRESSIONAL ELECTIONS:
THE MAIN SOURCE OF DIVIDED VOTING

Using a recent advance in ecological inference, we find that estimates of president-Congress ticket splitting at the national level mask tremendous variation in ticket splitting across congressional districts (most of whose boundaries change every 10 years) and states (whose boundaries are fixed). We even find substantial variation in the direction and frequency of ticket splitting across neighboring districts that are quite similar in terms of demographic composition and previous voting patterns. This suggests that congressional elections are a major source of ticket splitting. If divided government is the result of strategic balancing by voters, we would not expect such dramatic variation in ticket splitting from one jurisdiction to another, unless the desire for divided government varies just as dramatically across districts. We believe that to be unlikely, given that congressional districts are typically drawn to favor one political party or another rather than to contain a large number of moderate voters.

We find that the absence of competition in congressional races is a major source of ticket splitting in the United States. The direction and frequency of ticket splitting are strongly associated with incumbency, campaign spending, and candidate name recognition, all indicators of candidate quality in congressional contests. While presidential elections are often highly competitive, the reality of American national elections is that congressional campaigns (especially those for House seats) are usually lopsided contests, featuring a well-known, well-funded incumbent against a little-known, poorly funded challenger. In a given election cycle, the national party committees direct their vast campaign resources toward just a small fraction of competitive House races out of 435 nationwide. In the remaining noncompetitive House races, voters loyal to the losing party often face a Hobson's choice: vote for a popular candidate of the opposite party or vote for a weak candidate of their own party. In many cases, voters opt for the former or abstain.

It is important to keep in mind the basic distinction that presidential elections are national and congressional elections are primarily local. As a result, incumbency can trump partisanship in congressional elections, but party affiliation often trumps incumbency for the presidency. Presidential elections are the most competitive (that is, uncertain), and House elections are the least competitive, since the winner can usually be identified months before Election Day. From 1954 to 1996, running incumbents won 92.8 percent of the time in the House and 83.7 percent of the time in the

Senate but only 50 percent of the time for the presidency.[1] If we increase the denominator in these computations from the traditional one of only running members to all seats, the reelection rates fall a bit in the House (84.6 percent) and the Senate (68.3 percent) but drops even more dramatically for the presidency (33.3 percent). Incumbent presidents are at least as apt to lose as to win, but members of Congress must face unusually difficult circumstances to suffer defeat. Because presidential elections are more competitive and more visible, voters' decisions are more likely to turn on partisanship, important campaign issues, ideological concerns, events, and personal evaluations of the candidates. Though there is evidence that national issues play some role in congressional contests, voters are generally concerned with picking the "best" candidate based on a few simple criteria such as name recognition and ideological proximity. The chosen candidate is often an incumbent. The compound effect of parochialism and noncompetitive congressional districts produces many split tickets.

Rather than reflecting a full expression of voter preferences, divided government is driven partly by the constraints of the limited choices facing voters. Even if voters wished to balance their congressional and presidential votes, the absence of serious competition in most House elections limits opportunities to do so. Many voters face a limited choice in House elections because of the strategic decisions made by potential candidates and campaign donors well in advance of the election (Jacobson and Kernell 1983). Potential candidates often wait until an incumbent retires or is weakened by scandal, for example, before running for Congress. Similarly, many political action committees and other donors are loathe to give money to a candidate with little chance of winning. Thus, voters often split their ballots because the congressional candidate from their party (if there is one) has no political experience, little campaign money, and little appeal to voters.

A number of studies have demonstrated the virtues of competitive campaigns and elections, including increased media coverage (Westlye 1991), higher voter turnout (S. Patterson and Caldeira 1983; G. Cox and Munger 1986), an increased emphasis on substantive issues by candidates and voters (Kahn and Kenney 1999; Westlye 1991), and increased voter learning (Kahn and Kenney 1999). In competitive campaigns, when at least two candidates make serious efforts to communicate with voters, voters are more likely to cast ballots in line with their issue preferences and party affiliations.

If congressional elections become more competitive in the future, we expect ticket splitting to decline further. But we are not holding our breath. We envision three institutional changes (all remote) that would produce more competitive congressional elections. First, the adoption of a constitutional amendment imposing congressional term limitations might increase competition by forcing incumbents to leave office earlier than expected. However, congressional support for such an amendment has dwindled, and there are many good arguments against term limits (Hibbing 1991; Jacobson 2001, 262–64). Second, the reapportionment and redistricting processes following each national census could increase the number of competitive districts. However, given that most congressional district lines are drawn to protect incumbents and create safe seats for one party or the other, and given the increasing technical sophistication of redistricting planners in both parties, we are not optimistic that redistricting will increase competition. In fact, incumbent protection has been the general pattern in most congressional redistricting plans enacted after the 2000 census (Giroux 2001). Third, campaign reforms that help challengers finance campaigns and communicate with voters (such as free air time, or public financing of campaigns) will make congressional elections more competitive. However, the leading campaign finance reform at this time (the McCain-Feingold law), does little to increase electoral competition, aside from modest increases in contribution limits. Furthermore, by banning soft money donations to political parties, the McCain-Feingold reform may hinder party efforts to assist challengers. Some critics of divided government have offered other constitutional reforms (such as changing House terms to four years and allowing members of Congress to serve in the president's cabinet) designed to strengthen parties and reduce the likelihood of divided government (Sundquist 1986; Cutler 1989). However, these reforms would not improve competition in congressional campaigns, and thus will not reduce the frequency of ticket splitting or the likelihood of continued divided government.

Local competition and candidate quality also help explain why voters switch parties in midterm House elections. Campaign spending and incumbency influence the frequency with which voters deviate from previous voting behavior in midterm elections. A party is likely to lose votes in a midterm election if it fields a weaker candidate than in the previous election and if the incumbent is a member of the opposite party. Again, the movement of voters is often shaped by politicians' strategic decisions made months before Election Day.

Congressional elections are the usual source of ticket splitting, an argument that runs contrary to a certain amount of conventional wisdom. Journalistic accounts have often focused on presidential voting as an important source of ticket splitting, as indicated by common references to "Reagan Democrats" and "Clinton Republicans" (Balz and Broder 1996; Walker 1996). In addition, party-line voting is not much higher in presidential contests than in House and Senate elections (Stanley and Niemi 2000). How do our findings square with this information? The answer is that presidential coattails, while weaker than they once were, are alive and well (J. Campbell 1997; Jacobson 2001). Most voters who defect from their identified parties in presidential elections also defect in House and Senate elections (Jacobson 2001, 151). As a result, party defection in the presidential contest tends to produce a straight party ballot in national contests, while party defection in congressional races tends to produce a split ticket. Put another way, the increase in president-Congress ticket splitting in the 1960s and 1970s coincided with a substantial increase in party defection in congressional voting. In contrast, major-party defection in presidential voting did not increase steadily during the same period. This is not to say that presidential candidates have no effect on ticket splitting. In chapters 4–6, we find that presidents and presidential candidates do indeed influence ticket splitting and midterm voting. However, congressional contests are responsible for far more ticket splitting than are presidential campaigns.

Our findings are consistent with other research on American elections. For example, we find that the effect of congressional incumbency on ticket splitting increased dramatically during the 1960s and 1970s, the same period during which other measures document an increase in the incumbency advantage (Gelman and King 1990; Jacobson 2001). This coincides with a period during which congressional elections became more "candidate centered" (Wattenberg 1991b), as congressional candidates began running more as individuals than as party representatives. This suggests that the increase in ticket splitting in the 1960s and 1970s resulted largely from a growing incumbency advantage, reinforcing our point about the importance of congressional elections in understanding ticket splitting.

At the same time, regional differences in ticket splitting, evident in the 1950s, have largely disappeared. At one time, the South was unique in having a large number of voters choosing Republican candidates for president and Democrats for Congress (RD splitting). This southern exceptionalism gradually vanished in a manner consistent with a top-down party realignment increasing Republican strength in the South (Aistrup 1996; Brunell and Grofman 1998). Republican candidates became competitive in the South first in presidential contests, then in many Senate races, and finally in House races. This explains why RD splitting was more common in House elections than in Senate elections (see fig. 6.3). Now that Republicans are competitive in all national contests in the South, RD splitting is no higher in the South than in other regions of the country.

CANDIDATES AND IDEOLOGY

The preceding discussion is not intended to suggest that localism and a lack of competition in congressional elections are the only factors that facilitate divided voting. While we fail to find evidence consistent with a policy-balancing explanation of divided government, issues and candidate positions still play an important role. Our robust finding is that ticket splitting is more frequent when candidates' positions are nearer to one another and nearer to the ideological center. When candidates take extreme positions, ticket splitting is less common. We find a similar pattern in midterm elections. Incumbents who hold marginal seats and who are closely aligned with the president's agenda risk larger voter defections than do other representatives. In contrast, incumbents who maintain a safe distance from the president tend to minimize their losses in midterm elections.

We believe this occurs for two reasons. First, in the spatial logic of Downs (1957), when candidates adopt moderate positions, they distance themselves from their national party and increase the chances of attracting moderate voters from the opposite party. This also explains why party organizations often try to recruit and promote moderate candidates for Congress at the expense of candidates with more extreme ideological records. Second, when candidates and parties adopt moderate positions, they tend to blur the ideological differences between the parties. This makes party affiliation a less useful voting heuristic, easing the way for voters to cross party lines. We will subsequently discuss these points in more detail.

It is possible that policy-balancing voters are more comfortable splitting their votes between moderate candidates from both parties than splitting their votes between ideological extremists. Voters might be less certain about policy outcomes negotiated by elected officials occupying opposite poles on the ideological spectrum (Lacy and Niou 1998). However, this argument inverts the original motivation for policy balancing: the need to strike a balance between ideologically extreme parties and their elected officials.

Issues and ideology appear to be taking on greater importance in divided voting today. Since House elections have not become more competitive (and are not likely to do so), ticket splitting might be expected to continue at relatively high levels. However, president-House ticket splitting has decreased since the early 1990s (see fig. 1.1). Furthermore, other measures of divided voting, such as split Senate delegations and president-Senate splits used in chapter 6, indicate similar declines in the 1990s. By some measures, including ticket splitting, split districts, and split Senate delegations, the 2000 national elections produced the lowest levels of divided voting in more than 30 years.

Evidence of declining divided voting runs against another strand of conventional wisdom. Many texts emphasize a theme of U.S. political parties in decline. According to this argument, electoral reform and the growth of the mass media have reduced parties' power to structure and determine the vote. For example, some argue that voters' "attachments to the parties are weak and getting weaker" (Lawrence 1999, 173). Martin Wattenberg, a strong proponent of the party-decline thesis, attributes it to "partisans' using their identifications less and less as a cue in voting behavior" (1998, 27). Thus, "electoral disintegration" has been occurring because party identification is now less likely to be used as a common referent to link votes across levels of government (Burnham 1970). Finally, another text even notes that "these changes are reflected in increased split-ticket voting" (T. Patterson 2001, 221).

Our evidence of increased straight-ticket voting suggests that the party-decline thesis commonly found in American government texts needs to be updated. Indeed, a growing group of scholars argue for revision. Some claim that party ties never weakened. Keith et al. (1992) argue that the increasing number of independents' are largely party "leaners," closet partisans who behave just as other party identifiers. Thus, independents are no more common today than they were in the 1950s. More recent evidence (Bartels 2000; Hetherington 2001; Jacobson 2001; Miller 1991) shows that the influence of partisanship on voting in national elections is on the rise over the past 20 years. The latter findings are largely consistent with the recent decline in divided voting that we document in this book.

While some observers have been slow to notice the recent decline in ticket splitting, it still requires an explanation. We argue that party and ideology have become more important in national elections because the two parties have become more ideologically distinct from each other. Each party's increasing homogeneity and growing ideological distance between the two parties in Congress during the past 20 years has been well documented (G. Cox and McCubbins 1993; Poole and Rosenthal 1997; Rohde 1991). At the same time, the correspondence between party identification and ideology has intensified (Abramowitz and Saunders 1998; Knight and Erikson 1997; Levine, Carmines, and Huckfeldt 1997). As ideological clashes in the nation's capital have highlighted the parties' policy differences, voters have come to see government and candidates in a more partisan and ideological light. This development has increased the salience of party labels in the voting booth, particularly when voters infer the ideological positions of lesser-known candidates. In addition, the increasing homogeneity of the parties means that there are fewer candidates trying to run away from their parties' positions (Brunell, Grofman, and Merrill 2001). Thus, party labels and issues are more likely to reinforce one another when voters cast their ballots.

There is an important link between elite partisanship and mass partisanship that too often is neglected (cf. Carmines and Stimson 1989; Coleman 1996; Jacobson 2000a; Zaller 1992). While the relationship between public and elite behavior is likely interactive, we believe that the public tends to follow elite behavior when it comes to party polarization. In particular, Key's (1966) "echo chamber" metaphor for public opinion helps us understand the rise and fall of ticket splitting. When parties offer clear and contrasting policies, as has been occurring with greater frequency in recent years, the public responds with clear issue-based votes. In contrast, when the parties offer vague or similar policy alternatives, as was characteristic of national politics in the early 1970s, voters are more likely to split their ballots, relying more on candidate traits, and it becomes easier to reconcile voting for both parties. Or as Macdonald and Rabinowitz put it, when the parties converge toward the political center, "established partisanship is a less valuable guide to selecting candidates" (1987, 788).

For instance, ticket splitting is more common among National Election Study (NES) respondents who see no real differences between the parties (see chap. 4).[2] Across the 1988, 1992, and 1996 presidential surveys, an average of 31.0 percent of those who did not see important party differences split their tickets across presidential and House elections, whereas just 19.5 percent of those who saw differences split their tickets. This difference is statistically significant ($p < .01$) for each of the individual election years as well as for the pooled data set. In addition, the percentage of NES respondents who perceived important differences between the parties reached a low point of 46 percent in 1972 (when president-Congress ticket splitting reached its zenith) but reached its current high point of 69 percent in 2000 (when ticket splitting dropped to relatively low levels).

If we are correct, we should observe a negative correlation between measures of party polarization at the elite level and measures of ticket splitting observed over several decades. This hypothesis is the opposite of that predicted by Fiorina's (1996) policy-balancing model, which argues that increasing party polarization should lead to more ticket splitting as a larger group of moderate voters inhabits the policy space between the two parties.

To test these competing hypotheses, we compute simple bivariate correlations between measures of party polarization and measures of divided voting. We employ two measures of party polarization drawn from congressional behavior: the percentage of party votes taken in the House during the Congress preceding each presidential election (Stanley and Niemi 2000),[3] and the mean distance between the legislative parties in the House measured by DW-NOMINATE scores (Poole and Rosenthal 1997). A third indicator of party polarization we use is Ginsberg's (1976) measure of conflict in competing national party platforms. This measure is derived from content analyses of party platforms in seven broad issue areas. The measure unfortunately does not exist after 1968, making the number of cases (five) too small to analyze in one instance.

Divided voting is examined using five measures featured prominently in this book. Three indicators assess president-House splitting: total president-House ticket splitting reported in NES surveys, total president-House ticket splitting according to our ecological inferences, and the national percentage of split districts (defined in chap. 2).[4] We also examine the number of states with split Senate delegations and split presidential and Senate results after each presidential election. Thus, explicit measures of candidate ideology used in previous chapters have been replaced with measures of party positions, and our conditional estimates of ticket splitting have been replaced with values representing total divided voting behavior.

Table 7.1 presents the aggregate-level correlations between party polarization and divided voting. All but one of the correlations are negative, and many are statistically significant at the .1 level (or close), even though they are based on a small sample of cases. Once again, party convergence rather than divergence appears to increase split-ticket voting. As differences or conflict between the parties diminish, ticket splitting becomes more likely. Other studies indicate that the negative bivariate associations in the table persist when controlling for other determinants of ticket splitting (Brunell, Grofman, and Merrill 2001; Kimball 1997). In addition, there is evidence of a negative correlation between party polarization and ticket splitting at the state level (Brown and Wright 1982).

To examine further just one of the relationships in the table, figure 7.1 plots the percentage of party votes taken in the House and the percentage of NES respondents who report casting split tickets over time from 1952 to 2000. The two lines generally move in opposite directions. As party voting dropped from the 1950s to the 1970s, ticket splitting increased. Then, as party voting rebounded in the 1980s and 1990, ticket splitting decreased. In addition, the low point in party voting (1972) coincides with the high point in ticket splitting. The crossing of the two trends indicates the rather remarkable observation that in 1972, party voting in the House was less common than was president-House ticket splitting. It is again fairly clear from this evidence that divided outcomes are most likely when party differences are minimized.[5]

Some studies suggest that a rise in voter partisanship will result from an increased party presence in financing and servicing congressional campaigns, from soft money, coordinated expenditures, issue ads, and the like

TABLE 7.1. Party Polarization and Divided Voting

Measure of Party Polarization	Total NES Ticket Splitting (1952–2000)	Total EI Ticket Splitting (1952–2000)	Number of Split House Districts (1900–2000)	Split President-Senate Outcomes (1916–2000)	Split Senate Delegations (1900–2000)
DW-NOMINATE distance between parties in House (1900–2000)	−.05 (13)	−.23 (13)	−.70** (26)	.11 (21)	−.63** (26)
Percentage of party votes in House (1900–2000)	−.39 (13)	−.48* (13)	−.58** (26)	−.13 (21)	−.57** (26)
Party platform conflict (1900-1968)	—[a]	—[a]	−.33 (18)	−.15 (13)	−.34 (18)

Note: Entries are correlation coefficients with number of cases in parentheses.
[a]Too few cases (5) to compute reliable correlations.
$*p < .10, **p < .05$, (two-tailed test)

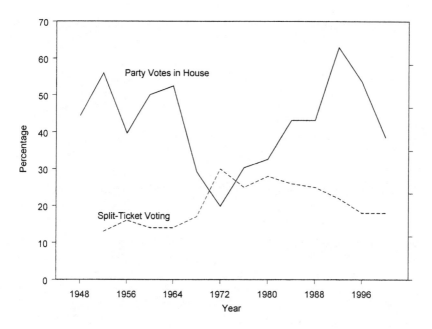

FIG. 7.1. Party voting and president-House ticket splitting by year

(Herrnson 2000; Menefee-Libey 2000). That is probably true. However, the increasing ideological homogeneity of the national parties has also increased the salience of party labels in national elections, spurring increased partisan behavior among voters.

THE FUTURE OF DIVIDED GOVERNMENT

Predicting the future of American politics is a tricky business. Given the current competitive balance between the two major national parties, predicting even the near future of divided government is tricky. It is worth emphasizing how evenly divided the two parties are. The last national election produced one of the closest presidential contests in the country's history. The same election produced an evenly divided Senate (until the Jeffords departure) and a slim five-seat GOP advantage in the House. Even president-Congress ticket splitting was evenly balanced between the two parties in 2000. Finally, in the three most recent national elections, the difference between the two major parties' share of House votes has been less than 1 percent, the longest such streak in more than 100 years. In such a competitive environment, even a small amount of ticket splitting may be enough to throw control of the government to one party.

In addition, events of the 1990s have forced scholars of American politics to rethink the causes and consequences of divided government. Two examples make this point. First, the idea of institutional matching (Jacobson 1991; Petrocik 1991), whereby Democrats better "fit" Congressional duties while Republicans are better suited for the presidency, was turned on its head, particularly in the 1996 elections, which produced a Democratic president and put Republicans in charge of the national legislature. This pattern persisted through the 106th Congress (1999–2000). Though one might argue that the 1994 election that led to the current configuration was a fluke, voters chose not to reverse it when given the opportunity in subsequent elections. The second theory undone by real politics is that of budget deficits. A common view holds that divided governments are more likely than unified governments to increase the deficit (Cutler 1989; McCubbins 1991; Sundquist 1988; cf. Fiorina 1996). While divided governments quadrupled the deficit in the 1980s and shut down the government twice in the 1990s, a Democratic president and Republican Congress agreed on a balanced budget in 1997 and presided over budget surpluses in 1999 and 2000. Though this book does not directly study the consequences of divided government, these events demonstrate that history has easily unraveled earlier assumptions about divided control. We should be cautious in extrapolating from our data to the future.

Nevertheless, we are prepared to make a few tentative speculations about the microfoundations of divided government in the twenty-first century. Though divided voting will wax and wane in frequency over coming years, we see no reason to expect that the way in which voters come to cast split tickets will change in any serious way. High levels of divided voting are associated with a lack of two-party competition in congressional elections and similar party platforms. Low levels of divided voting are the product of competitive elections and ideologically polarized parties. Thus, if we see more competitive congressional elections and continuing party polarization in the future, we expect ticket splitting to continue to decline. As we noted earlier, given a candidate-centered election environment, plus the strong hand of incumbents and parties in the redistricting process, we see little reason to expect more competitive House elections. Furthermore, the passage of the McCain-Feingold initiative banning soft money donations to national parties may hamper parties' efforts to contest elections vigorously. In that case, we can expect more ticket splitting as candidates wage campaigns with less party interference.

However, party polarization appears to be a likelier route to reduced divided voting. National leaders can pursue partisan or bipartisan approaches to governance. The partisan approach is characterized by sharp policy differences, as exemplified by the contentious debates over budget priorities during the 1990s and President George W. Bush's recent tax cut proposals. A bipartisan approach features more compromise and less party conflict, as in the 1997 budget agreement, efforts to beef up homeland security, and President Bush's education reform plan. If the future holds more bipartisan activity, and if the Republican Party moves back toward the center, then we should see an increase in divided voting. Conversely, if the future brings more sharp partisan conflict in Washington, we expect that divided voting will continue to decline. At this writing, we foresee more opportunities for ideological conflict over such matters as judicial nominations, tax cuts, budget priorities, and health reform than for bipartisanship. Thus, other things remaining the same—especially a strong role for parties in servicing and financing campaigns—we see little reason for divided voting to increase in the near future.[6]

ON MANDATES, MESSAGES, AND MASS MOTIVATION

We conclude by reminding ourselves of the differences between collective outcomes and individual action (Schelling 1978). Even if the preference aggregation process were clear, it is often misleading to infer from election results what voters intended to do with their ballots. We are not arguing that divided government is purely accidental or that voters never think about the composition of government when casting their votes. It is possible that some moderate voters split their ballots in a strategic fashion designed to create divided government. However, from our vantage point, these voters are so small in number and sufficiently constrained by the lopsided nature of the campaigns that they do not drive the engine that is producing divided government. The mandates that journalists and politicians glean from election results are only cryptically connected to voter motives. The messages sent by voters via ticket splitting and divided government have some content, but the desire to offset bipolar candidate offerings is not their major thrust. Most voters use Election Day to register a preference for the more appealing candidate, typically in terms of personal traits and policy positions. For most voters, this process produces a straight party ticket in national races. Occasionally, it produces a split ticket.

In chapter 1, we cited William Safire's advice to voters: split your ticket to keep policy centrist and incremental. Politicians on both ends of the political spectrum, Safire (2000) asserts, will refrain from pulling government too far to the left or right, a sort of mandate for moderation. While we have nothing to say about whether this is the right or wrong thing to do in a given election, we are skeptical of Safire's diagnosis on two counts. First, it is not clear that divided government produces moderate and incremental policy-making "between the 35-yard lines." Policy sometimes zigzags more wildly when parties share power, even if some politicians (like Bill Clinton in 1996) try to interpret divided government as a mandate for bipartisan cooperation. Second, even if a sizable number of voters casts strategic split tickets, as Safire suggests, it is unlikely that other voters are thinking about sending messages to the national government in favor of centrist policy. The large majority of voters choose the same party in presidential and congressional contests.

Policy-balancing theory is appealing as a romantic view that links voters to some of the founding principles of the United States such as separation of powers and checks and balances. While we disagree with policy-balancing theory, we do not intend to denigrate the sophistication of the American electorate. Contrary to many studies of congressional elections, we find, for example, that candidates' and parties' ideological positions are important to voters, but not in the way predicted by policy-balancing theories of divided government. Though we have not called them "informational shortcuts" (Popkin 1996), we believe that voters use relatively simple criteria such as candidate traits and simple ideological proximity when selecting candidates. Moreover, at a normative level, these criteria appear quite reasonable. Thus, despite continuing efforts to uncover the rationale behind ticket splitting, the main causes of ticket splitting and divided government—a blurring of party differences and a lack of competition in locally driven congressional campaigns—are not as closely linked to voter motivations as some might think.

Notes

1. The 1996 NES asked respondents the following question about the budget showdown: "Who do you think is more to blame for the federal budget deficit, the Clinton administration or the Republican Congress?" Seventy percent named the Republican Congress. For more detailed accounts of the budget negotiations, see Drew 1996; Maraniss and Weisskopf 1996; and Thurber 1996.

2. In an abstract sense, the "voters" did elect Bill Clinton, Trent Lott, and Newt Gingrich in 1996. However, these three politicians were not elected by the same voters. Most of the southern voters who helped elect Lott and Gingrich chose Bob Dole for president. Dole received almost twice as many votes as Clinton did in Gingrich's congressional district, and Dole outpolled Clinton in Lott's home state of Mississippi. In contrast, Clinton won most of the states in the Northeast, Midwest, and Far West, outside of the southern base represented by Lott and Gingrich.

3. Table 1.1 begins in 1826, roughly when a national two-party system first developed (Silbey 1996).

4. Since ticket splitting was almost impossible before the introduction of the Australian ballot just before the beginning of the twentieth century, figure 1.1 begins in 1900.

5. At least this is the conventional wisdom as W. Miller and Shanks (1996), Wattenberg (1998), and others present it. Keith et al. (1992) are more skeptical about the rise of independent affiliation.

6. In addition, Fiorina 1996 extends the treatment in Downs 1957, showing how the vote options in a two-party presidential system parallel those found in a three-party parliamentary system.

7. Kelly (1993) even takes issue with Mayhew's definition of significant legislation. Using a more stringent definition that shrinks the number of items considered, Kelly finds that divided governments are indeed less likely to legislate successfully. Weatherford (1994) offers an intriguing thesis that divided government disrupts the flow of legislation by increasing policymakers' uncertainty about future policy directions. According to this argument, gridlock is particularly likely early in a divided regime, but adjustment over time might make divided government more deliberative in later years.

8. Peterson and Greene (1994) go further, arguing that interbranch conflict declined from 1947 to 1990. This might be a result of growing homogeneity of American society and the decline of distributive politics. Ironically, the fading of constituent party bases tends to heighten partisanship.

9. However, divided government does not appear to reduce the likelihood of confirmation (Krutz, Fleisher, and Bond 1998).

CHAPTER 2

1. Some theorists advocate constitutional reforms (such as lengthening House terms to four years and allowing members of Congress to serve in the president's cabinet) intended to encourage single-party control of government. For a summary of these reform ideas, see Sundquist 1986, 1988, 1993; Cutler 1989; for critiques, see Menefee-Libey 1991; Petracca 1991; and Thurber 1991.

2. Interestingly, redistricting has been cited as a reason for the Republican takeover of Congress in 1994. In the South in particular, the creation of black (minority) majority districts reduced the number of Democratic voters in neighboring districts, making these other districts ripe for Republican victories (Cook 1994; Lublin 1997).

3. It is ironic that Fiorina's work on legislative professionalism was published in 1994, when Republicans captured many state legislatures and Congress, the most professional of all American legislatures (see Fiorina 1996, 150–51 for his explanation). For further debate on legislative professionalism and divided government, see Fiorina 1997; and Stonecash and Agathangelou 1997.

4. For alternate views, see Erikson 1989; and Sigelman 1990. For example, candidate quality in congressional elections is influenced by national conditions (Jacobson 1997). Further, the Republican Party has demonstrated over the past three presidential elections that it is capable of a divisive primary (and convention) season.

5. Split outcomes among subpresidential levels of government (Jacobson 1991; Soss and Canon 1995) increased substantially between the 1950s and 1980s.

6. Another view recognizes the recent experience with ticket splitting and divided government as part of a long-term realignment, particularly in the South (Brunell and Grofman 1998). Republican gains in the South, which first appeared several decades ago in presidential elections, did not appear in subpresidential races until much more recently (Aistrup 1996; Bullock 1988), producing split results in the interim. Along similar lines, Gimpel (1996) traces divided voting to different issue cleavages between the parties at the national and state levels. Ticket splitting has generally been more common among southern voters (Alvarez and Schousen 1993), although this relationship has weakened in recent elections (Garand and Lichtl 2000) as Republican candidates became more competitive in southern subpresidential elections.

7. Even if Keith et al. (1992) are right that independents have not grown in number, ticket splitting increased, so party attachments could not have remained constant over the past 50 years even if the distribution of self-identifications held steady.

8. Of course, one presidential candidate sometimes appears quite a bit weaker than his opponent. This should lead to more partisan defection and thus more split-ticket voting (as in 1972).

9. Prior to the 1990s, Republicans ran weaker candidates (in terms of prior political experience) in congressional elections. As a result, Republican voters might have

split their ballots by voting for more appealing and perhaps better-known Democratic candidates for Congress.

10. The penchant for reifying election outcomes is common, as is evidenced by those who look for policy "mandates." The 1996 case is particularly egregious since most estimates indicate that roughly 80 percent of the voters chose the same party for president and the House of Representatives. Thus, the overwhelming majority of voters revealed a preference for one-party government.

11. Alternative explanations for midterm losses abound. In the original surge-and-decline theory (A. Campbell 1960), presidential elections are high-salience races that induce independents (who tend to vote a straight ticket for the party of the winning presidential candidate) to turn out. In contrast, midterm elections are low-salience races in which only core partisans vote, thus eliminating the advantage that the president's party enjoyed two years earlier. Kernell (1977) argues that the midterm is really a referendum on the president's performance and that midterm losses reflect inevitable negative evaluations of the president. Tufte (1978) adds the nation's economic performance to the presidential-referendum argument. Oppenheimer, Stimson, and Waterman (1986) argue that the more seats the majority party has (the more "exposed" it is), the more susceptible it is to midterm losses (see also Jacobson 2001; Marra and Ostrom 1989). A revised surge-and-decline theory (J. Campbell 1993) combines several of these elements but argues that higher turnout among the advantaged party's members accounts for the surge in presidential elections. In any case, there is some controversy as to which of these explanations (including the balancing model) accounts for midterm losses (Niemi and Weisberg 1993).

12. A 1996 postelection study of voters found that only 2 percent of ticket splitters volunteered a balancing rationale when asked why they split their ballots (Tarrance and DeVries 1998, 25).

13. Born (2000b) finds evidence of policy balancing in the 1996 national elections but not in any other presidential elections since 1972.

14. It is unclear how the two studies reach such different conclusions. Schmidt, Kenny, and Morton (1996) only examine sitting senators running for reelection, whereas Nicholson and Segura examine all contested races. Perhaps it is easier for voters to balance between two sitting senators with known records than to balance a sitting senator with a relatively unknown candidate running for an open seat.

15. It is difficult to find a relationship between a trust-in-government scale and ticket splitting because at least two components of the trust measure—a policy dimension (Miller 1974) and a party loyalty dimension (Citrin 1974)—do not reflect Fiorina's (1992) concept of disenchantment with both parties. An adequate test of the government-degeneration hypothesis might involve a reconsideration of the party neutrality/negativity dichotomy presented by Wattenberg (1998). One such attempt finds that ticket splitting is associated with neutral attitudes toward parties but not with negative feelings toward both parties (Kimball 1997).

16. More efforts have been made recently to incorporate contextual variables in voting analyses using survey data (e.g., Bobo and Gilliam 1990; Box-Steffensmeier, Tate, and Kimball 1997; Huckfeldt and Sprague 1987).

17. Johnston and Pattie (1999) find that spending in local campaigns is highly predictive of ticket splitting in three non-U.S. democracies.

18. Our emphasis on spatial proximity theory is also at odds with a directional theory of voting (Matthews 1979; Rabinowitz and MacDonald 1989). Directional models argue that voters focus on the direction candidates would move policy (in relation to the status quo, for example) rather than the specific positions of candidates. Thus, voters may prefer extreme candidates on their side of the ideological spectrum rather than candidates closer to their own positions. In contrast to the proximity logic we use, for example, a directional model holds that "voters in the center do not have high affect for centrist candidates" (Rabinowitz and MacDonald 1989, 114). While directional models may explain presidential coattails in on-year elections and midterm losses in off-year elections in terms of a shift in the status quo (Merrill and Grofman 1999), it is unclear how the directional model accounts for ticket splitting in a single election.

19. Presidential candidates sometimes draw substantial numbers of voters across party lines, as in the case of Reagan Democrats in the 1980s. For examples in the Clinton era, see Balz and Broder 1996; and Walker 1996.

20. Since 1960, a majority of ticket splitters defected in the House race, with the exception of 1972, when only about 40 percent of ticket splitting was driven by the House contests because of the lopsided presidential election. Even this exception fits within the broader theoretical viewpoint that lack of competition, in this case at the presidential level, is responsible for most ticket splitting and thus divided government. It is likely that many moderate Democrats voted sincerely for Nixon and a Democratic congressional candidate.

CHAPTER 3

1. Some scholars have measured ticket splitting by examining actual ballots or ballot records, computerized records of each ballot cast (Bain 1996; Blunt 2000; Gitelson 1978; Gitelson and Richard 1983). These data are extremely attractive, but they are not available in many jurisdictions (Bain 1996), and managing the millions of observations required to analyze them is daunting (see Blunt 2000). Thus, studies of ballot records have been confined to single counties or communities.

2. Technically, estimates may be unbiased if reporting errors are random. Systematic misreporting in a particular direction induces bias.

3. Exit polls underestimate ballot roll-off and thus likely underestimate ticket splitting.

4. Cowart 1974 and Fiegert 1979 discuss the use of ecological inference to estimate ticket splitting but ultimately conclude that the dominant methods at the time—all variants of Goodman's regression—have serious limitations.

5. We ignore votes for third-party candidates in years when few voters choose such candidates. In most cases, this is a safe assumption. For example, in 1988, 98.7 percent of presidential votes, 98.3 percent of Senate votes, and 98.5 percent of House votes went to the two major parties. We account for third-party presidential candidates when they exceed 5 percent of the popular vote (1996, 1992, 1980, and 1968) by adding another column to table 3.1.

6. We assume that presidential nonvoters also abstain from the congressional contest, an assumption that is rarely violated (Burden and Kimball 2001).

7. King's software and related documentation are available for free at <http://gking.harvard.edu>.

8. This is analogous to the assumption in medical imaging that tumors occur in a single cluster rather than being randomly spread around a large area (King 1997, chap. 6).

9. With King's *EzI* program, we used the EI command to make the first-stage estimates and the EI2 command to make the second-stage estimates. See King 1997, chap. 15, for a more detailed description of this technique.

10. According to our estimates, Democrats were somewhat more likely than Republicans to abstain from the House contest. In addition, ballot roll-off was quite high in some congressional districts, especially where an incumbent ran unopposed or faced token opposition. As it turns out, our results did not change substantially when we did not control ballot roll-off. For an example that controls for roll-off in studying racially polarized voting, see Palmquist and Voss 1996.

11. King (1997, 283) recommends this option when there are "unanimous" districts whose values are likely to be generated by a different process than that which governs the rest of the data.

12. In addition, King's method and our application (Burden and Kimball 1998) have been criticized on the grounds that repeated analyses of the same data can produce different ecological estimates (Cho and Gaines 2001; Altman and McDonald 2002). However, variation in repeated estimates of ticket splitting is small in our data and does not change the substantive conclusions reported in this book or in our earlier work (Burden and Kimball 2001; Altman and McDonald 2002). Finally, Herron and Shotts (forthcoming) criticize the use of King's ecological inference estimates as dependent variables in a regression analysis.

13. Specifically, we use the South as a covariate for β_i^w in both stages of estimation, assuming that roll-off and ticket-splitting patterns are unique among Republican presidential voters in the South.

14. Due to the declining exceptionalism of the South in recent elections (see Chapter 4), we do not use the South as a covariate for ticket splitting estimates after 1988. Given the increasing effect of incumbency on ticket splitting in recent elections, we also experiment with incumbency as a covariate. This approach produces similar estimates of ticket splitting as those reported in the book. King's technique includes a nonparametric estimation option that relaxes the TBVN assumption. We generated similar estimates of ticket splitting when using this nonparametric version.

15. The deterministic bounds for Maryland's sixth district are somewhat different than the bounds reported earlier in this chapter (in discussing table 3.1). The earlier calculations assumed extreme ballot roll-off patterns (e.g., only Bush voters abstaining from the House contest), while these calculations are based on our first stage estimates, which indicate more equal roll-off rates for both parties.

16. The slope of each tomography line is $-X_i/(1 - X_i)$. Thus, data with wide variation in X across units will have many different sloping tomography lines.

17. We incorporate the standard errors in subsequent analyses by giving greater weight to districts with more informative bounds.

18. An equivalent assumption is used to apply the method of bounds to estimate voter transition rates and class voting (Achen and Shively 1995, chap. 8). Incorporating this assumption into King's method (by adjusting the prior values of the quantities to be estimated or by culling simulated values that violate the assumption) is a possible avenue for updating our analysis. We simply used the assumption as a diagnostic device to make sure that the district-level estimates and the simulated values did not appear above the diagonal in the tomography plot. Our estimates never violated the assumption.

19. As King (1997, 202, 238) points out, the estimated mode need not fall within the unit square. In cases where the mode or much of the contour lines falls outside the unit square, then much of the TBVN distribution masses along the edge of the square, thereby reducing the variance in the estimated quantities of interest. Such heavy truncation, as in our data, also helps King's basic ecological inference method produce accurate estimates, even in the presence of aggregation bias (King 1997, chap. 11).

20. These estimates differ slightly from those published in Burden and Kimball 1998 because several errors in the original 1988 data set identified by Cho and Gaines (2001) were corrected in the interim.

21. Chapter 6 also examines president-Senate ticket-splitting in 1988 in more detail. Since there were only 33 Senate races in 1988, the 1988 House data were included in the estimation so that the likelihood function could borrow strength from the added observations to improve the Senate estimates.

22. Cho (2001) suggests a switching regression model. Also, Johnston and colleagues (Johnston and Hay 1984; Johnston and Pattie 2000) have used an alternative ecological inference method to estimate the frequency of ticket splitting. Their "entropy-maximizing" procedure incorporates the method of bounds (like King) but uses survey data to further narrow the district-level bounds. They have used the same method on our data to estimate president-Congress ticket splitting in 1988, and their estimates are highly correlated with ours (personal correspondence, July 3, 2000).

23. We find the same pattern when comparing our estimates to the BCR measure using data from other elections and when examining president-Senate splitting.

24. Feigert (1979) finds a similar relationship between the BCR measure and ballot roll-off.

25. Our estimates of on-year to off-year voter transitions (drop-off and party defection) analyzed in chapter 5 resemble those drawn from NES panel studies.

CHAPTER 4

1. In the 1990s, the Democrats also captured the White House in two consecutive elections. As we discuss later, this is another reason why RD ticket splitting declined.

2. We count the 11 former states of the Confederacy plus Kentucky and Oklahoma as the South.

3. In 1956, 27 states had a ballot that allowed voters to pull a single lever or check a box to vote a straight ticket. Today, only 16 states have a straight party option on the ballot. South Dakota, Georgia, Illinois, and Michigan were the most recent states to

eliminate straight party voting, and other states are considering legislation to remove it from their ballot.

4. Our measure of ballot format is not as nuanced as Rusk's (1970), but we believe that it captures the most important variation across states.

5. Using tobit in place of ordinary least squares (OLS) to account for censoring of the dependent variable does not change the results in any substantive way. We exclude uncontested races from most analyses to limit our focus to cases where voters have a choice between casting a split ballot or a straight party ballot. Weighted least squares (WLS) is another alternative to OLS estimation since our district-level estimates of ticket splitting have varying levels of uncertainty associated with them. In fact, King (1997) suggests weighting ecological estimates by the inverse of their standard errors in subsequent analyses. As reported in other work (Burden and Kimball 1998), OLS and WLS estimation produce similar substantive findings with respect to the determinants of ticket splitting. Finally, there is some evidence that WLS is inappropriate in this situation (Lewis 1999). Thus, we report only OLS results here.

6. The electoral costs of being a party leader in Congress have been experienced by others, such as Tom Foley and Newt Gingrich.

7. The effect of campaign spending on RD splitting is also weaker in years when the Democrats captured the White House.

8. These results should be interpreted with some caution since we have not attempted to account for the pooled nature of the data, which often violates the assumptions of OLS (Stimson 1985). Since district boundaries are redrawn every ten years, there are no consistent geographic units, which complicates applying the standard corrections for pooled data. Fortunately, the results do not change when clustering (by state or year), using fixed or random effects, or FGLS to estimate the results presented in table 4.5.

9. W-NOMINATE is a maximum likelihood technique that uses roll-call data ("yeas" and "nays") to estimate the ideal points of legislators. It relies on a multidimensional spatial model in which legislators take roll-call positions that are nearest their ideal point, with some error, thus making it probabilistic. As is common practice, we use first-dimension W-NOMINATE scores, which explain more than 80 percent of the variance in roll-call voting patterns. We prefer W-NOMINATE scores to interest group ratings (e.g., ADA) because W-NOMINATE scores, which are based on hundreds of roll calls, are less likely to suffer from the "artificial extremism" found in interest group ratings, which are based on 20 to 30 roll calls (Burden, Caldeira, and Groseclose 2000; Snyder 1992). W-NOMINATE scores for legislators cannot be compared over time and thus we only evaluate them in cross-sectional analyses (e.g., a single election year). When comparing legislators' positions over time (as in chapter 6), we use first-dimension DW-NOMINATE scores, a dynamic version of W-NOMINATE scores that allow comparisons across years (see McCarty, Poole, and Rosenthal 1997). For a given Congress, DW-NOMINATE and W-NOMINATE scores are highly correlated (Pearson's r values above .9). W-NOMINATE and DW-NOMINATE data are publicly available from Dr. Keith Poole at the University of Houston <http://voteview.uh.edu/default_nomdata.htm>.

10. These results could be consistent with policy-balancing theories if one allows the ideological position of the balancing voter to shift from district to district, just as

the position of the median voter probably varies across districts (Grofman et al. 2000). For example, a slightly right-of-center voter may be inclined to balance a Republican presidential vote with a vote for a moderate incumbent House Democrat. Similarly, a somewhat left-of-center voter may balance a Democratic presidential vote with a vote for a moderate Republican incumbent. In addition to the other constraints imposed by the electoral system, this diversity of preferences may limit the extent to which balancing voters can "coordinate" to produce divided government (Mebane 1999).

11. The declining regional disparity in ticket splitting is even more dramatic if all House races are examined. When uncontested races are included in the analysis, RD splitting was about 50 percent higher in the South during the 1950s, then declines almost monotonically to zero in 1996. The incumbency effect hovers around .2 from 1952 to 1964, then jumps to approximately .4 for elections from 1972 to 1988, and then drops back to .2 in 1992 and 1996. The 1968 election appears to be the first where incumbency has a larger effect on RD splitting than does the South.

12. Two states redrew district lines during these intervals. In those cases, we matched each new district with its closest counterpart under the old map. If doing so proved impossible, we dropped the district from the analysis.

13. Results are available from the authors.

14. Sigelman, Wahlbeck, and Buell (1997) use the same model to examine ticket splitting in 1992. Their findings are quite similar to ours.

15. There are many ways one might operationalize this concept, and we have tried most of them, never finding support for balancing theory. For example, a dummy variable for respondents who place themselves between the two major parties is also not related to ticket splitting. A more sophisticated testing that counts only moderates who scored above the mean on political knowledge, interest in politics, and efficacy (the 10 percent or so of moderates with the wherewithal to balance) also finds no support. We also exclude a measure of one's strength of partisanship from the model to avoid confounding the effect of ideological moderation (the two variables are correlated). The results do not change when strength of partisanship is added to the model.

CHAPTER 5

1. Leaners are treated as party identifiers in table 5.1. Survey respondents were coded as Republican, independent, or Democratic in each election. Those who moved to a different category between elections were coded as having changed their party identification.

2. J. Campbell (1993) also understates the effect of voter defection because he uses voters' current party identification as the baseline for measuring vote defection. Given that some voters might change their reported party identification in response to short-term political forces and to remain consistent with their current voting behavior, this method will uncover less party switching than actually occurs (Born 1990, 642 n.30). One of the advantages of the NES panel data is that they allow the use of past voting behavior as the baseline for measuring party defection and subsequent voter turnout.

3. Data are not available for races in states that do not report election results for

uncontested seats (Florida, Arkansas, and Oklahoma). In addition, we exclude Louisiana's House races from our analysis because most seats are won in the open primary elections. Louisiana also underwent a major redistricting before the 1994 elections. No other major redistricting occurred in any other states during the election cycles we examine. Finally, we exclude Vermont's at-large seat (discussed subsequently) for the 1988–90 and 1992–94 election cycles. As a result, our 1992–94 analysis excludes 15 districts, our 1988–90 analysis excludes 22 districts, and our 1984–86 analysis excludes 21 districts.

4. Again, we ignore votes for independent and third-party candidates. Of the elections we examine in this chapter, no more than 3.6 percent of votes nationwide were cast for third-party or independent candidates. The lone exception is Vermont's at-large seat, held by independent candidate Bernard Sanders since 1990 (he also ran for the seat as an independent in 1988 and lost, capturing 37.5 percent of the vote). Thus, we exclude the Vermont case from our analysis in years when Sanders ran for the seat.

5. As table 5.2 implies, our estimation also assumes that there are no midterm voters who abstained from the previous on-year election (or that these new voters are equally divided between the two parties). It appears that very few people sit out the presidential election and then vote in the following midterm. For example, only 37 respondents (2 percent of the total) in the 1994 NES survey reported voting in 1994 but not in 1992. King (1997) reports similar figures for Fulton County, Georgia.

6. Because the Democrats started out with a majority of voters in each case, the relatively modest party differences in abstention rates (in percentages) are even larger when measured in terms of the raw number of voters.

7. We could have generated voter abstention estimates for 1990 and 1986 from vote recall questions routinely included in NES surveys. However, vote recall questions are unreliable and understate the frequency of changing behavior (Benewick et al. 1969; Converse 1962; Himmelweit, Biberian, and Stockdale 1978; Weir 1975).

8. To simplify the presentation, we also drop the South variable. When it was included in the analyses in table 5.7, its effect was not significant and did not alter the other findings.

9. The explained variance when regressing the multiplicative term on its two components is .99.

10. The incumbent's ideological extremism does not appear to be related to voter defection. When we insert the incumbent's W-NOMINATE score in place of presidential support in table 5.7, the estimated coefficients for the W-NOMINATE variables are not significant in 1990 or 1994.

11. The same pattern is found among Democratic defectors in the 1994 election.

CHAPTER 6

1. See Crook and Hibbing 1997 and Brunell and Grofman 1998 for empirical analyses of this electoral reform's effects on the Senate.

2. This does not mean that the House membership never changes. Because open seats appear in different districts each election cycle, there can be a fair amount of

gradual turnover in House seats. Mann (1992) notes that 50 to 75 percent of House and Senate members are replaced every 12 years.

3. A reasonable baseline for comparison is 50 percent, which is the percentage that would be reelected under random voting or perfectly competitive elections. Senate incumbents perform half again better than the baseline, and House incumbents do nearly twice as well.

4. However, in states with only one House district—where both the representative and the senators have the same geographic constituencies—senators remain less secure (Krasno 1994; Lee and Oppenheimer 1999). Thus, constituency size alone does not account for differences in House and Senate elections.

5. Maximum likelihood estimates are asymptotically efficient, consistent, unbiased, and normally distributed, which means that one should have greater confidence in results (other things being equal) when a sufficiently large sample is used to produce them (King 1989).

6. We have excluded elections in Louisiana as a result of its unusual nonpartisan primary system. The 1968 elections also have been omitted because George Wallace beat both major-party candidates in most southern states. A handful of Senate races were uncontested and, as in the House analysis, have been temporarily removed at the estimation stages of King's ecological inference procedure.

7. We show in chapter 7 that the ideological polarization of state delegations is unrelated to the frequency of split delegations, a necessary condition for balancing theory to hold. Further, it seems clear in cases where seat changes occur that candidate-level factors are most important (Abramowitz and Segal 1992; Krasno 1994; Westlye 1991). Finally, the number of split delegations cannot exceed the number of senators in the minority party in the Senate, causing a sort of ceiling effect.

8. Some advocates of policy balancing (Lacy and Niou 1998) argue that increased policy distance between candidates increases a voter's uncertainty about potential policy outcomes, thus reducing the desire for policy-balancing behavior.

9. See note 9 in chapter 4 for a more detailed description of DW-NOMINATE scores.

10. As Fiorina notes, "unless we have data on both the Democratic incumbent and her Republican challenger, and unless we can put the presidential candidates and the voters on the same scale, we cannot differentiate among such different situations and hence decide whether ticket-splitting is consistent with an ideological consistency or ideological balancing model" (1996, 155). The SES data satisfy these criteria.

11. Keith Poole has also produced W-NOMINATE estimates for presidents' positions based on their stated preferences about key congressional votes. Measuring the distance between senators and presidents for each year would produce similar results because presidents' positions are constant.

12. State electorate ideology—measured using the Erikson, Wright, and McIver data; Berry et al. data; or SES state means—are excluded here because they clutter the models and are never statistically significant. There is no evidence here that moderate states cast more split tickets.

13. A model of the Republican share of the vote using the relative-distance mea-

sure produces coefficients that are exactly opposite those in the first column and is thus redundant.

CHAPTER 7

1. Presidential elections where an incumbent was constitutionally barred from seeking reelection (1960 and 1988) are omitted. Nixon, Reagan, and Clinton won second terms, while Ford, Carter, and Bush failed. Although this is a small number of cases from which to draw inferences, it is all that is available.

2. The NES question is: "Do you think there are any important differences in what the Republicans and Democrats stand for?"

3. A "party vote" occurs when a majority of the Democrats oppose a majority of the Republicans. The percentage reflects the proportion of total roll calls that were party votes.

4. In this instance, split-ticket voting is computed only among major party voters. Expanding the measure to include minor-party voters does not change the substantive interpretation of the correlations, though they become somewhat less significant.

5. We have also examined the placements of the political parties in the NES surveys, a more direct measure of public awareness of party polarization. This measure has the drawback of being included only in eight presidential-year surveys (1972 to 2000). Nevertheless, the ideological distance between the parties has increased since 1972. In addition, mean party distance is again negatively correlated with total ticket splitting, whether the measurements are drawn from the NES or from our overall ecological inference estimates.

6. We also find that ticket splitting is slightly less common in states with a straight party device on the ballot. Four states removed these mechanisms from the ballot since the mid-1990s, and several other states are considering doing so. These changes in ballot format will make ticket splitting easier, but the overall impact should be small.

References

Abramowitz, Alan I. 1981. "Choices and Echoes in the 1980 U.S. Senate Elections: A Research Note." *American Journal of Political Science* 25:112–18.

Abramowitz, Alan I., and Kyle L. Saunders. 1998. "Ideological Realignment in the U.S. Electorate." *Journal of Politics* 60:634–52.

Abramowitz, Alan I, and Jeffrey A. Segal. 1992. *Senate Elections.* Ann Arbor: University of Michigan Press.

Abramson, Paul R., and William Claggett. 1991. "Racial Differences in Self-Reported and Validated Turnout in the 1988 Presidential Election." *Journal of Politics* 53:186–97.

Achen, Christopher H., and W. Phillips Shively. 1995. *Cross-Level Inference.* Chicago: University of Chicago Press.

Aistrup, Joseph A. 1996. *The Southern Strategy Revisited.* Lexington: University of Kentucky Press.

Alesina, Alberto, Morris Fiorina, and Howard Rosenthal. 1994. "Why Are There So Many Divided Senate Delegations?" Manuscript. Harvard University.

Alesina, Alberto, and Howard Rosenthal. 1989. "Partisan Cycles in Congressional Elections and the Macroeconomy." *American Political Science Review* 83:373–98.

Alesina, Alberto, and Howard Rosenthal. 1995. *Partisan Politics, Divided Government, and the Economy.* New York: Cambridge University Press.

Alt, James E., and Robert C. Lowry. 1994. "Divided Government, Fiscal Institutions, and Budget Deficits: Evidence from the States." *American Political Science Review* 88:811–28.

Altman, Micah, and Michael P. McDonald. 2002. Improving the Accuracy of Ecological Inference. Manuscript.

Alvarez, R. Michael, and Matthew M. Schousen. 1993. "Policy Moderation or Conflicting Expectations? Testing the Intentional Models of Split-Ticket Voting." *American Politics Quarterly* 21:410–38.

Asher, Herbert B. 1988. *Presidential Elections and American Politics.* 4th ed. Chicago: Dorsey Press.

Asher, Herbert. 1995. *Polling and the Public.* 3d ed. Washington, DC: Congressional Quarterly Press.

Bader, John B. 1994. "Congressional Party Leadership and Policy Priorities under Divided Government, 1969–1990." Paper presented at the annual meeting of the American Political Science Association, New York.

Bain, Henry. 1996. "The Scholarly Recount: A Useful Addition to the Methods of Voting Research . . . with an Example." *PS: Political Science and Politics* 29:495–501.

Balz, Dan, and David S. Broder. 1996. "Dole's Weakness Creates 'Clinton Republicans.'" *Washington Post*, October 4, A1.

Barone, Michael, and Grant Ujifusa. 1989. *The Almanac of American Politics 1990.* Washington, DC: National Journal.

Barro, Robert. 1991. "Comments on McCubbins." In *Politics and Economics in the Eighties*, ed. Alberto Alesina and Geoffrey Carliner. Chicago: University of Chicago Press.

Bartels, Larry M. 2000. "Partisanship and Voting Behavior, 1952–1996." *American Journal of Political Science* 44:35–50.

Beck, Paul Allen. 1997. *Party Politics in America.* 8th ed. New York: Longman Press.

Beck, Paul Allen. 1999. "The Changing American Party Coalitions." In *The State of the Parties*, ed. John C. Green and Daniel M. Shea, 3d ed. Lanham, MD: Rowman and Littlefield.

Beck, Paul Allen, Lawrence Baum, Aage R. Clausen, and Charles E. Smith Jr. 1992. "Patterns and Sources of Ticket Splitting in Subpresidential Voting." *American Political Science Review* 86:916–28.

Benewick, R. J., A. H. Birch, J. G. Blumler, and A. Ewbank. 1969. "The Floating Voter and the Liberal View of Representation." *Political Studies* 17:177–95.

Bennett, Stephen Earl, and Linda L. M. Bennett. 1993. "Out of Sight, Out of Mind: Americans' Knowledge of Party Control of the House of Representatives." *Political Research Quarterly* 21:67–80.

Berry, William D., Evan J. Ringquist, Richard C. Fording, and Russell L. Hanson. 1998. "Measuring Citizen and Government Ideology in the American States, 1960–1993." *American Journal of Political Science* 42:327–48.

Binder, Sarah A. 1999. "The Dynamics of Legislative Gridlock, 1947–1996." *American Political Science Review* 93:519–34.

Binder, Sarah A. 2001. "Congress, the Executive, and the Production of Public Policy: United We Govern?" In *Congress Reconsidered*, ed. Lawrence C. Dodd and Bruce I. Oppenheimer, 7th ed. Washington, DC: Congressional Quarterly Press.

Binder, Sarah A., and Forrest Maltzman. 2002. "Senatorial Delay in Confirming Federal Judges, 1947–1998." *American Journal of Political Science* 46:190–99.

Bloom, Joel David. 1994. "The Rational Act of Ticket Splitting?" Paper presented at the annual meeting of the Midwest Political Science Association, Chicago.

Blunt, Christopher C. 2000. "Incumbency, Issues, and Split-Ticket Voting." Paper presented at the annual meeting of the American Political Science Association, Washington, DC.

Bobo, Lawrence, and Franklin D. Gilliam Jr. 1990. "Race, Socioeconomic Status, and Black Empowerment." *American Political Science Review* 84:377–94.

Born, Richard. 1990. "Surge and Decline, Negative Voting, and the Midterm Loss Phenomenon: A Simultaneous Choice Analysis." *American Journal of Political Science* 34:615–45.

Born, Richard. 1994. "Split-Ticket Voters, Divided Government, and Fiorina's Policy-Balancing Model." *Legislative Studies Quarterly* 19:95–115.

Born, Richard. 2000a. "Congressional Incumbency and the Rise of Split-Ticket Voting." *Legislative Studies Quarterly* 25:365–87.

Born, Richard. 2000b. "Policy Balancing Models and the Split-Ticket Voter, 1972–1996." *American Politics Quarterly* 28:131–62.

Bowling, Cynthia J., and Margaret R. Ferguson. 2001. "Divided Government, Interest Representation, and Policy Differences: Competing Explanations of Gridlock in the Fifty States." *Journal of Politics* 63:182–206.

Box-Steffensmeier, Janet M. 1996. "A Dynamic Analysis of the Role of War Chests in Campaign Strategy." *American Journal of Political Science* 40:352–71.

Box-Steffensmeier, Janet M., Gary C. Jacobson, and J. Tobin Grant. 2000. "Question Wording and the House Vote Choice: Some Experimental Evidence." *Public Opinion Quarterly* 64:257–70.

Box-Steffensmeier, Janet M., Katherine Tate, and David C. Kimball. 1997. "Linking Representation and House Member Behavior." Paper presented at the annual meeting of the American Political Science Association, Washington, DC.

Boyd, Richard W. 1985. "Electoral Change in the United States and Great Britain." *British Journal of Political Science* 15:517–39.

Boyd, Richard W. 1986. "Electoral Change and the Floating Voter: The Reagan Elections." *Political Behavior* 8:230–44.

Brace, Kimball W., ed. 1993. *The Election Data Book: A Statistical Portrait of Voting in America, 1992.* Lanham, MD: Bernan Press.

Brady, David W., John F. Cogan, Brian J. Gaines, and Douglas Rivers. 1996. "The Perils of Presidential Support: How the Republicans Took the House in the 1994 Midterm Elections." *Political Behavior* 18:345–67.

Brady, David W., Joseph Cooper, and Patricia A. Hurley. 1979. "The Decline of Party in the U.S. House of Representatives." *Legislative Studies Quarterly* 4:381–407.

Brady, David W., and Craig Volden. 1998. *Revolving Gridlock: Politics and Policy from Carter to Clinton.* Boulder, CO: Westview.

Broder, David S. 1996. "Does Clinton Want to Govern?" *Washington Post*, February 4, C7.

Brody, Richard A. 1991. *Assessing the President: The Media, Elite Opinion, and Public Support.* Stanford, CA: Stanford University Press.

Brody, Richard A., David W. Brady, and Valerie Heitshusen. 1994. "Accounting for Divided Government: Generational Effects on Party and Split-Ticket Voting." In *Elections at Home and Abroad*, ed. M. Kent Jennings and Thomas E. Mann. Ann Arbor: University of Michigan Press.

Brody, Richard A., and Lawrence S. Rothenberg. 1988. "The Instability of Partisanship: An Analysis of the 1980 Presidential Election." *British Journal of Political Science* 18:445–66.

Brown, Robert D., and Gerald C. Wright. 1992. "Elections and State Party Polarization." *American Politics Quarterly* 20:411–26.

Brunell, Thomas L., and Bernard Grofman. 1998. "Explaining Divided U.S. Senate Delegations, 1788–1996: A Realignment Approach." *American Political Science Review* 92:391–400.

Brunell, Thomas L., Bernard Grofman, and Samuel Merrill III. 2001. "Explaining the Proportion of Split House and President Outcomes, 1900–1996." Paper presented at the annual meeting of the Public Choice Society, San Antonio, TX.

Bullock, Charles S., III. 1988. "Regional Realignment from an Officeholding Perspective." *Journal of Politics* 50:553–74.

Bullock, Charles S., III, and David W. Brady. 1983. "Party, Constituency, and Roll-Call Voting in the U.S. Senate." *Legislative Studies Quarterly* 8:29–43.

Burden, Barry C. 1997. "Deterministic and Probabilistic Voting Models." *American Journal of Political Science* 41:1150–69.

Burden, Barry C. 1998. "Candidates' Positions in Congressional Elections." Ph.D. diss., Ohio State University.

Burden, Barry C. 2000. "Voter Turnout and the National Election Studies." *Political Analysis* 8:389–98.

Burden, Barry C., Gregory A. Caldeira, and Tim Groseclose. 2000. "Measuring the Ideologies U.S. Senators: The Song Remains the Same." *Legislative Studies Quarterly* 25:237–58.

Burden, Barry C., and Steven Greene. 2000. "Party Attachments and State Election Laws." *Political Research Quarterly* 53:57–70.

Burden, Barry C., and David C. Kimball. 1997. "Breaking up Isn't So Hard to Do: Ecological Inference and Split-Ticket Voting in the 1988 Presidential Election." Paper presented at the annual meeting of the Midwest Political Science Association, Chicago.

Burden, Barry C., and David C. Kimball. 1998. "A New Approach to the Study of Ticket Splitting." *American Political Science Review* 92:533–44.

Burden, Barry C., and David C. Kimball. 2001. "Proper Replication in the Study of Ticket Splitting." Manuscript.

Burnham, Walter Dean. 1965. "The Changing Shape of the American Political Universe." *American Political Science Review* 59:7–28.

Burnham, Walter Dean. 1970. *Critical Elections and the Mainsprings of American Politics.* New York: Norton.

Butler, David, and Bruce Cain. 1992. *Congressional Redistricting: Comparative and Theoretical Perspectives.* New York: Macmillan.

Cain, Bruce, John A. Ferejohn, and Morris P. Fiorina. 1987. *The Personal Vote: Constituency Service and Electoral Independence.* Cambridge: Harvard University Press.

Cameron, Charles M. 2000. *Veto Bargaining: Presidents and the Politics of Negative Power.* New York: Cambridge University Press.

Campbell, Angus. 1960. "Surge and Decline: A Study in Electoral Change." *Public Opinion Quarterly* 24:397–418.

Campbell, Angus, Philip E. Converse, Warren E. Miller, and Donald E. Stokes. 1960. *The American Voter.* New York: Wiley.

Campbell, Angus, and Warren E. Miller. 1957. "The Motivational Basis of Straight and Split Ticket Voting." *American Political Science Review* 51:293–312.

Campbell, James E. 1993. *The Presidential Pulse of Congressional Elections.* Lexington: University Press of Kentucky.

Campbell, James E. 1996. *Cheap Seats: The Democratic Party's Advantage in U.S. House Elections*. Columbus: Ohio State University Press.

Campbell, James E. 1997. "The Presidential Pulse and the 1994 Midterm Congressional Election." *Journal of Politics* 59:830–57.

Cho, Wendy K. Tam. 1998. "Iff the Assumption Fits . . . : A Comment on the King Ecological Inference Solution." *Political Analysis* 7:143–63.

Cho, Wendy K. Tam. 2001. "Latent Groups and Cross-Level Inferences." *Electoral Studies* 20:243–63.

Cho, Wendy K. Tam, and Brian J. Gaines. 2001. "Reassessing the Study of Split-Ticket Voting." Manuscript.

Coleman, John J. 1996. *Party Decline in America: Policy, Politics, and the Fiscal State*. Princeton: Princeton University Press.

Coleman, John J. 1997. "The Importance of Being Republican: Forecasting Party Fortunes in House Midterm Elections." *Journal of Politics* 59:497–519.

Converse, Philip E. 1962. "Information Flow and the Stability of Partisan Attitudes." *Public Opinion Quarterly* 26:578–99.

Cook, Rhodes. 1994. "Democrats' Congressional Base Shredded by November Vote." *Congressional Quarterly Weekly Report*, December 1, 3517–18.

Cowart, Andrew T. 1974. "A Cautionary Note on Aggregate Indicators of Split Ticket Voting." *Political Methodology* 1:109–30.

Cox, Gary W., and Jonathan N. Katz. 1996. "Why Did the Incumbency Advantage in U.S. House Elections Grow?" *American Journal of Political Science* 40:478–97.

Cox, Gary W., and Samuel Kernell, eds. 1991. *The Politics of Divided Government*. Boulder, CO: Westview.

Cox, Gary W., and Mathew D. McCubbins. 1993. *Legislative Leviathan: Party Government in the House*. Berkeley: University of California Press.

Cox, Gary W., and Michael C. Munger. 1986. "Closeness, Expenditure, Turnout: The 1982 U.S. House Elections." *American Political Science Review* 83:217–32.

Cox, James, Gregory Hager, and David Lowery. 1993. "Regime Change in Presidential and Congressional Budgeting: Role Discontinuity or Role Evolution?" *American Journal of Political Science* 37:88–118.

Crook, Sara Brandes, and John R. Hibbing. 1997. "A Not-So-Distant Mirror: The Seventeenth Amendment and Congressional Change." *American Political Science Review* 91:845–53.

Cummings, Milton C., Jr. 1966. *Congressmen and the Electorate: Elections for the U.S. House and the President, 1920–1964*. New York: Free Press.

Cutler, Lloyd. 1989. "Now Is the Time for All Good Men." *William and Mary Law Review* 30:391.

De Vries, Walter, and Lance Tarrance. 1972. *The Ticket-Splitter: A New Force in American Politics*. Grand Rapids, MI: Eerdmans.

Dewar, Helen. 1996. "Balance of Power Appeals to Many Voters." *Washington Post*, October 27, A1.

Downs, Anthony. 1957. *An Economic Theory of Democracy*. New York: Harper and Row.

Drew, Elizabeth. 1996. *Showdown: The Struggle between the Gingrich Congress and the Clinton White House*. New York: Simon and Schuster.

Duncan, Otis Dudley, and Beverly Davis. 1953. "An Alternative to Ecological Correlation." *American Sociological Review* 18:665–66.

Durr, Robert H., John B. Gilmour, and Christina Wolbrecht. 1997. "Explaining Congressional Approval." *American Journal of Political Science* 41:175–207.

"Economists for Clinton." 1996. *Economist*, October 5.

Edwards, George C., III, Andrew Barrett, and Jeffrey Peake. 1997. "The Legislative Impact of Divided Government." *American Journal of Political Science* 41:545–63.

Epstein, David, and Sharyn O'Halloran. 1996. "Divided Government and the Design of Administrative Procedures." *Journal of Politics* 58:373–97.

Erikson, Robert S. 1988. "The Puzzle of Midterm Loss." *Journal of Politics* 50:1011–29.

Erikson, Robert S. 1989. "Why the Democrats Lose Presidential Elections—Toward a Theory of Optimal Loss." *PS: Political Science and Politics* 22:30–35.

Erikson, Robert S. 1990. "Roll Calls, Reputations, and Representation in the U.S. Senate." *Legislative Studies Quarterly* 15:623–40.

Erikson, Robert S., Gerald C. Wright, Jr., and John McIver. 1993. *Statehouse Democracy*. New York: Cambridge University Press.

Eubank, Robert B., and David John Gow. 1983. "The Pro-Incumbent Bias in the 1978 and 1980 National Election Studies." *American Journal of Political Science* 27:122–39.

The Federalist Papers. 1964. New York: Washington Square Press.

Feigert, Frank B. 1979. "Illusions of Ticket-Splitting." *American Politics Quarterly* 7:470–88.

Fenno, Richard F., Jr. 1978. *Home Style: House Members in Their Districts*. Boston: Little, Brown.

Ferejohn, John A. 1977. "On the Decline of Competition in Congressional Elections." *American Political Science Review* 71:166–76.

Ferejohn, John A., and Randall L. Calvert. 1984. "Presidential Coattails in Historical Perspective." *American Political Science Review* 28:147–63.

Fiorina, Morris P. 1974. *Representatives, Roll Calls, and Constituencies*. Lexington, MA: D. C. Heath.

Fiorina, Morris P. 1981. *Retrospective Voting in American National Elections*. New Haven: Yale University Press.

Fiorina, Morris P. 1989. *Congress: Keystone of the Washington Establishment*. 2d ed. New Haven: Yale University Press.

Fiorina, Morris P. 1994. "Divided Government in the American States: A Byproduct of Legislative Professionalism?" *American Political Science Review* 88:304–16.

Fiorina, Morris P. 1996. *Divided Government*. 2d ed. Needham Heights, MA: Allyn and Bacon.

Fiorina, Morris P. 1997. "Professionalism, Realignment, and Representation." *American Political Science Review* 91:156–62.

Forgette, Richard, and Glenn J. Platt. 1999. "Voting for the Person, Not the Party:

Party Defection, Issue Voting, and Process Sophistication." *Social Science Quarterly* 80:409–21.

Franklin, Mark N., and Wolfgang P. Hirczy de Miño. 1998. "Separated Powers, Divided Government, and Turnout in U.S. Presidential Elections." *American Journal of Political Science* 42:316–36.

Freedman, David A., Stephen P. Klein, Michael Ostland, and Michael R. Roberts. 1998. Review of *A Solution to the Ecological Inference Problem. Journal of the American Statistical Association* 93:1518–22.

Frymer, Paul. 1994. "Ideological Consensus within Divided Party Government." *Political Science Quarterly* 109:287–311.

Frymer, Paul, Thomas Paul Kim, and Terri S. Bimes. 1997. "Party Elites, Ideological Voters, and Divided Party Government." *Legislative Studies Quarterly* 22:195–216.

Galderisi, Peter F., ed. 1996. *Divided Government: Change, Uncertainty, and the Constitutional Order.* Lanham, MD: Rowman and Littlefield.

Garand, James C., and Marci Glascock Lichtl. 2000. "Explaining Divided Government in the United States: Testing an Intentional Model of Split-Ticket Voting." *British Journal of Political Science* 30:173–91.

Gelman, Andrew, and Gary King. 1990. "Measuring Incumbency without Bias." *American Journal of Political Science* 34:1142–64.

Gerber, Alan. 1998. "Estimating the Effect of Campaign Spending on Senate Election Outcomes Using Instrumental Variables." *American Political Science Review* 92:401–12.

Gianos, Phillip L. 2000. "Bipartisan Legislative Delegations and the Mean-Seeking Hypothesis: The Case of Washington, 1948–96." *Legislative Studies Quarterly* 25:499–515.

Gimpel, James. 1996. *National Elections and the Autonomy of American State Party Systems.* Pittsburgh: University of Pittsburgh Press.

Ginsberg, Benjamin. 1976. "Elections and Public Policy." *American Political Science Review* 70:41–49.

Giroux, Gregory L. 2001. "Remaps' Clear Trend: Incumbent Protection." *Congressional Quarterly Weekly Report,* November 3, 2627–32.

Gitelson, Alan R. 1978. "An Analysis of Split-Ticket Voting Patterns at the Macroanalytic Level." *Political Methodology* 4:445–59.

Gitelson, Alan R., and Patricia Bayer Richard. 1983. "Ticket-Splitting: Aggregate Measures versus Actual Ballots." *Western Political Quarterly* 36:410–19.

Gleckman, Howard. 1996. "Split Decision." *Business Week,* November 18, p. 38.

Goeas, Ed, and Brian C. Tringali. 1993. "Here's Looking at You: Battleground Analysis Can Help You Focus on Swing Voters." *Campaigns and Elections* 14:47–48.

Goodman, Leo. 1959. "Some Alternatives to Ecological Correlation." *American Journal of Sociology* 64:610–24.

Gosnell, Harold. 1937. *Machine Politics: Chicago Model.* Chicago: University of Chicago Press.

Gow, David John, and Robert B. Eubank. 1984. "The Pro-Incumbent Bias in the 1982 National Election Study." *American Journal of Political Science* 28:224–30.

Green, Donald Philip, and Jonathan S. Krasno. 1988. "Salvation for the Spendthrift Incumbent." *American Journal of Political Science* 32:844–907.

Green, Donald Philip, and Jonathan S. Krasno. 1990. "Rebuttal to Jacobson's 'New Evidence for Old Arguments.'" *American Journal of Political Science* 34:363–72.

Grofman, Bernard, William Koetzle, Michael P. McDonald, and Thomas L. Brunell. 2000. "A New Look at Split Ticket Outcomes for House and President: The Comparative Midpoints Model." *Journal of Politics* 62:34–50.

Gronke, Paul. 2000. *The Electorate, the Campaign, and the Office: A Unified Approach to Senate and House Elections*. Ann Arbor: University of Michigan Press.

Groseclose, Tim, and Nolan McCarty. 2000. "The Politics of Blame: Bargaining before an Audience." *American Journal of Political Science* 45:100–119.

Hetherington, Marc J. 2001. "Resurgent Mass Partisanship: The Role of Elite Polarization." *American Political Science Review* 95:619–31.

Herrnson, Paul S. 1997. *Congressional Elections: Campaigning at Home and in Washington*. 2d ed. Washington, DC: Congressional Quarterly Press.

Herron, Michael C., and Kenneth W. Shotts. Forthcoming. *Political Analysis*. "Using Ecological Inference Point Estimates in Second Stage Linear Regressions."

Hibbing, John. 1991. *Congressional Careers*. Chapel Hill: University of North Carolina Press.

Himmelweit, Hilde T., Marianne Jaeger Biberian, and Janet Stockdale. 1978. "Memory for Past Vote: Implications of a Study of Bias in Recall." *British Journal of Political Science* 8:365–75.

Hodgett, Alistair, and Keith Tarr-Whelan. 1997. "England Swings." *Campaigns and Elections* 18:8–9.

Howell, William, Scott Adler, Charles Cameron, and Charles Riemann. 2000. "Divided Government and Legislative Productivity of Congress, 1945–1994." *Legislative Studies Quarterly* 25:285–312.

Huckfeldt, Robert, and John Sprague. 1987. "Networks in Context: The Social Flow of Political Information." *American Political Science Review* 81:1197–1216.

Huntington, Samuel P. 1950. "A Revised Theory of American Political Parties." *American Political Science Review* 40:669–77.

Ingberman, Daniel, and John Villani. 1993. "An Institutional Theory of Divided Government and Party Polarization." *American Journal of Political Science* 37:429–71.

Jackson, John S., III. 1997. "The 1996 Congressional Elections." In *America's Choice: The Election of 1996*, ed. William Crotty and Jerome N. Mileur. New York: McGraw-Hill.

Jacobson, Gary C. 1990a. "The Effects of Campaign Spending in House Elections: New Evidence for Old Arguments." *American Journal of Political Science* 34:334–62.

Jacobson, Gary C. 1990b. *The Electoral Origins of Divided Government*. Boulder, CO: Westview.

Jacobson, Gary C. 1997. *The Politics of Congressional Elections*. 4th ed. New York: Longman.

Jacobson, Gary C. 2000a. "Party Polarization in National Politics: The Electoral Connection." In *Polarized Politics*, ed. Jon R. Bond and Richard Fleisher. Washington, DC: Congressional Quarterly Press.

Jacobson, Gary C. 2000b. "Reversal of Fortune: The Transformation of U.S. House Elections in the 1990s." In *Change and Continuity in House Elections*, ed. David W. Brady and Morris P. Fiorina. Stanford, CA: Stanford University Press.

Jacobson, Gary C. 2001. *The Politics of Congressional Elections*. 5th ed. New York: Longman.

Jacobson, Gary C., and Samuel Kernell. 1983. *Strategy and Choice in Congressional Elections*. 2d ed. New Haven: Yale University Press.

Jacobson, Gary C., and Douglas Rivers. 1993. "Explaining the Overreport for the Incumbent in the National Election Studies." Paper presented at the annual meeting of the Western Political Science Association, Pasadena, CA.

Jennings, M. Kent, and Gregory B. Markus. 1984. "Partisan Orientations over the Long Haul: Results from the Three-Wave Political Socialization Panel Study." *American Political Science Review* 78:1000–1018.

Johnston, Ronald J., and A. M. Hay. 1984. "The Geography of Ticket Splitting: A Preliminary Study of the 1976 Elections Using Entropy-Maximizing Methods." *Professional Geographer* 36:201–6.

Johnston, Ronald J., and Charles Pattie. 2000. "Ecological Inference and Entropy-Maximizing: An Alternative Estimation Procedure for Split-Ticket Voting." *Political Analysis* 8:333–45.

Johnston, Ronald J., and Charles Pattie. 1999. "Constituency, Campaign Intensity, and Split-Ticket Voting: New Zealand's First Election Under MMP, 1996." *Political Science* 51:164–81.

Jones, Bradford S., and Barbara Norrander. 1996. "The Reliability of Aggregated Public Opinion Measures." *American Journal of Political Science* 40:295–309.

Jones, Bryan D., James L. True, and Frank R. Baumgartner. 1997. "Does Incrementalism Stem from Political Consensus or from Institutional Gridlock?" *American Journal of Political Science* 41:1319–39.

Jones, Charles O. 1994. *The Presidency in a Separated System*. Washington, DC: Brookings Institution.

Kahn, Kim Fridkin, and Patrick J. Kenney. 1999. *The Spectacle of U.S. Senate Campaigns*. Princeton: Princeton University Press.

Keith, Bruce E., David B. Magleby, Candice J. Nelson, Elizabeth Orr, Mark C. Westlye, and Raymond E. Wolfinger. 1992. *The Myth of the Independent Voter*. Berkeley: University of California Press.

Kelly, Sean Q. 1993. "Divided We Govern: A Reassessment." *Polity* 25:475–84.

Kernell, Samuel. 1991. "Facing an Opposition Congress: The President's Strategic Circumstance." In *The Politics of Divided Government*, ed. Gary W. Cox and Samuel Kernell. Boulder, CO: Westview.

Kernell, Samuel. 1978. "Explaining Presidential Popularity." *American Political Science Review* 72:506–22.

Kernell, Samuel. 1997. *Going Public: New Strategies of Presidential Leadership*. 3d ed. Washington, DC: Congressional Quarterly Press.

Key, V. O. 1964. *Politics, Parties, and Pressure Groups*. 5th ed. New York: Crowell.

Key, V. O., Jr., with Milton C. Cummings Jr. 1966. *The Responsible Electorate: Rationality in Presidential Voting, 1936–1960*. Cambridge: Harvard University Press, Belknap Press.

Kimball, David C. 1997. "The Divided Voter in American Politics." Ph.D. diss., Ohio State University.

King, Gary. 1989. *Unifying Political Methodology: The Likelihood Theory of Inference*. Princeton: Princeton University Press. Reprint, Ann Arbor: University of Michigan Press, 1998.

King, Gary. 1997. *A Solution to the Ecological Inference Problem: Reconstructing Individual Behavior from Aggregate Data*. Princeton: Princeton University Press.

King, Gary, Robert O. Keohane, and Sidney Verba. 1994. *Designing Social Inquiry: Scientific Inference in Qualitative Research*. Princeton: Princeton University Press.

King, Gary, Michael Tomz, and Jason Wittenberg. 2000. "Making the Most of Statistical Analyses: Improving Interpretation and Presentation." *American Journal of Political Science* 44:341–55.

Kitchens, James T., and Larry Powell. 1994. "Ticket Splitting: Dead or Alive?" *Campaigns & Elections* 6:34–35.

Knight, Kathleen, and Robert S. Erikson. 1997. "Ideology in the 1990s." In *Understanding Public Opinion*, ed. Barbara Norrander and Clyde Wilcox. Washington, DC: Congressional Quarterly Press.

Krasno, Jonathan S. 1994. *Challengers, Competition, and Reelection*. New Haven: Yale University Press.

Krehbiel, Keith. 1998. *Pivotal Politics: A Theory of U.S. Lawmaking*. Chicago: University of Chicago Press.

Krosnick, Jon A., and Laura A. Brannon. 1993. "The Impact of the Gulf War on the Ingredients of Presidential Evaluations: Multidimensional Effects of Political Involvement." *American Political Science Review* 87:963–75.

Krutz, Glen S. 2001. "Tactical Maneuvering on Omnibus Bills in Congress." *American Journal of Political Science* 45:210–23.

Krutz, Glen S., Richard Fleisher, and Jon R. Bond. 1998. "From Abe Fortas to Zoë Baird: Why Some Presidential Nominations Fail in the Senate." *American Political Science Review* 92:871–82.

Lacy, Dean. 1997. "Back from Intermission: The 1994 Elections and the Return to Divided Government." In *Great Theatre: The American Congress in the 1990s*, ed. Herbert F. Weisberg and Samuel C. Patterson. New York: Cambridge University Press.

Lacy, Dean, and Emerson M. S. Niou. 1998. "Elections in Double-Member Districts with Nonseparable Preferences." *Journal of Theoretical Politics* 10:89–110.

Lacy, Dean, and Philip Paolino. 1998. "Downsian Voting and the Separation of Powers." *American Journal of Political Science* 42:1180–99.

Lang, Kurt, Gladys Engel Lang, and Irving Crespi. 1998. "Discerning the Mandate: Voter Intentions and Media Interpretations." Paper presented at the annual meeting of the American Political Science Association, Boston.

Laver, Michael. 1999. "Divided Parties, Divided Government." *Legislative Studies Quarterly* 19:5–30.

Laver, Michael, and Kenneth A. Shepsle. 1996. *Making and Breaking Governments: Cabinets and Legislatures in Parliamentary Democracies*. New York: Cambridge University Press.

Lawrence, David. 1999. *America: The Politics of Diversity*. Belmont, CA: Wadsworth.

Lee, Frances E., and Bruce I. Oppenheimer. 1999. *Sizing up the Senate: The Unequal Consequences of Equal Representation*. Chicago: University of Chicago Press.

LeoGrande, William M., and Alana S. Jeydel. 1997. "Using Presidential Election Returns to Measure Constituent Ideology." *American Politics Quarterly* 25:3–18.

Levine, Jeffrey, Edward G. Carmines, and Robert Huckfeldt. 1997. "The Rise of Ideology in the Post–New Deal Party System, 1972–1992." *American Politics Quarterly* 25:19–34.

Lockerbie, Brad. 1999. "The Partisan Component of the Incumbency Advantage, 1956–1996." *Political Research Quarterly* 52:631–46.

Lowry, Robert C., James E. Alt, and Karen E. Ferree. 1998. "Fiscal Policy Outcomes and Electoral Accountability in American States." *American Political Science Review* 92:759–74.

Lublin, David. 1997. *The Paradox of Representation*. Princeton: Princeton University Press.

Macdonald, Stuart Elaine, and George Rabinowitz. 1987. "The Dynamics of Structural Realignment." *American Political Science Review* 81:775–96.

MacKuen, Michael B., Robert S. Erikson, and James A. Stimson. 1989. "Macropartisanship." *American Political Science Review* 83:1125–42.

Maddox, William S., and Dan Nimmo. 1981. "In Search of the Ticket-Splitter." *Social Science Quarterly* 62:401–8.

Mann, Thomas E. 1978. *Unsafe at Any Margin: Interpreting Congressional Elections*. Washington, DC: American Enterprise Institute.

Mann, Thomas E. 1992. "The Wrong Medicine." *Brookings Review* 10:23–25.

Mann, Thomas E., and Raymond E. Wolfinger. 1980. "Candidates and Parties in Congressional Elections." *American Political Science Review* 74:617–32.

Maraniss, David, and Michael Weisskopf. 1996. *"Tell Newt to Shut Up!"* New York: Simon and Schuster.

Markus, Gregory B. 1974. "Electoral Coalitions and Senate Roll Call Behavior: An Ecological Analysis." *American Journal of Political Science* 38:595–607.

Matthews, Steven E. 1979. "A Simple Direction Model of Electoral Competition." *Public Choice* 34:141–56.

Mattei, Franco, and John S. Howes. 2000. "Competing Explanations of Split-Ticket Voting in American National Elections." *American Politics Quarterly* 28:379–407.

Mayer, William G. 1996. *The Divided Democrats: Ideological Unity, Party Reform, and Presidential Elections*. Boulder, CO: Westview.

Mayhew, David R. 1974. *Congress: The Electoral Connection*. New Haven: Yale University Press.

Mayhew, David R. 1991. *Divided We Govern*. New Haven: Yale University Press.

McAlliser, Ian, and Robert Darcy. 1992. "Sources of Split-Ticket Voting in the 1988 American Elections." *Political Studies* 40:695–712.

McCarty, Nolan M., Keith T. Poole, and Howard Rosenthal. 1997. *Income Redistribution and the Realignment of American Politics.* Washington, DC: AEI Press.

McCubbins, Mathew. 1991. "Government on Lay-Away: Federal Spending and Deficits under Divided Party Control." In *The Politics of Divided Government,* ed. Gary W. Cox and Samuel Kernell. Boulder, CO: Westview.

McCue, Kenneth. 2001. "The Statistical Foundations of the 'EI' Method." *American Statistician* 55:106–11.

McFeatters, Dale. 2000. "A Guide for Ill-Informed Voters." Scripps Howard News Service, syndicated column, October 25.

Mebane, Walter R., Jr. 2000. "Coordination, Moderation, and Institutional Balancing in American Presidential and House Elections." *American Political Science Review* 94:37–58.

Menefee-Libey, David. 2000. *The Triumph of Campaign-Centered Politics.* Chatham, NJ: Chatham House.

Merrill, Samuel, III, and Bernard Grofman. 1999. *A Unified Theory of Voting: Directional and Spatial Models.* New York: Cambridge University Press.

Miller, Arthur H., Martin P. Wattenberg, and Oksana Melanchuk. 1986. "Schematic Assessments of Presidential Candidates." *American Political Science Review* 80:521–40.

Miller, Warren E., and J. Merrill Shanks. 1996. *The New American Voter.* Cambridge, MA: Harvard University Press.

Miller, Warren E., and Donald E. Stokes. 1963. "Constituency Influence in Congress." *American Political Science Review* 57:45–57.

Mondak, Jeffrey J., Carl McCurley, and Steven R.L. Millman. 1999. "The Impact of Incumbents' Levels of Competence and Integrity in the 1994 and 1996 U.S. House Elections." In *Reelection 1996,* ed. Herbert F. Weisberg and Janet M. Box-Steffensmeier. New York: Chatham House.

Moore, David W. 1996. "Clinton Loses Advantage in Budget Dispute." *Gallup Poll Monthly,* January, 11–14.

Moore, David W., and Lydia Saad. 1995. "Americans Still Favor Independent and Third-Party Candidates." *Gallup Poll Monthly,* July, 2–5.

Morgan, William. 1995. "Institutional Ownership of Issues, Party Ownership of Issues, and Divided Government." Paper presented at the annual meeting of the Midwest Political Science Association, Chicago.

Nicholson, Stephen P., and Gary M. Segura. 1999. "Midterm Elections and Divided Government: An Information-Driven Theory of Electoral Volatility." *Political Research Quarterly* 52:609–29.

Nie, Norman H., John R. Petrocik, and Sidney Verba. 1976. *The Changing American Voter.* Cambridge: Harvard University Press.

Norpoth, Helmut. 2001. "Divided Government and Economic Voting." *Journal of Politics* 63:414–35.

Norpoth, Helmut, and Bruce Buchanan. 1992. "Wanted: The Education President: Issue Trespassing by Political Candidates." *Public Opinion Quarterly* 56:87–99.

Oppenheimer, Bruce I., James A. Stimson, and Richard W. Waterman. 1986. "Interpreting U.S. Congressional Elections: The Exposure Thesis." *Legislative Studies Quarterly* 11:227–47.

Page, Benjamin I. 1978. *Choices and Echoes in Presidential Elections*. Chicago: University of Chicago Press.

Palmquist, Bradley, and D. Stephen Voss. 1996. "Racial Polarization and Turnout in Louisiana: New Insights from Aggregate Data Analysis." Paper presented at the annual meeting of the Midwest Political Science Association, Chicago.

Patterson, Samuel C., and Gregory A. Caldeira. 1983. "Getting Out the Vote: Participation in Gubernatorial Elections." *American Political Science Review* 77:675–89.

Patterson, Samuel C., and Gregory A. Caldeira. 1988. "Party Voting in the United States Congress." *British Journal of Political Science* 18:111–31.

Patterson, Samuel C., and Gregory A. Caldeira. 1990. "Standing up for Congress: Variations in Public Esteem since the 1960s." *Legislative Studies Quarterly* 15:25–47.

Patterson, Samuel C., and David C. Kimball. 1998. "Unsympathetic Audience: Citizens' Evaluations of Congress." In *Great Theatre: The American Congress in the 1990s*, ed. Herbert F. Weisberg and Samuel C. Patterson. New York: Cambridge University Press.

Patterson, Thomas E. 2001. *The American Democracy*. 5th ed. New York: McGraw-Hill.

Peterson, Paul E., and Jay P. Greene. 1994. "Why Executive-Legislative Conflict in the United States Is Dwindling." *British Journal of Political Science* 24:33–55.

Peterson, Paul E., and Mark Rom. 1988. "Lower Taxes, More Spending, and Budget Deficits." In *The Reagan Legacy*, ed. Charles O. Jones. Chatham, NJ: Chatham House.

Petracca, Mark P. 1991. "Divided Government and the Risks of Constitutional Reform." *PS: Political Science and Politics* 24:634–37.

Petrocik, John R. 1991. "Divided Government: Is It All in the Campaigns?" In *The Politics of Divided Government*, ed. Gary W. Cox and Samuel Kernell. Boulder, CO: Westview.

Petrocik, John R., and Joseph Doherty. 1996. "The Road to Divided Government: Paved without Intention." In *Divided Government: Change, Uncertainty, and the Constitutional Order*, ed. Peter F. Galderisi. Lanham, MD: Rowman and Littlefield.

Poole, Keith T. 1998. "Recovering a Basic Space from a Set of Issue Scales." *American Journal of Political Science* 42:954–93.

Poole, Keith T., and Howard Rosenthal. 1984. "The Polarization of American Politics." *Journal of Politics* 46:1061–79.

Poole, Keith T., and Howard Rosenthal. 1997. *Congress: A Political-Economic History of Roll Call Voting*. New York: Oxford University Press.

Popkin, Samuel L. 1996. *The Reasoning Voter*. 2d ed. Chicago: University of Chicago Press.

Poterba, James. 1994. "State Responses to Fiscal Crisis: The Effects of Budgetary Institutions and Politics." *Journal of Political Economy* 102:799–821.

Rabinowitz, George, and Stuart Elaine MacDonald. 1989. "A Directional Theory of Issue Voting." *American Political Science Review* 83:93–121.

Rivers, Douglas. 1998. Review of *A Solution to the Ecological Inference Problem* by Gary King. *American Political Science Review* 92:442–43.

Robinson, William S. 1950. "Ecological Correlations and the Behavior of Individuals." *American Sociological Review* 15:351–57.

Rohde, David W. 1991. *Parties and Leaders in the Postreform House.* Chicago: University of Chicago Press.

Rohde, David W., and Dennis M. Simon. 1985. "Presidential Vetoes and Congressional Response: A Study of Institutional Conflict." *American Journal of Political Science* 29:379–427.

Rusk, Jerrold G. 1970. "The Effect of the Australian Ballot Reform on Split Ticket Voting, 1876–1908." *American Political Science Review* 64:1220–38.

Saad, Lydia. 1995. "Budget Standoff Not Welcomed by Most Americans." *Gallup Poll Monthly,* November, pp. 5–8.

Safire, William. 2000 "The Clothespin Vote." *New York Times,* November 6, A39.

Samuelson, Robert J. 1996. ". . . By a Shrewd Electorate." *Washington Post,* November 13, A23.

Schelling, Thomas C. 1978. *Micromotives and Macrobehavior.* New York: Norton.

Scheve, Kenneth, and Michael Tomz. 1999. "Electoral Surprise and the Midterm Loss in U.S. Congressional Elections." *British Journal of Political Science* 29:507–21.

Schick, Allen. 1993. "Governments versus Budget Deficits." In *Do Institutions Matter? Government Capabilities in the United States and Abroad,* ed. R. Kent Weaver and Bert A. Rockman. Washington, DC: Brookings Institution.

Schmidt, Amy B., Lawrence W. Kenny, and Rebecca B. Morton. 1996. "Evidence on Electoral Accountability in the U.S. Senate: Are Unfaithful Agents Really Punished?" *Economic Inquiry* 34:545–67.

Segura, Gary M., and Stephen P. Nicholson. 1995. "Sequential Choices and Partisan Transitions in U.S. Senate Delegations." *Journal of Politics* 57:86–100.

Shapiro, Catherine R., David W. Brady, Richard A. Brody, and John A. Ferejohn. 1990. "Linking Constituency Opinion and Senate Voting Scores: A Hybrid Model." *Legislative Studies Quarterly* 15:599–621.

Shively, W. Phillips. 1985. "A Strategy for Cross-Level Inference under an Assumption of Breakage Effects." *Political Methodology* 11:167–79.

Shively, W. Phillips. 1991. "A General Extension of the Method of Bounds, with Special Application to Studies of Electoral Transition." *Historical Methods* 24:81–94.

Shively, W. Phillips. 1992. "From Differential Abstention to Conversion: A Change in Electoral Change, 1864–1988." *American Journal of Political Science* 36:309–30.

Shugart, Matthew Soberg. 1995. "The Electoral Cycle and Institutional Sources of Divided Presidential Government." *American Political Science Review* 89:327–43.

Sigelman, Lee. 1990. "Toward a Stupidity-Ugliness Theory of Democratic Electoral Debacles." *PS: Political Science and Politics* 23:18–20.

Sigelman, Lee. 1991. "Turning Cross Sections into a Panel: A Simple Procedure for Ecological Inference." *Social Science Research* 20:150–70.

Sigelman, Lee, Paul J. Wahlbeck, and Emmett H. Buell Jr. 1997. "Vote Choice and the Preference for Divided Government: Lessons of 1992." *American Journal of Political Science* 41:879–94.

Silbey, Joel H. 1996. "Divided Government in Historical Perspective, 1789–1996." In *Divided Government: Change, Uncertainty, and the Constitutional Order*, ed. Peter F. Galderisi. Lanham, MD: Rowman and Littlefield.

Silver, Brian D., Barbara A. Anderson, and Paul R. Abramson. 1986. "Who Overreports Voting?" *American Political Science Review* 80:613–24.

Smith, Charles E., Robert D. Brown, John M. Bruce, and L. Marvin Overby. 1999. "Policy Balancing and Voting for Congress in the 1996 National Election." *American Journal of Political Science* 43:737–64.

Smith, Mark A. 1997. "The Nature of Party Governance: Connecting Conceptualization and Measurement." *American Journal of Political Science* 41:1042–56.

Soss, Joe, and David T. Canon. 1995. "Partisan Divisions and Voting Decisions: U.S. Senators, Governors, and the Rise of a Divided Federal Government." *Political Research Quarterly* 48:253–74.

Stanley, Harold W., and Richard G. Niemi. 1999. *Vital Statistics on American Politics, 1999–2000*. Washington, DC: Congressional Quarterly Press.

Stimson, James A. 1985. "Regression Models in Space and Time: A Statistical Essay." *American Journal of Political Science* 29:914–47.

Stonecash, Jeffrey M., and Anna M. Agathangelou. 1997. "Trends in the Partisan Composition of State Legislatures: A Response to Fiorina." *American Political Science Review* 91:148–55.

Sundquist, James L. 1988. "Needed: A Political Theory for the New Era of Coalition Government in the United States." *Political Science Quarterly* 103:613–35.

Sundquist, James L. 1986. *Constitutional Reform and Effective Government*. Washington, DC: Brookings Institution.

Sundquist, James L., ed. 1993. *Beyond Gridlock? Prospects for Governance in the Clinton Years—and After*. Washington, DC: Brookings Institution.

Tarrance, V. Lance, Jr., and Walter De Vries, with Donna L. Mosher. 1998. *Checked and Balanced: How Ticket-Splitters Are Shaping the New Balance of Power in American Politics*. Grand Rapids, MI: Eerdmans.

Thorson, Gregory. 1998. "Divided Government and the Passage of Partisan Legislation, 1947–1990." *Political Research Quarterly* 51:751–64.

Thurber, James A. 1996. *Rivals for Power*. Washington, DC: Congressional Quarterly Press.

Tomz, Michael, Jason Wittenberg, and Gary King. 1999. "Clarify: Software for Interpreting and Presenting Statistical Results." Version 1.2.1. Harvard University, June 1. <http://gking.harvard.edu>.

Verhovek, Sam Howe. 2000. "Primary Vote Bolsters House Democrat G.O.P. Saw as Vulnerable." *New York Times*, October 2, A24.

Voss, D. Stephen, Andrew Gelman, and Gary King. 1995. "Preelection Survey Methodology: Details from Eight Polling Organizations, 1988 and 1992." *Public Opinion Quarterly* 59:98–132.

Walker, Martin. 1996. "The Clinton Republicans." *Los Angeles Times*, August 18, 1.

Wattenberg, Martin P. 1991a. "The Republican Presidential Advantage in the Age of Party Disunity." In *The Politics of Divided Government*, ed. Gary W. Cox and Samuel Kernell. Boulder, CO: Westview.

Wattenberg, Martin P. 1991b. *The Rise of Candidate-Centered Politics*. Cambridge: Harvard University Press.

Wattenberg, Martin P. 1998. *The Decline of American Political Parties, 1952–1996*. Cambridge: Harvard University Press.

Weatherford, M. Stephen. 1994. "Responsiveness and Deliberation in Divided Government: Presidential Leadership in Tax Policy Making." *British Journal of Political Science* 24:1–31.

Weir, Blair T. 1975. "The Distortion of Voter Recall." *American Journal of Political Science* 19:53–62.

Weisberg, Herbert F., and Charles E. Smith Jr. 1991. "The Influence of the Economy on Party Identification in the Reagan Years." *Journal of Politics* 53:1077–92.

Westlye, Mark C. 1991. *Senate Elections and Campaign Intensity*. Baltimore: Johns Hopkins University Press.

White, Halbert. 1980. "A Heteroskedasticity-Consistent Covariance Matrix Estimator and a Direct Test for Heteroskedasticity." *Econometrica* 48:817–30.

Wolfinger, Raymond E., Steven J. Rosenstone, and Richard A. McIntosh. 1981. "Presidential and Congressional Voters Compared." *American Politics Quarterly* 9:245–56.

Woolley, John T. 1991. "Institutions, the Election Cycle, and the Presidential Veto." *American Journal of Political Science* 35:279–304.

Wright, Gerald C. 1978. "Candidate Policy Positions and Voting in Congressional Elections." *Legislative Studies Quarterly* 3:445–64.

Wright, Gerald C. 1989. "Level-of-Analysis Effects on Explanations of Voting: The Case of the 1982 U.S. Senate Elections." *British Journal of Political Science* 19:381–98.

Wright, Gerald C. 1990. "Misreports of Vote Choice in the 1988 NES Senate Election Study." *Legislative Studies Quarterly* 15:543–63.

Wright, Gerald C. 1993. "Errors in Measuring Vote Choice in the National Election Studies, 1952–1988." *American Journal of Political Science* 39:291–316.

Wright, Gerald C., and Michael B. Berkman. 1986. "Candidates and Policy in United States Senate Elections." *American Political Science Review* 80:567–88.

Wright, Gerald C., John P. McIver, Robert S. Erikson, and David B. Holian. 2000. "Stability and Change in State Electorates, Carter through Clinton." Paper presented at the annual meeting of the Midwest Political Science Association, Chicago.

Wrighton, J. Mark, and Peverill Squire. 1997. "Uncontested Seats and Electoral Competition for the U.S. House of Representatives." *Journal of Politics* 59:452–68.

Zaller, John R. 1992. *The Nature and Origins of Mass Opinion*. New York: Cambridge University Press.

Zuckerman, Mortimer B. 1996. "The Power of the Center." *U.S. News and World Report*, November 18, 96.

Zupan, Mark. 1991. "An Economic Explanation for the Existence and Nature of Political Ticket Splitting." *Journal of Law and Economics* 34:343–69.

Index

accountability, 9–10

advertising, in campaigns, 25, 76, 115, 143

aggregate data, 33, 35, 68, 99; measure of ticket splitting and, 41–42, 43–45, 51, 53, 55, 60–62. *See also* survey data

Alesina, Alberto, 24, 136

American Voter, The (Campbell et al.), 77

"anchor" senators, 150–52

Australian ballot, 18, 41

ballot format, ticket splitting due to, 18, 40, 41, 49, 141, 176n. 3, 181n. 6; in president-House elections, 74, 77, 81–82, 91, 103

ballot roll-off, 44, 51, 52, 53, 62, 99, 175n. 10

Bartlett, Roscoe, 94, 96

BCR (Burnham-Cummings-Rusk) measure, 44, 60–62, 65, 99

Beck, Paul Allen, 13

Berry, William D., 132, 140, 141

Bersticker, Albert, 24

bipartisanship, 2, 157, 169, 170

bivariate normal distribution, 56–57. *See also* TBVN (truncated bivariate normal) distribution

Brady, David W., 137

Broder, David S., 24, 25

Brunell, Thomas L., 137

budget battle (1995–96), 1–2

budgeting, 8–9, 30, 168

Buell, Emmett H., Jr., 101

Bullock, Charles S., III, 137

Burnham, Walter Dean, 43, 44, 61. *See also* BCR (Burnham-Cummings-Rusk) measure

Bush, George, Sr., 8, 12, 36, 62–63, 69; 1988 election of, 46–48, 53, 56, 57, 59, 130; voters and, 56, 57, 70, 82

Bush, George W., 12, 169

Byron, Beverly, 46–48

campaign issues. *See* issues

campaigns, 13, 115; candidate-oriented, 75, 115, 134, 136, 153; finance reform for, 160, 168; presidential, 22, 35

campaign spending, 16, 34–35; on advertising, 25, 76, 115, 143; DR (Democratic-Republican) vote splitting and, 92–95; incumbency and, 40, 80–81, 101; midterm elections, 116–17; president-Senate vote splitting and, 140–49; RD (Republican-Democratic) vote splitting and, 76–77, 80–81, 87, 97

Campbell, Angus, 77, 111

candidate-oriented campaigns, 75, 115, 134, 136, 153

candidates, 22, 28, 31, 74–75, 96; appeal of, 68, 141, 169; campaign spending by, 34–35, 92, 143; ideology of, 32–33, 39, 145, 147–49, 156; independent, 3–4, 163; moderate, 156, 170; presidential, 99, 101, 104; quality of, 32, 73, 92, 94, 155, 158; visibility of, 23. *See also* incumbency advantage

checks and balances, 19, 25, 31

Clinton, Bill, 11–12, 25, 35, 119, 148;